HOW TO FEEL HUMAN

T V Smith

Published 2009 by arima publishing

www.arimapublishing.com

ISBN 978 1 84549 360 8

© T V Smith 2009

All rights reserved

This book is copyright. Subject to statutory exception and to provisions of relevant collective licensing agreements, no part of this publication may be reproduced, stored in a retrieval system, or transmitted in any form or by any means, without the prior written permission of the author.

Printed and bound in the United Kingdom

Typeset in Garamond 11/14

This book is sold subject to the conditions that it shall not, by way of trade or otherwise, be lent, re-sold, hired out, or otherwise circulated without the publisher's prior consent in any form of binding or cover other than that which it is published and without a similar condition including this condition being imposed on the subsequent purchaser.

arima publishing
ASK House, Northgate Avenue
Bury St Edmunds, Suffolk IP32 6BB
t: (+44) 01284 700321

www.arimapublishing.com

CONTENTS:

1. CZECH IN
2. MIND THE GENERATION GAP
3. BLOODY XMAS
4. PLAN A
5. TV SMITH DISCOVERS AMERICA
6. EAT!
7. THE EMERGENCY SANDWICH
8. BACK IN THE U.S.A.
9. FIESTA!
10. HOW TO FEEL HUMAN
11. GO WEST. NO VEST
12. CULTURE SLUSH
13. A VEGETARIAN IN SPAIN
14. IN THE MIDDLE OF NOWHERE IN THE MIDDLE OF NORWAY
15. IF YOU GO DOWN TO THE WOODS…
16. EL TV
17. A DUCK FLIES IN
18. THE RETURN OF THE EMERGENCY SANDWICH

Most of the photos are from my own collection, others were given to me by friends along the road, many of who also ended up unwittingly appearing as characters in this book. Thanks for being a part of it!

1. CZECH IN (2001)

2nd August

I'm bored. I've been here for hours, no one else speaks English, I don't speak Czech, and I don't know what's going on.

Yesterday I didn't even think I'd be coming. Air tickets hadn't arrived so I emailed my promoter Petr to ask if the tour was off—it had already been cut down from ten days to three, after all, and I'd only heard about that last week. Petr phoned back and told me in broken English that the organisers of the Trutnov festival which I'm supposed to be playing in three days time should have sent the tickets weeks ago. Apart from that, all he knows is that the flight was booked with Swissair, so I should contact them. I phone the airline and they tell me my schedule: a 6:20 a.m. flight to Prague, which means I'll have to get up at four in the morning and take a twenty quid cab to Heathrow. Also, the Swissair desk at the airport won't be open that early so I need to take the tube into town now and pick up the tickets from the central London office.

So I landed in Prague this morning, and from there Petr drove me here to his club in Teplice where I'll be playing later, and I've been hanging around all day on my own in the band room upstairs. Late afternoon I go down and sit in the bar, but the conversation goes on around me in Czech and after a while I wander outside in the sunshine, not knowing what to do with myself. A guy from a band called Squad 96, who I remember from the last time I was here because he speaks English, notices me as he goes into the bar and asks, 'What are you doing out here on your own?'

I say, 'Where would you like me to be on my own?'

The sound engineer arrives at around eight in the evening and proceeds to build the P.A. with two colleagues, a process which takes a couple of hours. Shortly before eleven there are still only eight people in the club. Petr apologises for the turnout and tells me that most of the potential audience has already left for the festival, which starts tomorrow morning. 'Not worry,' he says, 'Just play fifteen minutes if you feel like. Whatever you want. I must go in town now meet someone.'

I play for an hour, then sit outside on the benches with the entire audience. The guy from Squad 96 does all the translating. At one point he asks, 'Don't you get lonely touring by yourself?'

I hate to admit it, but sometimes, on days like these, I do.

3rd August

I wake up in the room above the club to find I'm not as lonely as I thought—two guys from Squad 96 are also sleeping there.

The plan for this evening is that I'll play support for Czech band Brutus, but I don't know what time we leave or even where the gig is; I looked up the name of the town on the map before I left England and couldn't find it. Meanwhile I have the rest of the day to myself with nothing to do.

Towards six Petr arrives back at the club and we set off. Along the way he tells me there has been a change of plan. Instead of playing the gig with Brutus, we're going to drive straight to Trutnov and see if I can play there tonight as well as tomorrow. Apparently there are three and a half thousand people at the festival already, the best turnout of any year in its ten year history.

We power down the motorway, then through twisty country roads, Petr making frequent calls on his mobile as he drives. After a while he puts together enough English to tell me a little about his history. Back in the early eighties, he was one of the first promoters of punk music in the former Communist-ruled Czechoslovakia. At first the authorities approved of punks because they had short hair—no more liberal long-haired hippies! Then, when they realised what the punks were actually singing about they saw it as a threat and tried to ban it. Petr continued to put on gigs regardless, until the Communist regime found a simple way to stop him: they threw him in jail.

Trutnov is way over near the Polish border, where the land is heavily forested and begins to rise up to the mountains. As we approach, the weather turns ugly. Black clouds hang over the hilltops and rain slashes down as we edge the minibus through the crowds of bedraggled people milling around the festival site and park up among the tall fir trees around the back of the stage. There is no undercover backstage area, and all the musicians are sheltering from the rain in cars and minivans parked chaotically in the mud.

Apparently all those mobile phone conversations I didn't understand during the journey have achieved something: I'm already on the running order, scheduled to play in about an hour, and from the stage I can hear it being announced that I have arrived. Petr produces a bottle of red wine, pushes the cork through with a knife, puts the Clash on the car stereo and we sit there for a while, the rain hammering on the roof drowning out the sound of the band on stage. Suddenly a thunderstorm breaks out right overhead. Lightning cracks around us and the sky rips open with thunder. I sprint out through the rain to the back of the stage to see how the crowd is taking it, and I'm amazed to see that most of them are staying to watch the band. It's an impressive sight; a vast amphitheatre filled with thousands of drenched people, the tree-lined hills rising up on all sides lit up by the near-continuous flashes of lightning.

Dashing back to the van I'm grabbed by a member of a band called Zona A who were on the same bill as me last time I played in the Czech Republic.

'Hey TV! Do you want to drink some red wine with us?' he shouts, as thunder booms overhead. 'Come and drink some red wine!' He grabs me by the arm and we skid through the mud to a large car already packed with people. Five of them cram into the back and I'm honoured with the passenger seat to myself, next to the driver.

'Hah, TV, you are in First Class!' laughs one of the girls in the back. 'Now you have to plug in your laptop!'

Someone produces a litre bottle of red wine given by a friend in a group from Italy called The Twinkles, and we pass it around while The Clash plays on the car stereo. Well, you can't have too much Clash. Or red wine; when the bottle runs out another one appears. Then another. It's quite a party but there doesn't seem to be any music coming from the stage any more...I'd better go out and investigate.

The rain is easing off a little, but the mixing desk has got a soaking so the band have had to stop until it has dried out. The organisers say it should take about twenty minutes, then the band will finish off their set and I'll be on straight after that. So, back to the car with Zona A and their friends, where another bottle has appeared. How much did The Twinkles bring with them?

Among the trees behind us I notice someone attempting to move a large camper van out into the steep forest track, which now resembles a fast-moving stream. The van slithers sideways in the mud down the slope towards a tree and breaks off a large branch, leaving the splintered remains poking into the side of the van and wedging it firmly where it is. Everyone stands around in the rain pondering the situation, but there doesn't seem to be any way to move the vehicle without ripping a hole through the bodywork. The driver comes over to our car, shrugs his shoulders and takes a glug of the wine. Then a soaked figure comes running through the mud triumphantly waving a saw and proceeds to shin up the tree and cut the jagged branch back to the trunk. The driver jumps back in and pulls the van safely into the path to a cheer from the onlookers. What a great show!

Unlike my show, which is cancelled.

4th August

I rouse from bed in my spartan room in a characterless tower block hotel at eleven and find a note from Petr telling me I'll be playing at ten this evening and he'll be back to pick me up at seven. What am I going to do until then? I go down to Reception, but breakfast is over, the restaurant is closed, the receptionist doesn't speak any English and there is no one else around. I can't phone Petr because I don't have any Czech money. The festival is too far away to walk.

I'm sitting in the lobby pondering the situation when to Petr's van pulls up outside. He's come to tell Zona A what time they will be playing. They were scheduled to go onstage a couple of hours ago, but he couldn't wake them. Fortunately, his return gives me the opportunity to go back to the festival, which has got to be better than hanging around the hotel all day. As we walk down to the minivan, the various members of Zona A and entourage are hanging over the balcony four floors above in various states of undress, waving and chanting 'TV! TV!'

The festival site is damp and muddy, shrouded in mist, but for the moment the rain is holding off. I haven't eaten since yesterday afternoon so I go to look for something now. The only vegetarian thing I can find is in a dingy little caravan with a fat guy sitting in the back, his vest and shorts covered with flour. He is kneading dough, which he then pummels into flat breads and puts into a deep fat fryer, scooping them out a few seconds later and placing them on a draining rack. At the front of the caravan, another guy in a dirty T-shirt sits low behind a serving hatch, reaches round to grab one of the breads, brushes it with an oil and garlic mix from a bowl under the counter, then squeezes tomato ketchup over it, finishing off with a sprinkling of cheese. As he makes mine, he quickly stuffs a handful of cheese in his mouth and a few stray bits fall out and land on the bread. It's a good job I'm hungry.

I walk up the hill to the rim of the amphitheatre to see how the stage looks from the audience's perspective, and bump into a couple of people from Skeptic Eleptic, a band I first met six weeks ago when they supported me at a gig in Austria. They tell me they had a seven hour drive to get here, but were rewarded last night with the best gig they've ever played, a couple of hours before the music got rained off. As I walk back down the hill, I'm recognised by a German band called Happy Cocks who also played yesterday while the weather was still good. They also had a seven hour journey to get here, in a car so old and unreliable that they had to carry a spare engine in the back. I hear a cheery voice calling me and see Kathy, the drummer from Sunderland band Distortion, who have just arrived at the site. They got to Trutnov yesterday night after being stranded in Amsterdam airport because they weren't given the ticket for their connecting flight when they left Britain. Their luggage was pulled off the plane and they had to hang around for three hours until the problem was sorted out. When they eventually arrived in Prague no one was there to pick them up. By the time someone came hours later the storm was in full swing, trees were down all over the road and tractors and bulldozers were out in force to clear a way for the traffic to get through.

Backstage, Zona A introduce me to the Twinkles, who provided the red wine last night. They had a two day trip to get here, stopping the night in Vienna on the way. Their gig was rained off, and they tell me that the organisers are trying to put all of the bands who couldn't play yesterday on today instead. This has left the running order in chaos: The Twinkles have already been moved back twice this afternoon and my start time of ten is looking decidedly unlikely.

Stage manager Tom tells me that the weather isn't the only problem. It seems that the festival has been getting a bad reputation this year: some punks wrecked the train they came in on yesterday, a Mercedes got mysteriously damaged, and a new statue in the town centre of local mythical character Krakonos was destroyed in the night. I've seen pictures of Krakonos on a postcard: he's a big bearded guy with a big hat and a big stick and he lives in the mountains. There may be more to the legend than that, I don't know.

Petr's been gone from the site for a while but now arrives back and lays out some bread and cheese on the folded-down seat in the back of his van, which serves as an impromptu picnic for us and all the other people he knows as they wander past. My start time has come and gone and there's still no sign of me getting to play. Still more bands have appeared on the running order in front of me, many of them distinctly average-sounding—'tired heart music' as Petr describes it—and no one has thought of asking them to play shorter sets. The evening is rapidly getting cooler so I sit in the back of the van trying to stay warm. There's a break in the clouds and for a moment a full moon peeks through but then is rapidly swallowed up and the rain starts again.

Mutiny's afoot. The Twinkles have set up their equipment behind the stage five times already and been put off each time. They're not happy about it. English band Vice Squad arrive and can't understand what's going on. They were supposed to be headlining at eleven—onstage right after me—but have just heard that their start time has been put back to the early hours of the morning. Members of another English band, the Varukers, are wandering around the backstage area giving the organisers murderous looks. Suddenly the guitarist from Vice Squad sweeps past. 'Right, we're telling them that if we don't play at twelve, we're leaving!'

'Don't say that!' I plead, 'You'll bump me even further back!'

The organisers finally seem to get some sense of the bad feeling in the air. Tom comes up to me apologising profusely and says the Varukers will play next, then Vice Squad, then me. After that the Twinkles will finally get to see if their two day car journey was worth it, then any other bands left can take the festival through to the morning.

At shortly after one Vice Squad start and I watch from the back of the stage for a while. At the midway point I go to tune up and am momentarily panicked when I see Petr's van has disappeared—with my guitar in it—until someone tells me that he's just gone to take Distortion back to the hotel and will be back any minute.

It's 2:15 in the morning and I'm just about to get onstage. There are a couple of thousand people still out there, even though it's so late. I'll play until at least three, then I'll have go straight back to the hotel as I need to wake up at seven to be in Prague in time for the flight back to England, which will include a three hour stopover in Zurich, finally getting me home in the early evening.

After two days of hardcore punk bands, what will this audience think of me, alone up there with just an acoustic guitar? I've been waiting three days for this. I hope I have the energy. I hope they understand some English. I can see some faces I recognise from previous gigs among the crowd jostling at the front of the stage and a few people have spotted me plugging in my guitar and are shouting out song titles and cheering. I walk up to the microphone and say, 'Hello! My name is...KRAKONOS!!' and get a big laugh.

It's going to be good.

2. MIND THE GENERATION GAP (2001)

<u>4th December</u>
The tickets for Finland don't arrive in time so I have to get to the airport at 8:00 a.m. to get replacements issued, which takes the woman behind the desk approximately thirty-two seconds and costs me exactly thirty-two pounds. The flight is pretty full and I have to do some fast talking at check-in to persuade them to let me carry the guitar on board and not have it dumped in the hold with the rest of the baggage. As I get on the plane, one of the air hostesses points at the guitar case and says, 'Is that going to be a problem?'

I meet her eye. 'Only if I play it.'

There are TV screens on board showing all the information you could possibly need: time at destination, distance to destination, outside air temperature, flying speed. Our current altitude flickers between 61 and 62 feet—strange, as we haven't taken off yet.

The captain announces, 'The weather in Helsinki is nice. The temperature is about minus three.'

Make your mind up.

For this short tour a Finnish band called Nollaseiska will be backing me. An agent over there sent me their recent indie chart number one single and told me that the band would like to learn the songs from my last album and play them with me. The agent would find the gigs, book me into hotels, and pay me. I said, 'Okay.'

I have never met the band, but I can see from the record sleeve that they are distressingly young. Guitarist Jippo is at the airport to meet me in his dad's big old tan Chevy. We cruise around the icy Helsinki streets for a while trying to find a music shop so we can buy guitar stands and drumsticks, Jippo glancing anxiously at his watch because he has to return the car to his stepmother so she can get to her Egyptian dancing class.

'I am going to have to drive fucking fast to get it back in time,' he worries.

'Not too fast!' I admonish, like a parent.

I check into the Hotel Finn—how do they come up with these names?—then a couple of hours later take the train to a rehearsal studio a few kilometres out of town to meet the rest of the band and run through the songs we will be playing together.

I make the band rehearse for nearly five hours until they are all exhausted. I'm not going to let them get away with being so young. Then lead guitarist and singer Janne drives us back to Helsinki in his Ford Fiesta, 'the oldest, rustiest car in the world.' We get six people and three guitars in it and all cringe when a police car goes past.

5th December

I take the midday train into Tampere to see my friends Punk Lurex OK who are making their new record in a studio near the venue I'll be playing tonight. As I walk in they are working on a song that is a pastiche of 70's Finnish music. 'The rest of the album isn't like this,' they hurry to assure me. People always come and visit the studio just when you're working on the weird track.

I sit in on the session for a while, feeling a bit out of place. Last time I was here Punk Lurex and I were making an EP together, and it feels strange not being involved. Friend and label boss Jukka arrives and we wander out through the snow to his flat so I can pick up some more copies of the EP to sell at gigs. As I enter the flat behind Jukka there is a small screech from inside and Jukka asks me to wait by the door for a moment. His wife Merja likes to do the housework in the nude.

I walk back through the park, avoiding the ducks sitting morosely on the path, deprived of their pond, which is iced-over and shining a luminescent torquoise as the sun sets. The frantic clatter of nearby games of ice hockey echoes around me in the still of the twilight. I drop back into the studio to pick up my bag and guitar, and find Punk Lurex working on a reggae track. They assure me that the rest of the album isn't like this. Then I meet up with the tour agent, Ekku, and go for a quick drink with him in my old Tampere haunt, the Telakka club, to talk about future plans for me in Finland.

I'll be playing tonight in the Tulliklubbi, which is just across the car park from the Telakka, so I leave my guitar there before heading off across town to check in to my hotel. Alas, it's a hostel—a narrow bed, a chair and a sink in a tiny room, with shower and toilet down the corridor. I drop off my bag and get back to the club to find the band have set up and are ready to soundcheck.

Jukka arrives and introduces me to a friend of his who also runs an independent label. He used to release records by Russian punk bands pre-*glasnost*, not easy as they were usually forbidden to leave the country. When he wanted to get one of his groups to play Helsinki he got round the problem by faking an official invitation from a fictitious 'Communist Party of Finland.' The band were given permission to play, but before they left the KGB invited them in for a little chat and told them: 'Go, but remember—if you don't come back, we know where your families live.'

In the dressing room as stage time approaches, Nollaseiska are pacing around looking worried. Janne says, 'I'm so nervous I think I'm gonna puke.'

'Just give it your best,' I tell them sagely, the voice of experience. 'It's going to be great.'

They do, and it is.

The only problem is, after two encores we have played everything we learned but the audience wants more. After ten minutes they are still cheering and I am still trying to push my way through them to the dressing room at the back of the hall, explaining as I go that we don't know any more songs.

I sit at a table with Tiina, Piise and Kukka from Punk Lurex, Tommi and Annastina from the Helsinki crew, and Jukka and Merja. Tiina says it was a great gig but admits to being a little jealous seeing me up onstage with 'those young guys.' We figure that the youngest of Nollaseiska must be Janne and speculate about just how young he might be. I say I intend to find out over the next few days and will let her know as soon as I do. Just then drummer Ronski walks past. 'Look!' says Tiina. 'That one's almost an adult!'

A friend of Punk Lurex wanders over and asks if we'd like to go out to his place on the edge of town for a sauna. The band don't seem too enthusiastic. When I talk to the guy he admits that he once invited them out there after he'd had a few too many drinks. He left them in his house and went outside to fire up the sauna in the cabin. When he didn't return they went to look for him and discovered him fast asleep, lying on his side by the woodpile with his head frozen to the bench. He had to rip out one side of his hair to free himself. I tell him that I'll give the sauna a miss.

As I'm formulating plans with Punk Lurex to go to a club, Nollaseiska bassist Heikki comes over to say he's going to call it a night and go to bed. I say, 'Good boy.'

It's Finnish Independence Day tomorrow, a national holiday, so tonight everyone's out on the town and all the clubs have long queues outside, no fun when it's sub-zero. When you finally get in there are more queues to order a drink, and by closing time at four in the morning we've only managed to get one beer each. Piise and Tiina, who both live out of town, now find they are just two among hundreds of revellers roaming the streets looking for a taxi, of which there are none to be found.

Well, it wouldn't be polite to leave them out in the snow, so all three of us end up back in my hostel room. A beer would be nice right now, but of course there are none to be had. For a joke I point at the cupboard under the sink and say, 'I'll just check the mini-bar.' I open the door with a flourish and find there are three bottles of beer in there.

Unfortunately all three are empty, with the caps put back on. Someone has a very cruel sense of humour.

I pour out three plastic beakers of water from the tap. Live a little! Tiina asks me what time Nollaseiska will be calling to wake me up, and speculates as to whether they will just bang on the door and shout, 'Oi, Grandad!' or tap very gently so as not to startle me. Old people get startled very easily, har, har.

It's past six. The three of us doze where we sit for a while until the morning buses run, then Piise heads for home and Tiina and I slither over the icy pavements to the only place that is open to serve coffee, a bar on the main street. The hardened drinkers are already in there, sitting grimly behind tables lined up with beers and shot glasses.

I head back to the hostel to find Nollaseiska just checking out. We have an eight hour drive to Oulu ahead of us and I have had no sleep. Good to know that I can still set an example to the kids.

6th December

There are nine of us and all the equipment in a mini van with a dodgy gearbox. We drive straight to a kebab place round the corner where everyone else eats a lot of meat and I have another coffee, then we go to a garage so I can get something vegetarian. They don't have anything vegetarian.

On the way out of Tampere we get stuck in the Independence Day parade which is making its way in. Finally we get free from the throng and put on some speed. Only another seven and a half hours to go!

Mid-afternoon we pull into a rest stop in the middle of nowhere. This far North the sky is already dark, a blackness so intense that it overwhelms the limpid light from the service station even before it reaches the surrounding snow-covered fields and forests.

The rest station has a theme, and the theme is 'bells.' There are bells everywhere. There is an enormous bell suspended inside a green fluorescent 'U' as you drive in. By the car park there is a three storey gantry, with bells as tall as a man hanging from it, five in each row; next to it, a half-size version carrying half-size bells. Bells lie haphazardly around, partially buried in the snow, and there is a parade of smaller bells flanking the path to the restaurant and shop. Inside you have to be careful where you sit or you will accidentally nudge the curtains of bells suspended behind you and set them a-ringing.

They sell postcards featuring the bells.

A small cheese roll costs £1.20.

Outside we gather in a little puddle of light around the van preparing to leave when giant speakers hidden inside a ten foot high tripod of handbells next to us blast into life filling the car park with a punishingly-loud amplified mournful synthesiser tune using every minor chord available, while the handbells trip automatically, playing along.

It really is very, very tacky.

Years later we reach Oulu at eight in the evening. We fuel up on coffee in the bar downstairs where the owner shows me his collection of early nineteenth century handcuffs and shackles. During the soundcheck Jippo sings backwards in Finnish.

We are all ravenous. The club was supposed to have prepared some food but there's not much sign of it arriving yet. Jippo comes back from downstairs and tells me that the cooking might be underway soon: 'There is a woman walking around the kitchen holding an onion.'

The club is open until four, and not much seems to be happening yet, so Jippo, Janne and me go to visit Nina, an old friend of the band who lives nearby. Nina has a small, pleasant apartment on the fourth floor with a balcony looking out over the rooftops of Oulu. When she moved from Helsinki two years ago she was quite excited about coming to the picture postcard snowy North but she hadn't counted on her first winter here being the coldest ever recorded. The temperature fell to minus twenty-five degrees and when she went outside her eyelashes frosted over. Now she's at college studying film and television. She shows me a small piece of wood with three converging wires attached to it which she built in the part of her course covering special effects. With this piece of wood, she claims, she can 'explode things.'

I throw down the challenge. 'Go on then, explode something.'

She shakes her head. 'Not in my flat.'

This is the first rule of exploding things: never in your own flat.

I ask if she has a marker pen so I can write out the setlists for tonight, but she can only find a calligraphy pen. The setlists look pretty nice.

We get a frantic phone call from the club to say they are waiting for us to start, and we leave in a hurry.

Another good gig. Now the first one is out of the way the band is much more confident and they are running around all over the stage. Throughout the set, a bald guy in a suit standing right in front of me keeps shouting for 'One Chord Wonders.' I'm amazed that anyone has heard of the song way up here so when I see him in the bar afterwards I go up to him and say, 'Hey, how come you know One Chord Wonders?'

He stares at me blankly. 'I don't.'

Then I notice there is another bald guy in a suit standing at the other end of the bar.

If I hurry back to my hotel now I could get five hours sleep.

7th December

I'm outside the locked front door of the club when the mobile rings. It's Jippo asking, 'Where are you?'

They don't believe the old guy can have got out of bed in time.

'I'm right outside the club.'

'Uh, okay—I'll come down and let you in.'

While we're waiting for the rest of the band I change the strings on my guitar and accidentally stab my finger. I feel the end of the string slide in like a needle, producing an impressive amount of blood. This is not what you want first thing in the morning.

It's another seven hour drive today. We stop briefly at a pizza place on the way out of town, but it's full and we don't have time to wait. But my, they smelled good.

We get into Joensuu at around seven. There's a heavy snow falling and a hush lies over the large town square by the club. While the band greet their mates I go to check in to my hotel, just a five minute walk away. There's enough time to rinse out a T-shirt and hang it over a radiator, then I head back to the club, where the gear is now set up.

After soundcheck, Jippo tells me that he wants me to come and meet his grandma, who's heard all about me and is going to cook some vegetarian food specially. While we're eating, she shows us the local newspaper which says I was once in the 80's band 'The Adtverds.'

Back in the cramped dressing room, a lot of Nollaseiska's friends are passing through, including one drunk guy who was crazy-dancing at soundcheck. He is asking everyone for some of their beer and doing quite well out of it. He is also talking drivel very s-l-o-w-l-y so I keep my head down and try to ignore him, but he soon notices me.

'Hey, old guy!' he calls.

He has my attention. 'Yes?'

'Why are you so *serious?*'

'I don't know. Why are you so drunk?'

Another friend of the band walks in. They tell me he can do incredible impressions of rally cars and trucks.

'Okay,' I say, 'do a rally car.'

'What type?' he asks.

There's more than one?

He chooses an Audi Quatro from the early eighties, one of his favourites. It's extraordinary; his throat wobbles and his cheeks blow out and suddenly there's the sound of a car powering through the dressing room. I almost jump out of the way.

Next he does a McLaren, including pit stop, and a large truck going up through the gears. For an encore he reverses it, complete with warning beeps. We give him a round of applause.

Drunk guy is not happy about no longer being the centre of attention and turns on Rally Car guy. 'Hey! Give me your beer,' he demands.

Rally Car guy thinks about it. 'Normally I would,' he explains. 'But it's mine.'

Things quieten down in the dressing room eventually and I have a chat with Janne, who tells me he moved from Joensuu to Helsinki in 1997, when he was 18. I discreetly send an SMS to Tiina: 'He's 22!'

We have a great gig, marred for me only when one one of the audience grabs the microphone stand and hauls himself up on stage to sing along, pushing his full weight down on to my injured finger which gets trapped in the microphone clip.

Long after the club has cleared Janne, Jippo and I sit with some beers on sofas at a low table talking about how much fun we've had over the last few days, while across the room the three girls who have been running the bar count the takings. Jippo decides it's time I learned another Finnish expression.

'You have to say this when you see a beautiful woman...*Hallo pulu!*'

'Hallo pulu?'

'No—hallo pulu.'

'That's what I said...hallo pulu.'

'There's no "h" in pulu. Hallo pulu.'

'I didn't say an "h". I said hallo pulu.'

'No I can still hear an "h." It's pulu.'

'Oh, so more like a "b"? Bulu.'

'Well, *more* like that, but it's still a "p". Pulu.'

'Pulu. Pulu.'

'Make the "p" with your lips. Look—pulu.'

'Pulu.'

'No, pulu.'

'Pulu...'

I notice the three girls have stopped counting the money and are falling about with laughter. For the last five minutes I have been attempting to say, 'Hello pigeon.'

We all get given drinks on the house, and Jippo finds the CD player and puts on some music. We're there quite a while.

Then I'm somehow walking back to my hotel across the main square, minus seven showing on the thermometer, fine snow falling all around me. I don't seem to have my hat any more.

8th December

The snow has stopped and stars glisten and twinkle in the black expanse of the sky. I am standing high up on the hillside, looking down into the warm amber glow of the town square, where tiny figures move about, preparing the fireworks display, which is just about to start. The first rocket soars above the rooftops and explodes silently, blooming into a thousand vivid colours that shoot outwards then swirl back on themselves, coalescing into the shape of an aeroplane that floats in a lazy spiral back down towards the snow-covered fields below me. It would all be so perfect if it wasn't for that noise, that *peeping* sound disturbing the mood...*peep, peep...peep, peep...*

I switch the alarm off, roll out of bed and force myself into the shower.

The van arrives at the hotel to pick me up, and I see Jippo waving my hat out of the window. 'Hello pulu!' he yells.

It's another seven hour drive, through endless forests under a heavy grey sky threatening more snow. There's nothing to do but gaze out of the window, and snooze occasionally with my head resting on my bag. At one point the road becomes exceptionally wide and Jippo tells me that it was designed to be an emergency landing strip for aircraft. For hundreds of kilometres we have seen only forests and frozen lakes. What kind of emergency could there possibly be?

Much later, Jippo suddenly says, 'You know that film, Titanic?'

'Yeah.'

'I saw it about four years ago, and I just realised—it wasn't so bad.'

Funny what the mind turns to on these long journeys.

We make it to Helsinki in time for an interview I've been asked to do at five, then we soundcheck. The Semi-Final club has replaced its old filthy linoleum floor with a new one made of asphalt so it feels like you are standing in the road.

Janne complains that his hangover from yesterday is just starting to come on and he's going to go home for a couple of hours. Jippo is intending to visit his mother and suggests I come along, but I turn the offer down because I am secretly scared she will be younger than me. Instead I walk back to the Hotel Finn to check in. A temporary thaw has started, snow melt gurgling down the drainpipes and across the pavements.

At the hotel I take another shower and change my clothes to fool myself into thinking I am feeling fit. It works. By the time I get back to the club at nine I'm raring to go. Unfortunately there's a sign on the door saying the gig won't start until twelve, but there are already a few people I know in so I hang around with some of them. Just before ten, while drinks are still half-price, my friends buy enough beer to completely cover the table we are sitting at, and they suddenly become quite popular.

The band arrive back with some bad news: their van has broken down, the 1,400 kilometres we have travelled over the last few days finally proving too much for it. The good news is that it happened here in Helsinki, not in some God-forsaken snowy wilderness.

The Semi-Final club is filling up and the feeling in the air is that this is going to be a good one. With a popular Swedish rock band playing in the larger venue upstairs we had been worried that no one would come to our gig but by show time the place is packed.

It's probably the best gig with a band I've ever had. These are my friends now, not just some strangers who decided to play my songs. The last few days have sharpened us all up, we're playing well together, cranking up the energy level together, and the audience love it.

Afterwards, it's sad to realise that it's all over, just as it was all working so well. We should be going out for another two weeks of dates, we should be ripping through Europe showing 'em what a real band can be like...instead we're hugging each other, saying goodbye, promising we're going to do this again sometime, somehow, somewhere.

Jippo leans back to me as his girlfriend drags him away. 'I'm gonna *miss* you...'

I'm going to miss you too, guys.
Good news from the North: the kids are alright.

3. BLOODY XMAS (2001)

19th December

Looks like everyone's leaving London for Christmas: eight in the morning and four packed queues at the check-in desks, preceded by a lengthy queue to join the queues. Like waiting for a ride at a theme park, but without the smiles. After an hour and a half shuffling forward with my bag and guitar, my flight is about to start boarding but unfortunately there are four Chinese men front of me trying to check in. They clearly understand no English and are having some difficulty with the security questions.

'Did you pack your bags yourselves?' asks the lady behind the desk.

They look at each other baffled, so she tries another tack.

'Could anybody have possibly put anything in your bags?'

No response.

'Your bags.' She points. 'Someone else, could they, er...anything...put in them?'

The men nod and grin in an attempt to be friendly. My flight leaves in twenty minutes.

When I eventually get to the desk, I have to do a lot of persuading before the woman will let me take my guitar on board, then she makes some kind of mistake which freezes up the computer and has to call for help. Finally checked in, I grab my guitar and run through the airport, getting to the gate just as the flight is closing. So much for the idea of buying a few Christmas presents from Duty Free.

When my bag doesn't come up on the carousel at Dusseldorf I stand there while the room empties around me, unable to believe it. I watch the belt go around until it clunks to a stop, then trudge with a heavy heart to the Lufthansa desk where a stern woman takes the details. She tells me the bag is certain to turn up in the next few days.

'I have to get it back today,' I plead. 'I'm a musician and there are things I need in it for a concert tonight.' The sequencer I use for backing tracks on some of the songs is in there. It could be the first ever case of an airline losing an entire band.

She is not interested. She is busy filling out a form.

'What was the last thing you packed in the bag? What will we see when we open it?'

'Well, there's a red folder with some papers in it.'

'Do any of the papers have your name on them?'

'Um. No, I don't think so.'

She sniffs. 'I don't see what can be so important about a folder with some papers in it that you must have it to play your concert.'

And a Merry Christmas to you too.

At least I have my guitar. I should go direct to Aachen for the gig, but I get off the train in Dusseldorf and take a taxi to the office of JKP, my German record label, where I hang around until the next flight from London comes in—but the bag isn't on it. The baggage handlers in London tell me they think they have found it, but it won't arrive in Dusseldorf until 10:30. By then I will be on stage.

I arrange for the bag to be delivered to the JKP office so I can pick it up tomorrow on the way to the next gig in Iserlohn, then I dash back to the station. The train I hoped to catch is cancelled and when the next one arrives there are so many people on it that I have spend the whole hour and a half journey standing.

Klaus and his girlfriend Melanie are at the station to meet me. We hurry into a taxi and rush down to the Wild Rover, the Irish bar where I'm playing tonight. I wait around for a couple of hours getting increasingly worried as the place remains resolutely empty. Everyone's out last-minute bloody Christmas shopping. By showtime there are still only twenty people in, but it's a nice intimate gig and my voice feels in great shape so I play for an hour and fifty.

Afterwards I have a drink with the bar manager. He tells me about a friend of his who went home to visit Ireland recently. He had his guitar with him and had to do some quick thinking at the check-in desk to stop it being put in the hold with the rest of the bags. Although it was a fairly basic cheap guitar he invented a story about it being an irreplaceable and expensive hand-built custom original, far too fragile to survive the journey unless it went in the cabin with him. On board, he stowed his guitar in the overhead locker, settled back into his seat and enjoyed some of the free hospitality during the flight. When he got off the plane at the end he was wandering happily across the tarmac towards the terminal when a stewardess came running after him with the guitar case... 'I think you forgot *this*...'

<u>20th December</u>

I go to the baker's to buy some *Brötchen*, then down the road to Melanie's flat to have breakfast with her and Klaus. There's a light flurry of snow in the air and as I walk along I nibble at a still-warm slice of *Stollen*, a traditional German Christmas cake filled with gooey marzipan that the bakers were handing out for free. Who knows, by the end of today I may even have my toothbrush back.

After breakfast Klaus prints out the directions to Iserlohn from his computer routefinder program. Last time I was here it led us disastrously astray, but he tells me he has 'changed the settings.' Unfortunately we have to go via Dusseldorf to pick up my bag and we miss one vital turning on the way and get hopelessly lost. We drive around in circles for a while, blocked from where we want to go by an endless succession of one-way streets, and by the time we finally get to the JKP office Klaus and I are both fuming. At least the bag has arrived. We should get straight off to Iserlohn but instead I go into the washroom to have a shave and brush my teeth. There's no warm water so the shave is a bit of a disaster—I come out with a couple of nicks on my chin that won't stop bleeding, and I have to keep dabbing at them with paper tissues. This is not what you want when you go to visit your record label.

We're running very late by the time we hit Iserlohn. The new settings on the computer programme don't work and we come into town a different way than we expected and have no idea how to find the Lindehof bar where I should be playing. The streets are clogged with traffic as people do their Christmas shopping, and to make it worse it's now dangerously icy, snow packed high at the edges of the street. Finally we get to within metres of the Lindenhof but there's nowhere to park. The one-way system funnels us off in the wrong direction and suddenly we are miles away and don't know how to get back to where we just came from.

We turn into a street that seems to be heading in the right direction and crawl along under strings of gaily coloured Christmas lights, weaving between the last of the pedestrians heading home with their bundles of gifts, until we reach a sign saying 'No Cars.' We have been driving around Iserlohn for over an hour. Klaus stops the car and we sit there for a moment, our heads in our hands, and weep with frustration.

'Let's just fucking go back to Aachen, fuck the gig.' I say. But we know we would never find the road out. We will be in Iserlohn for ever.

Ten minutes later we summon the strength to try again. Hey, we recognise this street. Hey, there's the Lindenhof! Hey, there's a parking space!

After all that, not many people in, but a pretty good gig, and on the way back the new settings work and we are in Aachen by five in the morning.

21st December

A biggie today—supporting a rare concert by The Boys at a large venue in Dusseldorf called Tor Drei. People are coming from all over Germany for it, including my friend PamP, who named his band 'Garden Gang' after a Boys song and is really looking forward to seeing them for the first time. He's driving all the way from Bavaria for the show.

It's exciting to walk into a great venue like this and know that in a few hours I'm going to be up on the stage. The Boys are soundchecking now and there's already a buzz in the air. The event has been billed as a 'Xmas Punk Rock Party' and 850 tickets have been sold in advance, which means at least a thousand people in tonight.

A couple of hours before I'm due to start PamP phones to tell me he's held up in an enormous traffic jam on the autobahn, still a hundred kilometres away and nothing's moving. He set off first thing this morning, but South Germany has seen heavy snowfalls and the roads are in chaos.

I watch a bit of the support band and I'm itching to get going. I hit the stage running and have a terrific gig. Well, that's me done. Support slots are great: now I can relax, have a few drink and enjoy The Boys.

In the hall there's still no sign of PamP but he could be anywhere in this crowd. No reply from his mobile.

Celebratory mood in the air. The Boys play a great set, then they come back onstage for the encores as their festive alter-egos the Yobs, dressed up in Santa costumes. I almost feel a bit Christmas-y.

PamP rings. He is stuck behind a lorry that couldn't make the hill ahead of him and has slewed sideways and blocked the road. It's sixteen hours since he left home.

Hmm. Most of The Boys and me are supposed to be staying at drummer Vom's place but I'm told he was seen leaving about half an hour ago. I'm starting to think about a back-up plan when his wife Mary appears, stressed out from running the merchandise stand, and assures me we'll be getting a taxi with her. I round up Matt and Cas from the band so we can travel together. Cas is wandering around with a bleary drunken smile on his face and takes some persuading to get into the taxi. When we arrive at Vom's he's reluctant to get out. Matt and I fetch our guitars from the boot and carry them into the house then return to find he has shut the doors of the taxi and is having a little lie down.

Downstairs Vom is entertaining the rest of the band in his very own Pub. He's converted the cellar and stands proudly behind the bar serving up the beer. We are all given silly hats and have to put them on. It's Christmas.

Oops, 7:30 in the morning.

22nd December

At midday I phone up Klaus and arrrange to meet for the drive to tonight's gig in Dortmund, He tells me PamP finally arrived after 24 hours on the road. It's a long way to come to miss a gig.

Over the high ground towards Dortmund the snow starts coming down and the roads gradually turn white, so we breathe a sigh of relief when we finally drive down into the city where the weather is a bit milder and the streets haven't iced over yet. A Christmas market has been set up in the town centre and is alive with people, noise and lights, but we are unable to penetrate the pedestrianised zone around it to reach the Platzhirsch, where I'll be playing, and end up having to park up and walk.

At the end of the narrow bar is an arch leading to a tiny room with some musical equipment strewn about. It's planned that four bands will play here, then I'll go on at around one in the morning. It's billed as a 'Punk Rock Party around the Christmas Tree' but if there was a Christmas tree here there would be no room for the party.

Berze, who booked the gig, comes to say hello. I immediately start trying to negotiate my way down the billing as I really don't want to hang around here longer than I have to, but unfortunately nobody else wants to go on late either because they all want to get drunk. We finally agree that I'll go on third.

A couple of hours later the room is heaving with people craning over each others' shoulders to try and get a glimpse of the band through the arch, the mass of bodies damping the sound from the little P.A. speakers so that halfway down the bar all you can hear is a muffled drone. A little doorway to the left of the arch leads down some steps to the toilets and I find a cramped but relatively quiet corner down there among some broken tables and chairs where I can sit, out of the heat and smoke. Every time someone comes down to use the loo they glance over at me sitting on my own. I feel like the toilet attendant.

The audience is starting to get lively up there now. One pogo-er misses his footing and comes crashing down the stairs followed by a cascade of bottles. When it's my turn to play I go back upstairs, but the band who should go on after me ask if they can go on now because one of them has a birthday today and they need to start drinking. I say okay. I meet a girl fan from Austria who gives me my first Christmas present—a box of dainty, delicate Christmas biscuits.

Start time finally arrives and I wade my way through the sweaty mass of bodies to see what I can do about a soundcheck. I drag the tables holding the P.A. speakers as far back into the room as the short cables will allow to create some space for a few more people. Unfortunately they all pile straight in so then I can't get to the mixing desk any more and have to keep pushing through them to try and get my sound set up. There are three hundred knobs on the mixing desk and no light. Nearly ready to go, I glance down to see I am splashing blood all over the place. A sliver of glass from a broken bottle on the floor has sliced into my middle finger and now I have a half inch cut right where I press down on the guitar. Klaus fetches me a toilet roll to try and clean it up but I am bleeding like a stuck pig. This is not what you want just before a gig.

I'm playing now and the crowd is surging forward around me. About 120 people are crammed into the bar, but only the thirty who have pushed their way into the back room can see anything. It's a rowdy audience, which makes for an exciting if uncomfortable gig. People keep grabbing the microphone to sing along but then don't put it back to my height so I have to sing at a crouch. The support band has made good on their promise to start drinking; one of them is in the front row waving around a bottle of wine, most of it spilling on the people around him. At one point his cheeks puff and he vomits a frothy mouthful on the floor in front of me. Then he carries on dancing.

As soon as the gig finishes I pack together my gear in record time and Klaus and me get the hell out of there, and follow Berze up six flights of stairs to his girlfriend Natje's clean and quiet flat where we can sit down and get some peace. I wash the gore off my hands—*I went to Dortmund for Christmas and all I got was blood poisoning!*—and wipe down the guitar and cables. My bag and jacket which were lying on the floor by the mixing desk have both been soaked with beer, the dainty biscuits are just crumbs.

Natje's parents are visiting and her father, who is a professional chef, has cooked a vegetarian meal for us, a delicious stew of vegetables with baked feta on the top. Berze puts on some Tom Waits quietly in the background. Far below us we hear the sirens of the police arriving at the Platzhirsch. Klaus tells me something I hadn't noticed during the gig: the guy who puked on the floor subsequently fell in it. So there is some justice in the world.

We take a taxi back to Berze's place and I go to sleep in a very cold borrowed sleeping bag which rustles so loudly that every time I turn over I wake myself up.

23rd December

At breakfast Berze apologises for the fridge being full of fish but, well, his flatmate works in the fish market. All his friends are getting fish for Christmas.

We think about a visit to the Christmas market, maybe to drink a *Glühwein* or two before we head off to Oberhausen for the last date of the tour. It will be Christmas in two days, so this could be the ideal opportunity to get all those presents I haven't even thought about yet, but by the time we've gone back to the Platzhirsch to retrieve my guitar stand that disappeared in the scrum yesterday, Klaus and I have to hit the road. It's only a couple of hours to Oberhausen and the snow has held off so we make it by late afternoon in good time for soundcheck. There will be five bands playing tonight in a large venue for Moloko fanzine's Christmas party, with me playing a few songs between each of them while the onstage equipment is swapped around. Sounds chaotic.

I bump straight into Joseph from Blyth Power who is here tonight in his 'other job,' playing drums for the Whisky Priests. We compare our schedules for tomorrow. After the gig Klaus and I have to drive back to his place in Aachen, then I take the train to Dusseldorf airport first thing in the morning to get my Christmas Eve flight back home. It's even worse for the Whisky Priests. Straight after the gig they will get into the van and drive across Germany, Holland and France to get the six a.m. ferry to England. One of the band has to be dropped off in London to get a morning train heading North so that he'll be in time to catch the last connecting train to Berwick, his last hope of getting home for Christmas. Snow on the roads. Nail-biting stuff.

Joseph and I wander upstairs to the dressing room where there is a buffet laid out on a long table. I'm surprised to see him eating some scrambled egg—I'd always thought he was a vegan—even more surprised when I see there's ham in the egg. 'You're not even vegetarian?'

'Oh no,' he says cheerfully,' it's just that I've been in bands with vegetarians so long I've been tainted with the reputation. I'm carnivore central.'

Among the food are some little baskets of mini-choc bars. They all have different wrappers than the familiar English brands so you never know what you will find inside. Joseph suggests making up a chart comparing the different types of chocolate bar wrappers in different countries. Joseph's hobby is trainspotting.

Still no soundcheck, but I've been collared by one of the sound engineers who is in a band who are covering my song 'Bored Teenagers' for their new record and want me to sing along to it in German. *'Wir ha'm Langeweile...wir müssen uns die Zeit vertreiben...'* He plays the backing track to me through the P.A. system, and suggests he could set a microphone up right there and then in the hall and we could record it. I say I would rather get my soundcheck done first.

Soundcheck doesn't happen.

Back in the dressing room, band members are stuffing their bags with mini-choc bars as emergency Christmas presents. They'll need that chart.

I go to start the first of my four mini-concerts and it's soon clear that the idea of playing while the bands set up is a big mistake. I stand helplessly by the side of the stage while one four-piece band is clearing its gear off and another eight-piece band is trying to get their stuff on. The stage crew is too busy with them to get my guitar working. As a consequence I don't start my allotted four numbers until the next band is all ready to go. We don't save any time, and they have to stand behind me, instruments at the ready, all through my set.

Will they resist the temptation to play along?

No.

Do they know any of my songs, including the unexpected chord changes?

No.

Then I pace around the dressing room for nearly an hour, unable to relax because I know I've got to do it all over again another three times.

As soon as the last set is over Klaus and I head straight out to the car. I was supposed to be offstage at 11:15 on the original running order and we'd hoped to be back in Aachen soon after midnight for a goodbye-and-happy-Christmas drink with Melanie, but it's past one already. We set off confidently to negotiate the maze of autobahns around Dusseldorf but I read the map wrongly and before we know it we are driving along a narrow country road, no signposts to be found. I must adjust my settings.

In Aachen the streets are covered by deep packed ice and it's nearly four a.m. by the time we park up in the underground garage. Too late really, but we have to have a quick drink to mark the end of the tour, even though I'll need to be up at eight for the train. With luck I might even make it to the airport in time to buy some Christmas presents. Cigarettes, anyone?

4. PLAN A (2002)

PART 1: SWITZERLAND

19th April

Forgot to order a vegetarian meal with Swissair so breakfast on the plane is a mini croissant. And I mean mini.

Someone from England recognises me while I'm waiting for my bags at Zurich airport. He heard me on Tom Robinson's radio show a few nights ago and is intending to come to the gig tonight. He shows me a printout he's made with the address of the club—Almendstrasse—and asks me whereabouts in Zurich he'll find it. He's a bit surprised when I tell him that it's in Thun, a two hour drive away. Tomorrow.

I go through Customs and negotiate my new wheely bag around a crowd of journalists waiting for the arrival of Die Toten Hosen, who play the only Swiss gig of their European tour tonight. The reporters don't know or care that I'll be there too, guesting on a couple of songs.

René and Mariann are waiting for me, and drive me over to the venue. When the band turn up we try out the songs together at soundcheck, and for me it's a strange experience to be playing them in this huge venue—a cavernous old wooden ice hockey stadium—while ranks of security barriers are erected in front of the stage and gigantic lighting gantries are lifted into place on either side. When we finish, Mariann points out that it was not very punk rock of me to rehearse Gary Gilmore's Eyes with the most famous band in Germany while holding a mug of tea.

The doors are opened and as the first of the audience run down the hall to grab a space at the front, it starts to sink in that this is the biggest gig I've ever played. Come to think of it, there will be more people here than in all of my 150 solo gigs last year put together. Oh shit.

I watch most of the Toten Hosen's set from the guest area by the stage, while beside me limp bodies are hauled out of the sweaty crowd by the medical crew and laid on stretchers. I'm supposed to join the band towards the end of their show, and as the time gets nearer I slip into the dressing room to limber up a bit, and happen to notice a setlist showing the songs in a different order than we practised in soundcheck. Good job I saw that; it would be a bit embarrassing to come on in front of 12,500 people and start singing the wrong song.

In the end it goes fine, but by the time I'm warmed up, it's all over. I stand around in the aftershow party thinking, 'What happened there?'

Tomorrow the tour proper starts, and I'll be leaving the Toten Hosen to their stadium dates and be off performing on my own in rather more modest-sized clubs. I'll be out on the road for a month, just a couple of days off along the way, and with so many gigs ahead of me I plan to get some early nights on this tour: if not the first in bed—Plan A—then, at least—Plan B—not the last. At least sometimes. But by the time René and Mariann get me back to Winterthur and we've had something to eat and seen off a bottle of red wine, Plan A has already gone horribly wrong.

20th April

It's great to be back in the Café Mokka, one of my favourite venues. Since my last visit, the alleyway leading to the door of the club has acquired a set of brightly coloured fibre glass sofas and two life-size model horses. Inside, club manager Beat explains that he'd hoped to get two real horses for a Country'n'Western theme night tomorrow, but no one would hire out any so he's had to make do with fake ones. As I plug in my guitar for soundcheck, rain starts to bucket down outside. The barman unlocks a side door, then he and Beat carry the horses in from the alley, setting them down in front of the stage, where they gaze placidly over at me running through a couple of songs while the barman wipes them down with a cloth.

René has a surprise for me: he's had a backdrop for the stage made, and pretty good it looks too—a blow up of the cover of the latest album, a depressing grey beach with the word 'Useless' written above it. Fits in marvellously with the vases of brightly coloured plastic flowers that festoon the stage.

Shortly before showtime there are quite a few people in, including a couple from Hamburg who had asked me to play a birthday party today; when I said I couldn't because I was already booked in Thun they flew here instead. PamP and Andi from Munich, and my friend Max from Vienna are all here too.

So, the first real gig of the tour, and a nice one. The place is packed by the time I start and I sweat it out for well over two hours. I can see Beat behind the mixing desk at the far end of the club waving his arms in the air and banging along on some percussion. I play seven songs for encores then squeeze past the horses in the corridor and stagger up the back stairs to the dressing room, exhausted.

By the time I have recovered enough to go back down and pack away my guitar the audience has thinned out, and PamP, Andi and Max have already gone back to the hotel. Nice to know some people are good at Plan A.

21st April

René, Mariann and me have some time to spare before we need to set off for tonight's gig in a small bar in Aarau so we go into a café in the town and arrange our tourist programme over an expresso.

First, 'the oldest panorama in the world,' a circular brick building by the Thun lake, its interior painted with scenes of everyday life in the town over the last century. Closed. We walk back to the car through the lakeside park, the pungent scent of wild garlic wafting over us. When René and Mariann tell me that it's quite common to cook with wild garlic, *Bärlauch*, in Switzerland I get interested. I've smelled it enough times in the countryside in England but don't actually know what it looks like, so we leave the path and trample through the undergrowth, sniffing around until we find some.

Next: an exciting-sounding funicular railway ride up an Alp, a twenty minute drive away. Closed. The tourist leaflet boasts that the path alongside the railway has 11,674 steps, the longest staircase in the world, but adds that you're not allowed to climb them 'for safety reasons.' Lucky escape.

Instead we drive into Interlaken, a pretty town nestling in the mountains but spoilt by a profusion of burger bars and tourist shops selling cuckoo clocks. We sit in the Spring sunshine outside the most expensive hotel in town; I drink a green tea, and leaf through a newspaper left behind on the table. Inside is a rather lukewarm review of the Hosen gig in Zurich which says, *even the guest appearance of British punk legend TV Smith couldn't get the crowd going.*

While we're walking back to the car the promoter for tonight phones René to ask, will TV be wanting a stage?

A two hour drive to the venue in Aarau. Inside I spot the flyers for the gig: *Tonight—TV Smith. Two nights ago he appeared on stage with Die Toten Hosen in Zurich Hallenstadion.*

That's all it says.

Everyone here is very friendly and helpful, and soundcheck goes well on the makeshift stage. Behind me René struggles to hang up the backdrop. Pretty soon people start to trickle in, and by the time I start the little bar is comfortably full. It's a nice, intimate gig with a mixed crowd of the smartly-dressed and punk rockers.

Afterwards the punks chat with me and as the hour gets later and they get drunker they take over the bar stereo system and play their punk compilation albums, which inevitably include a few Adverts songs. Every time one of those turns up, the punks turn to me with open arms and expressions of wonder. At the end of the evening one of them puts a toothbrush through his pierced ear.

Back in Winterthur, aware that tomorrow is a day off, I rather neglect Plan A.

Up an Alp

22nd April

We have a long, lazy breakfast on the balcony, then wander into town to shop for ingredients for tonight's meal—Mariann is going to make a salad with the *Bärlauch*, and René is planning chestnut gnocchi.

As Plan A slips by we work out the tourist programme for tomorrow. Looks like there'll be a second chance to go up an Alp before the gig in St. Gallen—the 2,502 metre high Säntis is on the way. 'Maybe we'll also have time to go to the Cheese Museum,' says Mariann.

You have to hold on to your dreams.

23rd April

It's a steep stomach-churning climb in the cable car to the top of the mountain, then we crunch through the snow to the lookout point for a breathtaking panorama over six countries. Perfect peace up here—until the army manoeuvres begin out of sight over the ridge below us and explosions thunder around the mountains and jet planes roar overhead.

Safely back at the base station we get into the car and head off towards St. Gallen. On the slopes either side of the road dun-coloured cows lazily lick each others ears in the sunshine. The fields have a light yellow blush from the first of the Spring flowers. We stop off in Appenzeller to give me an idea of *Heiligen Welt* Switzerland, where picture postcard houses lie scattered over the hills, and all is clean, neat and tidy. René goes to buy the stinkiest cheese he can find in a delicatessen just over the road from a tourist shop selling plastic gnomes.

We drive into St. Gallen, find the club and take a quick photo as someone gets up on a stepladder and starts sliding the letters of my name into the billboard above the entrance door. Inside as we unfold the 'Useless' banner it's hard not to notice that after only two gigs it's reeking of stale smoke and alcohol.

Tuesday evening in St. Gallen and not many in the audience, but they seem to enjoy it so I play for two hours.

As we load up the car we vent the windows for a while to diminish the effects of the stink-cheese which has been sitting in the boot for the past few hours. What with the backdrop in there as well it's going to be a fragrant drive back to Winterthur.

And by the time we get there it's too late for Plan A.

Big in St Gallen

24th April

Not far to go for tonight's gig; it's just a couple of minutes down the road here in Winterthur, so there is time during the day to wander into town and see a symbolist exhibition in the Oskar Reinhardt gallery, which includes a couple of pictures by weird Belgian artist James Ensor.

My fourth time at the Gaswerk and the place is filling up early. That's good—this time I'll be playing early, opening for a young Swiss indie band who have just had a chart hit with a cover of Britney Spears' 'Oops I Did It Again.'

Terrific gig, the audience singing along all the way through. When the band come on after me they begin by giving me loads of compliments: 'Thanks to TV Smith—he's cool!'

They launch into the Britney cover and I slip into the dressing room. When I come back into the club later I see a bunch of people mimicking my guitar style, all with big grins on their faces. That makes me feel good.

25th April

Getting tired now. Should have paid more attention to Plan A. I sit in the car in a daze during the drive to Basel then shuffle blankly after René and Mariann to the venue. A quick expresso perks me up and I'm ready for soundcheck. Today the weather is just like summer and it's obvious things are going to get late as people laze outside in the warm evening. It's always the same: the more tired you are, the later the gig starts. To kill some time, the three of us go for a walk along the river and into the town centre, where we find a bar in a pleasant courtyard.

Back at the venue only forty or fifty people have gathered. They really enjoy the gig so I play around thirty songs, and it's after two by the time we knock back another expresso and hit the road for Winterthur. Don't these venues know about Plan A?

26th April

Today's gig on the Swiss tour is in Austria. Well, just—five hundred metres over the border in Dornbirn.

We arrive at the venue, a decent sized club on the outskirts of the town, at around 6:30 but nothing much is happening. Looks like it's going to be a late one again.

I sit around with René and Mariann in the upstairs dressing room and notice a few board games stacked up on a shelf. Desperate for something to do to pass the time, I investigate one called 'Charts—Der Big Deal mit dem Mega-Hits.' and leaf through the game cards which offer various cash penalties and rewards for your band along the way to the all important Mega-Hit. I read the playing instructions out loud, including one that states 'every band is given a start capital of $20 million.' Oh how we laughed.

The gig goes great until about halfway through, shortly after midnight, when the last bus for the town leaves, along with many of the audience.

A couple of hours back to Winterthur, where we make good inroads into an extremely large bottle of Chianti. Obviously Plan A is never going to work in Switzerland, I will try harder on the German tour that starts in a few days time.

27th April

Tonight's gig in Schaffhausen will be late but we have to turn up early as it's in a restaurant and I should soundcheck before the evening meals are served. Later on, the tables will be moved out of the way for the gig.

One advantage of turning up early is that there's time to eat, and here the food is great. I'm feeling tired, but an expresso wakes me up a bit, and while we're in expresso mode, René suggests a walk through the town to another café where they served a great one last time he was here. We're on an expresso crawl!

On the way back to the venue we pass a McDonald's. They are promoting a 'Seven Days, Seven Cheeses' menu, and it makes grim reading: all those classic Swiss cheeses reduced to something to slap in a fast food burger and renamed McEmmental, McRacclette, McAppenzeller™.

Upstairs in the dressing room, I sit on a sofa next to a forlorn looking cloth orangutan with sad eyes and get ready for the gig. Eventually promoter Flo lets me know that it's time to play. Last day of the tour and I'm over the fatigue now and really in the mood for it. Downstairs the restaurant is stuffed with people. On the way to the stage two German fans who have travelled from Hanover for tonight's gig say hello. A six and a half hour journey—I'd better be good.

I start off with an unplugged number, explaining to the crowd that the venue is just about small enough to give it a try. Perhaps I should have told Flo as well: he is down in the cellar changing a beer barrel when he hears me begin, unamplified. Thinking the P.A. isn't working, he comes running to the stage and pushes up all the faders on the mixing desk, creating howls of feedback.

I love these little packed gigs, everyone right in front of me, the energy bouncing back from them. I feel fit and in form and play for over two and a half hours.

Finally after six encores I get off the stage and push my way through the crowd towards the dressing room while people thank me and clap me on the back. Upstairs I sit gasping, drenched with sweat, and drink so much water my stomach bulges. From down in the venue I can hear an excited buzz of voices.

I swear that ape looks happy.

PART 2: GERMANY

30th April

One day at home—just enough time to put my clothes in the washing machine—and suddenly I'm off again for a three week tour of Germany.

I cause a bit of a rumpus on the escalators at Stansted airport when my new wheely bag falls over and causes a chain reaction below me, toppling bag-laden travellers like ninepins.

I'd been a bit nervous about finding my way around the German rail system on this tour, and spend some time reading the instructions on the ticket machine at Frankfurt airport's railway station. I must look like I know what I'm doing: a German guy comes up and asks me how the machine works so I end up having to explain it and put the money in for him, then miss my train by 53 seconds.

Matze and Nikko from support band Nichts Gelernt are at Mainz station to meet me. They drive us to tonight's gig, a little pub called 'Hafeneck,' today celebrating its fourth anniversary.

Already sold out with 130 advance tickets, it's difficult to see how everyone's going to fit in here. The room is small and not really designed for bands—it literally goes round a corner, with a tiny stage made of two wooden pallets at the bend and a P.A. speaker in each room. People are gathering outside as I soundcheck, standing around in the warm evening and occasionally nipping in to fetch a beer from the bar.

The gig starts and everyone squeezes in somehow. Nichts Gelernt's drumkit takes up the entire stage, the amps are balanced on the window sill, and the band members stand—slightly restricted in their movements—on the benches on either side.

After the band finishes, club owner Christoph gets up to sing some *chansons* accompanied by a piano player, then I start as soon as I can after that. It's a very exciting couple of hours, and the crowd won't let me get away without an encore despite the fact we are running slightly over the ten o'clock curfew, after which the neighbours tend to call the police.

By the time I've dried off and packed away my guitar the party is in full swing. Records are being played and the room is still packed. Everywhere I turn people want to talk to me and buy me drinks. A couple of punk girls with full mohicans grab Matze and me and insist on a round of Jägermeister—dangerous stuff—and as soon as it's down order another one. I try and surreptitiously slip away but there's not much room to escape in a bar this small. They soon catch up with me: 'TV—you forgot your Jägermeister...'

After a couple of hours it's hard to understand what people are trying to say over the volume of the records and the general hubbub in the room. There's no escape, not even in the toilets. There are two urinals there. The guy standing next to me gives me the quick up-and-down...

'TV Smiss...'

Slightly drunk, I revert to English. 'Excuse me. TV Smiss is having a piss.'

Oops. It's 4:30. What about Plan A? I collar Christoph's wife Susi and ask if she'll take me to their flat upstairs and show me where I'll be sleeping. She lets me in and leads me to their music room where a folding bed for me has been set up next to two grand pianos. When I ask Susi if she knows how to play, she sits down and, with apologies for not being note-perfect, delivers four atmospheric pieces by Chopin. After hours of ear-bending conversation and extreme volume hardcore punk I think Moonlight Sonata is the most beautiful and mysterious thing I have ever heard.

Still bloody noisy down there. Maybe I should call the police?

1st May

Hmm. No hot water, and no one else up yet. I have a shave and a quick wash but don't feel strong enough to risk a cold shower.

We all meet up again in the bar soon after midday and Christoph and Susi lay out a huge spread for breakfast put together from the leftovers of the feast they provided free for everyone who came to Sunday's 'official' birthday for the Hafeneck. Across the table

Matze tells me how shortly after I escaped upstairs last night one of the Jägermeister girls threw up on his trousers. They're coming to the Dusseldorf gig next week!

Susi says, 'I think that was the best party we've ever had here. And we've had A LOT of good parties here.'

Time to leave for Kassel. I tell Christoph and Susi that I hate goodbyes, give them both a hug, then roll my bag over the road to the Nichts Gelernt tourbus. Great idea these roller bags, until you try and cross tram lines.

It's a three hour drive to Kassel. When Nichts Gelernt originally asked if they could support me here at *Das Haus* I explained that the venue was no larger than an average living room. They said they wanted to do it anyway, but when we walk in they still seem taken aback at just how small it actually is.

It's going to be a late one, looks like I won't be on stage—er, there is no stage—looks like I won't be *starting* before midnight. Promoter Ede takes us to his nearby flat and that kills a couple of hours. It was planned that I would be sleeping here tonight, but Matze and Nikko say that they'll be driving back to Mainz after the gig and if I come with them it would take me a good deal of the way towards tomorrow's gig in Karlsruhe.

'But I don't have anywhere to stay in Mainz,' I point out.

'Christoph and Susi will put you up again,' says Matze. 'They'd be *delighted* to have you. I'll ring them up...'

Even at eleven when Nichts Gelernt are due to start the venue isn't full. Ede tells us that yesterday there was a big all-night party at *Das Haus* for International Workers Day, and most of the usual crowd are still at home with hangovers.

As soon as it's over we pack up rapidly, load up the van and leave at around 2:45. On the journey back we crack open a packet of biscuits and pass round three bottles of water. You people don't know what you're missing.

It's around six in the morning when I ring on Christoph and Susi's doorbell to wake them up so they can let me in to the flat. 'I told you I hate goodbyes,' I say. They lead me into the music room, then decide to have a little break from sleep and sit around a table with me for half an hour chatting, while outside the birds start singing.

2nd May

I've been shown the button I need to press to make the hot water work so this morning I get to have a shower. Downstairs I eat the leftovers of the leftovers for breakfast while Christoph tells me about the next show at the Hafeneck—a book reading by four authors, one of them a satirical writer called Bdolf. Bdolf—like Adolf, geddit?! The book reading will be a different kind of event to the gig the other night, with tables and chairs set out and everyone seated. Christoph looks a bit surprised when I ask him if there'll be candles on the tables. This is because I have mixed up the German word for 'candle' with the word for 'kitten.'

Christoph and Susi drive me to the station and we say our goodbyes again.

An hour and a half later I'm in Karlsruhe. I have an address for the club but no phone number so I load my gear into the back of a taxi and ask the driver to take me to Schwarzwaldstrasse. He says, 'This is Schwarzwaldstrasse.' I unload my gear again, and roll my bag down the road, keeping an eye out for any graffiti-covered buildings, the usual sign that I'm getting near the venue.

Smash Capitalism! Keep warm—burn the rich!

Looks like I'm there.

I've knocked on all the doors and rung all the bells and so far have only heard one distant voice from inside saying 'I haven't got a key,' when Tobi, one of my email contacts for the gig, arrives in his car. He lets me in and shows me round the venue: on the ground floor a large room with a stage where well-known bands play; down in the cellar a funky warren of little rooms you climb between through holes knocked in the walls, including one slightly larger room, big enough for a couple of hundred people at a squeeze, set up with a stage and P.A. system. This is where I'll be playing. Up on the top two floors are some rooms where people live, including an empty one with three mattresses on the floor which will be mine for the night. When I point out to Tobi that I don't have a sleeping bag he goes down to the car to fetch his for me. It's one of those heavy duty all-weather ones with arms and hood, like an enormous coat.

Everything sounds a bit dull and flat at soundcheck and when I stick my ear in front of the P.A. cabinet I notice that there's absolutely no sound coming from it, all we'd been hearing in the room was the sound of my onstage monitors. Soundman Franki tracks down the fault and before long we're up and running again. Co-promoter Heiko turns up along with support band Teenkrieg, who emailed me before the tour to ask if they could play a few numbers with me at the end of the gig and I said, why not? We try the five songs they've learnt at the end of their soundcheck and it all goes pretty well. Then it's upstairs to the main venue, which is currently being used as a refectory—a hearty vegetable stew with garlic bread has been prepared for everyone living in the house and all the musicians, and is also on sale for a negligible price to early arrivals for tonight's show.

By gig time the cellars downstairs are packed and I can hardly get a glimpse of Teenkrieg's set. It's already getting on for midnight when they finish so I get straight down to it. First time I've played in Karlsruhe and it won't be the last—the gig is great and the songs with the band go down a storm.

After the gig a spontaneous open mic event happens, where various members of the audience, most of them in states of extreme drunkenness, get on stage in twos and threes and wail whatever they like into the microphone. A lot of it seems to consist of good natured insults aimed at their friends and snatches of obscene songs. I learn a few new words. From my stool by the bar at the furthest end of the cellar from the stage, which I have decided to use as my dressing room, it's all quite funny.

Things get a bit hazy around now. Franki is behind the decks in his other role as DJ, playing some good records. His girlfriend Moni is working behind the bar and opens a bottle of wine, most of which seems to find its way into my glass. I ask Moni when they close here and she replies, 'When everyone has left.'

Upstairs, a mattress on the floor and a big-coat sleeping bag is waiting.

3rd May

Those members of the house who aren't too hungover gather round a table in the top floor for a communal breakfast, then I set off through the pouring rain with my guitar case and roller bag to the train station. Some of the puddles are coming up over the wheels.

I get in to Frankfurt at five, and just as the train comes to a stop, tonight's promoter Silke rings up, which is handy as I've just realised I don't have her phone number and have no idea how to get to the gig. The rain is still thundering down when she picks me up in her little car an hour later. She's only recently got the car, and is just discovering where it leaks.

We drive to the Elfer club, where it looks like it's going to be another late start. Meanwhile, in the dressing room Silke has prepared a local speciality for me and the support band: the famous Frankfurt seven herb green sauce.

Since you ask: parsley, borage, chives, dandelion and er, three others. Everyone in Frankfurt is an expert on the seven herb green sauce, but everyone has a different opinion. Okay—there are seven herbs, minimum, but you can have more than seven as long as it includes the basic seven. Basil? You can have basil in it, but not unless you've already got the basic seven. Marjoram? Not unless you've already got the seven. Garlic? You don't have garlic in green sauce! Should the chopped hard-boiled egg be in it, or on the side? It's a culinary minefield. One thing is for sure: you have it with boiled potatoes. Or rice.

The support band wave their forks in approval. '*This* is the genuine Frankfurt seven herb green sauce.'

The first time I played in Frankfurt there were fifteen people in the audience. Then I avoided it for a while. Last year I played here in the Elfer and the club was half full, tonight it's packed. We have a great gig.

Much later, we leave the car at the venue and get a taxi back to Silke's place where there is a fold-up bed for me.

4:59 lights out. So much for Plan A.

4th May

I'm at a magic show and sitting right up there on the side of the stage so I can see how all the tricks are done. Then I wake up.

The rain is holding off for the moment so Silke and I amble over to the nearby fruit and vegetable market to buy some things for breakfast. On some of the stands I see the packs of fresh herbs that go to make the green sauce, and when we get back to the flat I find the wrapper from yesterday and study it over breakfast. So here it is, definitively, the seven herbs required for the 'Echte Frankfurter Grüne Soße' (pay attention at the back):

Parsley, chervil, sorrel, pimpernel, chives, borage, cress.

'No basil?' says Silke's boyfriend.

No, *you can only put in basil if you've already got the seven.*

Silke takes a cab to the Elfer to pick up the car, then drives me to the station. We load up and head off in good time but on the way the engine keeps cutting out and finally refuses to start again, leaving us stranded in the middle of single-lane street we have driven up to avoid the massive traffic jam on the main streets caused by a demonstration by some neo-Nazis and the consequent counter-demonstration by anti-fascists. A line of cars builds up behind us while Silke desperately pumps the pedal. 'There's got to be a trick to it...'

Eventually a guy gets out of the car behind us, glances in the driver's window, says 'Oh, a woman,' and pushes us to the next junction so he can get past. I'm now late for my train. Silke tries the engine a few more times then looks across at me. 'You'd better go.'

I roll my bags in the pouring rain to the nearest U-Bahn, arriving at the main station thirty minutes later, wet, cold and flustered, and with a bad conscience about leaving Silke stranded.

I've just bought my ticket and am hurrying towards the platform when René phones to tell me he has just got to Stuttgart after a few hours drive from Switzerland; am I there yet? René booked the gig, so for today he is my official manager. I explain that I'm still in Frankfurt.

After a long boring train journey watching the rain pile down over the German countryside I wait shivering in Stuttgart station until René and Mariann arrive. We just have time to drop my bags off at the hotel before soundcheck. The room is clean, comfortable, and the first private space I've had for five days. There's also a very good view out of the window of the most boring office block in Germany.

Tonight's gig is in a very big club, slightly worrying as I'm not aware of having much of a following in Stuttgart. The stage is larger than the most of the clubs I usually play. All the same, I kind of like the place, and also like the look of the gigantic P.A. system—whether anyone comes or not at least it's going to sound good. Well, loud.

René has brought the backdrop with him in the car, so he and two of the guys from the club set about the complicated business of getting it hung from some lighting bars on the ceiling, which involves high ladders and wire cables. The backdrop is pumping out an even more pungent aroma of beer and smoke than the last time I used it but luckily the room is so large it should dissipate harmlessly. The club puts out some tables and chairs to fill out the space in front of the stage and the place begins to look pretty good.

Not many people in, but some nights I just feel right onstage, and this is one of them. I play my longest-ever set at 41 songs.

5th May

René, Mariann and me walk around chilly Stuttgart until we find a café that sells a good expresso. Then we hit the road for Munich and arrive in time for a quick wander around some of the tourist sights in the old-town centre which, despite my many previous visits here, I've never seen except on postcards.

I have a few technical problems in soundcheck which get me a bit twitchy but finally everything seems to be working. The room soon starts to fill, there's a really good buzz about the gig, and I end up playing only two songs less than yesterday.

After the gig, René and Mariann go off to their hotel, and my old friends from Garden Gang, PamP and Andi, drive me back to their flat in a village outside Munich, where they cook up a dish of veggie-*Wurst* and potatoes. Then we drink a couple of *Weizen* and suddenly it's 6:00 a.m. and the bloody birds are singing. Plan A is going very badly.

6th May

Ah, a day off. It's late afternoon before we all meet up with René and Mariann in Munich's Viktualenmarkt, its stalls overflowing with produce from the Bavarian countryside. We share a bottle of Prosecco in an organic shop and restaurant, then René and Mariann say their goodbyes—they have to drive home to Switzerland. I hate goodbyes. And they're taking the backdrop with them.

PamP and Andi walk me around a few of the tourist sights I missed yesterday, including the world-famous Frauenkirche.

'You know, all my life I've lived here and I've never once looked inside,' says PamP. We have a quick peek. He hasn't missed much. A sign on the wall says: 'This is a house of prayer. Please wear respectful clothing.' I am wearing my bleach-streaked jeans and 'Only One Flavour' jacket.

As evening falls, we have an extremely good meal in another organic veggie restaurant on the edge of the market, then drive back to PamP and Andi's place, where Plan A fails again.

7th May

Ah, another day off. The sun is shining over Bavaria so I sit outside for a few hours while my clothes are in the washing machine, then hang everything out to dry. I am ready for a fresh start.

8th May

PamP and Andi have decided to come to the next couple of gigs, so they will drive me up from Munich to Dusseldorf despite the bad experience they had last time they attempted this trip, just before Christmas when they came to see me supporting The Boys and got stranded on the motorway overnight in the snow. This time the sun is blazing and it's an uncomfortably hot and sticky drive.

Three hours down the autobahn and still only halfway there we pass Frankfurt airport, where I arrived for the start of this tour. I check my diary and see it was only nine days ago. Unbelievable. Feels like forever.

Over the next few days the three of us will be staying at Toten Hosen drummer Vom's place, and during the journey I tell PamP and Andi how nice it is there: a few weeks ago I was over doing some recording with him, and every day when we got out of the studio we went back to the house and straight down into his private bar in the basement, drank the free beer he gets delivered in a sponsorship deal and laughed ourselves stupid. Even though Vom won't be there this time because he's out on tour, his wife Mary has assured us that the bar will be open for business, so we've got that to look forward to when we get back from the gigs. Having played for many years herself in a band called B Bang Cider, Mary knows what it's like.

We're running late, so we head straight to the venue in Ratingen, just outside Dusseldorf, and get straight into soundcheck. There are already quite a few people hanging around outside the Lux, looks like we might get a good crowd in tonight. There are a lot of technical problems in soundcheck, but somehow everything ends up working and afterwards PamP and I dash off in the car to Vom's place so Mary can give us a key to get in after the show.

We make it back to the club just before gig time and the place is packed. It's a very exciting gig with a lively audience and I'm in good voice after the couple of days off, but there's no air conditioning in the room and I'm soaked with sweat after a couple of numbers. So much for the freshly-washed clothes.

Down in the dressing room I guzzle water and promoter Fichli and some friends come down and we hang around chatting for a while. Then PamP, Andi and me head back to Vom's place, tiptoe in so as not to wake Mary and young son Jez, and go straight down to the cosy bar where—finally—we can relax.

As Vom's not here I take the role of barman, get the beers out of the fridge and pass them round, then take my position on the bar stool. We clink the bottles, and sigh in relief to finally be sitting in peace and quiet. We don't think much about it when we notice a few ants flying around the lampshades over the bar. PamP takes another sip, glances upwards and says, 'One day a year they fly.'

Today's the day. Ten minutes later there is a whirling maelstrom of ants around us, diving into our hair and clothes, swimming in our beer. We can hardly see each other through the insect cloud. It's impossible to stay in the room so flapping our hands frantically over our heads we head for the door, grabbing some bottles from the fridge on the way. In a state of shock we sit outside onto the verandah where we talk in whispers for half an hour then head up to the top floor to bed.

9th May

There's no sign of them. Okay, a couple of dead ones on the bar, but apart from that, nothing—like one of those murder mysteries, where by the time the police arrive the body has disappeared. I expected a scene of chaos and destruction. Mary smirks mockingly. *Yeah, the big punk rocker worried about a few little ants.*

Late afternoon Mary drives us to the Coffey so Jez can watch the soundcheck—he's never seen his uncle Tim on stage before. It's a nice little cellar club with a decent P.A.—also pretty loud, and the sound engineer advises Mary to take Jez upstairs again to protect his ears. But I'm never happier than when I can hear everything loud. The sound is bouncing around the stone walls and I'm hearing exactly what the audience will be hearing. My only worry is that this little room will get too full later—there's a lot of interest in the gig.

I leave PamP and Andi to set up a merchandising stand in the upstairs bar, and go back to the house with Mary where I keep myself calm by sitting in the garden in the warm evening as the sun goes down. In genuine rock'n'roller style Mary opens a beer bottle with a cigarette lighter and I express my admiration.

'I've never been able to do that,' I say.

She says, 'Ten years in B Bang Cider.'

'Yeah—but I've been gigging for twenty-five years.'

She just looks at me. *'Ten years in B Bang Cider.'*

We leave the van at the house and get a taxi to the club. As expected, the gig is a sauna—so packed and hot that many people have to take time out during the set and grab some air upstairs before coming back into the cellar for another dose.

I've been making the occasional derogatory comment about Britney Spears-type pap pop music from the stage over the past few gigs, and at one point tonight some people near the front unroll a banner saying 'TV Spears we love you!' I have to stop the show and celebrate my first ever banner.

The crowd are really on my side and singing along to all the songs, which fills me with energy. I get a lot of requests and play most of them. There's no dressing room, so when I finally call it a night, I sit on the side of the stage dripping with sweat and trying to get my breath back while loads of people talk to me.

'It's amazing to see you up there playing for two hours,' says one guy.

'Two *and a half* hours,' I correct him.

Quite a crowd of people are coming back to Vom's bar, including Mary's old friend Monique, who is something of a rock'n'roll legend around here. As a large party of us stagger out into the streets of Dusseldorf to find some taxis she is a couple of steps ahead of me and shouting over her shoulder for the benefit of the entire town.

'An Englishman who speaks German....well, *really*!'

'I'm sorry.'

'It's just not right...YOU SHOULD BE ASHAMED OF YOURSELF!!'

Monique was also in B Bang Cider.

There are seven or eight of us around the bar, and PamP has barely uttered the words, 'It's a good job ants only fly one day a year,' when we notice the first one fluttering around the lampshade. Within ten minutes the air is thick with them. They tumble around in a silent swarm, blotting out the light, even worse than last night, but this time it's war: flying ants versus B Bang Cider. Mary and Monique sit either side of the bar, slapping the ants down with cigarette packets and dredging them off the bar to the floor. 'BASTARDS! BASTARDS!' shouts Mary.

Monique fetches a large white plastic bowl filled with water and puts it on the bar underneath the lamp and all the ants gather on the bright surface and march triumphantly around it, shortly before they get drowned. It's a scene of massacre, a thick scum of dead ants on the water, a black carpet of them on the bar surface and the floor. After half an hour of slaughter we are making some headway but somehow the party mood has gone.

10th May

I get up fairly early and spend some time gardening with Jez, which mainly consists of digging little holes with a toy spade and then saying, 'Whew, that was a lot of work!'

Tonight's gig is just down the road in Cologne in a venue called the Sonic Ballroom. Far from being a ballroom, the venue is actually a small bar without a stage or monitors, which I played on the last tour with Garden Gang supporting. Tonight, without drumkit and band amplifiers, there's more room than I remember and I feel quite comfortable set up in the corner between the P.A. speakers.

There are lots of people in the audience I recognise from previous gigs, including quite a few from Dusseldorf—surprising considering the notorious rivalry between Dusseldorf and Cologne. Someone from Dusseldorf innocently asks me to make a big announcement at the beginning of my set welcoming everyone from Dusseldorf to the gig, but I'm wise to it. I do get a bit involved in some inter-town drinking rivalry where both sides insist on buying me their local beer—*Altbier* and *Kölsch*—throughout the gig so I can pronounce on which I prefer. Diplomatically I drink quite a lot of both.

The gig is packed and I play forever.

Back at Mary's we venture down to the bar, take one look at the killing fields—the big white bowl of water with its inch-thick layer of ants floating on the surface, the black expanse of mangled bodies lying scattered over the bar and floor—and retreat upstairs to bed.

11th May

The gig planned for today in Oelde was cancelled a few weeks ago because the town council had double-booked the venue for a meeting and for some reason that took preference over me, but Vom is playing with the Hosen in Cologne tonight so PamP, Andi and me are going to drive over there to see the gig. Mary's not coming because she's going to see them tomorrow, and anyway she needs to stay home to clear up the corpses in the bar.

The venue in Cologne is a massive modern sports stadium ringed by multi storey car parks, 15,000 people packed in it. I go to watch the support band from side stage and get handed a piece of paper over the security barrier saying, 'TV Smith—we ™ you.' It's nice to feel ™ed. But a gig like this is a different world to the little club gigs I play. Tomorrow in nearby Leverkusen I know I will be lucky to get one percent of this crowd.

After the show I catch up with Vom and am surprised see that his eye is red and swollen—I hadn't noticed that from down in the audience. He tells me that his cymbal stand was placed too close to the drumkit on the stage and on the first beat of the first song he hit the cymbal and the drum stick rebounded straight into his eye. He's refused the offer to go to hospital because he just wants to get home after a week on the road, so after a couple of hours doing the requisite meet and greet in the aftershow party he sneaks out with me and PamP and Andi, hoping he won't get recognised on the way to the car. Wearing a Toten Hosen hat and carrying a Toten Hosen bag is probably not the best idea.

Pretty soon we're wandering round a vast concrete loading bay area, completely lost. When we eventually emerge into the car park and follow the signs to the floor where we parked, we find that we have reached the right number bay but are in the wrong car park, so have to walk past all the dispersing fans to the other side of the stadium. It's one of those nights.

But it's a quick trip back to Dusseldorf, and when we get into Vom's bar there are no ants.

12th May

Mary's taking Vom into hospital to get his eye checked out before he leaves on the tourbus, so I take on babysitting duties and watch the Thunderbirds film on video with Jez. Pretty exciting it is too.

PamP and Andi will be driving home today, leaving me to get around on my own, so as soon as Mary's back from the hospital I get in front of the computer and work out my train times and routing for the next few days. At around six I get on the train for Leverkusen, where I'll be playing tonight in the *Autonomes Zentrum*. One of the workers there, Matthias, picks me up from the station and explains that tonight is the first gig they've put on and really the place isn't finished yet. Uh oh.

It's a medium-sized room, walls and doorways still being knocked through, dust everywhere, a few old sofas along one wall, a makeshift bar along another. In one corner a threadbare red rug lies over the concrete floor. This is where I will play.

I attempt a soundcheck and it's not too bad—the only real problem is that I have to plug directly into the mixing desk which is sitting on the bar, far away from me. My guitar cable isn't really long enough and hangs across the room like a skipping rope.

Doesn't look as though there will be as many here tonight as at the last few gigs, although there are already a few people I recognise. One girl comes up and asks me where I'll be staying tonight, eying up the tatty sofas with concern.

'I'm not sure,' I say, 'With the promoter somewhere, I think. Hopefully not here!'

She wanders off, and in five minutes is back. 'It's all settled,' she says brightly. 'You can stay with my mother. I phoned her up and she says it's okay.'

Just then Henne, who booked the gig a few months ago before he moved to Bremen, arrives after a six hour journey in heavy traffic and assures me that the venue has a bed for me.

Time's getting on and there are still not many people in. Most of those who are here hang around in the fresh air outside, enjoying the last of the day's warmth as the sun goes down. Before I start to play, Mathias' girlfriend offers to show me the renovation the collective has been doing upstairs. They've been at it a year now but still haven't got the lights in, and we realise as soon as we get upstairs that it's now got quite dark and we can't see a thing. We feel a bit foolish stumbling around from room to room in the murk: '...and this will be the kitchen...I know it looks just like the office at the moment...well, it all looks the same at the moment...' They are planning some good things up here, though: information and advice centres, an office to help refugees. Unfortunately over the last year the number of helpers has been tailing off, and there's still a long way to go before everything's finished.

As it's pretty empty tonight I plan to play a shorter set, but then start taking requests and before I know it I've been on stage—I mean, on carpet—for two and a half hours. Oops, I did it again.

We take two carloads back to where I'll be staying the night and my heart sinks when I see a room full of mattresses and comatose bodies, but—no, Henne's as good as his word and there's an office with a bed in it where I'll be sleeping.

Seven or eight of us gather in the kitchen with a bottle of wine and some beers and I start to wind down. I have strange aches and pains over my body and discover a bump on my head that I don't remember getting.

Henne tells me about a recent trip he made to Italy with some friends. They planned to make an appearance at the Genoa anti-globalisation demonstration then tour around for a few days to see a bit of the countryside. They managed to avoid getting caught up in the violence at the demonstration but the next day were stopped in their camper van by the Cabinieri, who accused them of being involved in the riots. Their van was searched and the Cabinieri immediately noticed a red flag with a black star in the middle hanging from the back window and arrested Henne and his friends for being part of a terror group. The flag also had a skull and crossbones in the middle of the star—it's the official Toten Hosen logo. Henne was in prison for six weeks until the band's record company were able to convince the Italians that the flag was a piece of band merchandise, bought from them, and he was finally released. This year he may try a different country for his holidays.

During the course of the last few hours people have been trickling off to bed and Plan A has trickled off with them. Now it's time for me to slip away into the office, open my guitar case to air out the sweat, and lie down beneath the giant Taxi Driver poster.

13th May

It doesn't seem right—my favourite club in Hamburg, the Knust, torn down to be replaced by a mega-discotheque. Norbert, the promoter, managed to find me another venue but it's just not going to be the same.

After a freshly cooked tofu-heavy breakfast in Leverkusen, Henne and Matthias drive me to the station. There's a four and a half hour journey ahead of me, and the connecting train in Cologne is nearly an hour late, which leaves me a bit nervous about whether or not I'll make it in time for soundcheck. I grab a cab from Hamburg station but the driver hasn't heard of the Marquee club and I don't have a number for it so he drops me off in the Reeperbahn and I pull my wheelie bag around the neighbouring cobbled streets until I find it. Over cobbles, the wheelie bag becomes a drag-a-bag. Also, due to a basic design fault, every time I let go of it to check my directions, it falls over.

The Marquee is yer basic rock club, painted black, good stage and P.A., looks like it could hold a couple of hundred people. Inside, the manager introduces me to a Spanish punk band who were supposed to play last night but arrived too late, so could they possibly play before me tonight? I notice they already have their gear set up on the stage, so I say OK. They seem pleased: 'Oh, thank you Mister TV Smith, punk rock hero!'

Downstairs in the filthy dressing room the band have already laid waste to the bread rolls that have been put out for me, leaving just a couple of non-vegetarian salami ones.

I do my soundcheck, then rumble my bag back to the Reeperbahn, where the club has booked me a cheap hotel tucked in among the sex shops. Outside the window, the ledge is covered with two inches of bird shit, in the middle of which a bedraggled pigeon sits. Yes, life could be worse.

I wash out my sweat-soaked T-shirt from last night, hang it on a towel rail to dry, and pull a new one out of my bag. I meet two guys in a bar for a radio interview, then later when I head back to the club I find Norbert outside enjoying the fine evening weather—along with most of the audience. He mentions that he's also promoting a gig in the Tanzhalle, a couple of doors away, and there's some hot food there if I'm hungry. But it's too soon before going onstage. I take a last breath of the fresh evening air then go down to the filthy dressing room and round up the last few sips of water from the Evian bottles which had been left in the fridge for me, but have all been opened by the Spanish band and now lie scattered around the room, partly emptied.

Upstairs in the venue, it's already hot. I watch the band hurtle through their last few songs of bluesy speed rock to thin applause then get on stage as quickly as I can.

Okay—it's not the Knust, but a lot of the audience from the Knust shows are here and give me a great reception. I can also see some familiar people from Dusseldorf, and halfway through the gig they lift up a large sheet of cardboard saying 'HEY TV! HERE'S YOUR SECOND BANNER,' which makes me laugh. A few songs later a piece of paper towel is placed on the stage from the front row, written in lipstick on it: '3rd Banner. All good TV things are 3!'

I make it a long gig, nearly three hours again—because all good TV things are 3—but it's hot up there and by the last half hour it feels like my brain is banging around inside my skull.

I collapse in a pool of sweat in the squalid dressing room, where a second round of *Brötchen* had apparently been laid out but has been demolished by the other band while I was on stage. A large slug crawls over the threadbare carpet. My soaked clothes cling cold and clammy to my skin. There are no towels.

I've hardly gathered my breath before one of the band barges in, heads straight for the refrigerator and fills his pockets with the last remaining five bottles of beer.

'Hey, Mister TV Smith, I am stealing all your beer,' he says cheerfully.

Norbert comes in and tells me about the 'New Knust' he's planning. Boy, am I looking forward to that. My mind firmly fixed on Plan A, I turn down two offers of going out drinking and head back to the hotel where I rinse out tonight's T-shirt and hang it on the towel rail next to the other one. Checkout is at 11:00. I'll need to take a shower before I leave so I set my alarm for 10:30, then decide to treat myself to a lie-in and re-set it for 10:35.

It's 5:30. I'm too tired to sleep.

14th May
Someone knocks on my door at 10:00.
'WHAT?!!'

'Oh...sorry...' comes a voice from out in the corridor.

Not half as sorry as I am.

My trousers and T-shirts are still damp. I pack them into my baggage in a separate plastic bag and hope I'll have time to hang them out somewhere when I get to Paderborn later. Good job I brought that spare pair of trousers.

I grab a mozzarella and salad roll in Hamburg station. I'm so fatigued I'm not sure if I'm hungry or not but feel I ought to eat something.

When I reach Paderborn I check the map outside the station and decide that the venue, an Irish pub called Limerick's, looks near enough to walk. I didn't count on the pedestrian zone, which has a kind of crazy paving surface which sends my roller bag bucking all over the place and jumping out of my hand, after which it falls over, scattering pedestrians.

A young guy smelling strongly of sour alcohol falls into step beside me.

'Nice looking guitar,' he says, although I don't know how he can tell, as the guitar is still in its case. Then he proceeds to tell me about all his guitars. I roll erratically on and eventually he falls behind, carrying on the conversation to no one.

Limericks is shut, but pub manager Gareth's phone number is in the window so I ring him and he comes over and opens up. I mention my problem with the damp clothes and he sends one of the barmen over to the local laundrette to give them a quick spin in the tumble dryer. When he gets back I find that I have also tumble-dried the fee for last night's gig, which was still in my pocket.

I do a quick interview with a local paper then get on the stage for two hours fifty minutes, after which all my clothes are soaked again.

It's about 4:30 by the time I rumble over to Gareth's apartment to bed down in the living room on a mattress that has, as he says, 'seen a lot of use.'

15th May

Gareth and I grab a quick breakfast in a cafe in a nearby shopping centre, sitting at a table beneath a replica Statue of Liberty, then go back to the bar to pick up my stuff. It's too late to walk to the station, so I call a cab and get there with only a couple of minutes to spare, for a long journey on a stopping train. Marco meets me at Braunschweig and points out that I look tired.

Nearly a month on tour now.

Marco has a band called Tanzende Kadaver, and offered to find me a gig here on the understanding that his band could support and also play a few songs with me. Unfortunately it somehow didn't work out with the clubs he'd hoped to book us into and I've ended up back at the Haifischbar, which I played a couple of years ago with Garden Gang and is far too small for a band. The stage may be full tonight but the club probably won't be—all the promo material got lost in the post so the gig doesn't appear in any of the listings.

We arrive at the venue to find two of the band dragging a large sofa out of the venue. They see Marcus and me and set the sofa down in the doorway and start a long chat. It's already 7:30 and I'm a bit worried about soundcheck but no one seems particularly keen to start lugging that heavy sofa any further. Eventually it gets shoved to one side and the band load their gear in.

As the drummer puts together his kit, which fills the tiny stage, the venue manager explains that they have changed the P.A. since the last time I was here. The speaker system comprises two small monitor boxes sitting on the window ledge at the back of the stage. The mixing desk, a little disco console which used to be on the stage, is now at the far end of the bar, too far away for my cables to reach it so I have to plug my guitar into one of Tanzende Kadaver's amps. I'm almost relieved that no one is going to come.

I sit in the small sideroom that serves as a backstage drinking coffee and water while waves of fatigue wash over me. Through the narrow street level window I see the sofa go past. Who knows where?

There are a handul of people in by the time Tanzende Kadaver start. It's too loud for the P.A. system so you can't hear any vocals, the instruments meld into one mush of sound, and there are no lights on the stage, so they play in complete darkness. When they finish I step up onto the narrow strip of stage remaining in front of the drumkit and plug my guitar in. The floor is littered with broken glass and awash with beer—it's impossible to avoid it slopping all over my guitar strap and cable as I get ready to start. At least I'm near the end of the tour and they will only stink of beer for another two days.

I play a slightly shorter set than usual, only a couple of hours, and at the end Marco's band joins me but it's all a bit of a mess—the sound is terrible and some of the band seem to be having a problem keeping up so I cut it short after two numbers and speed back to the dressing room, which is now mysteriously also littered with broken glass and awash with recently-spilled beer. I dash forward to get my bag out of the way before the foaming tide reaches it.

Marco drives me back to his flat, which he's lending me for the night while he goes to sleep at his parents' place. He thoughtfully puts out a pair of earplugs for me in case I get disturbed by the trams outside the window in the morning, but the way I feel at the moment they could run straight through the bedroom and I wouldn't wake up.

16th May

Marco arrives with some *Brötchen* and a thermos of freshly-brewed coffee for breakfast. It's a sweltering morning outside, he tells me. Good timing for the refrigerator to break down; inside is a lettuce that can't be saved and a wedge of cheese we have to scrape the mould off.

I get on Marco's computer because I suddenly realise that I haven't heard from the punk festival in Ireland I'm supposed to be playing in a few days time. I don't even know where in Dublin it is—my head's been so full of the German tour that I've kind of forgotten life will go on afterwards. I don't have the email address of the promoter with me but I search for the website of the festival and find I am indeed on the bill, which is a relief as I bought the plane ticket four weeks ago before I left for Switzerland. The name and address of the venue are also on the site so one way or another I will be able to find it.

No need for a train today; Marco's driving to Hamburg anyway so he can drop me off in Bremen on the way. We sit in a traffic jam outside Hanover for a very long time as the temperature climbs to 29 degrees.

It gets a bit complicated in Bremen. Henne, who helped arrange the Leverkusen gig last week is also responsible for tonight's one in the Zakk, a small semi-legal bar and venue in the commune where he now lives. He was intending to come and pick me up at the station, but after Marco drops me off there I find that neither of the numbers he gave me after the Leverkusen gig work. This is what happens when you scribble down phone numbers at the end of an evening.

Nothing else to do but get in a taxi. The driver can't find the address on his map and has to enlist help from a colleague—then once we get going we drive straight into a traffic jam. I sit there, sticky and sweaty in the heat, watching people lazing in the sun on the grassy banks of the Weser outside, and the taxi fare rising inside.

Henne is devastated to hear the phone numbers didn't work, he's been waiting to come and get me. He shows me the little downstairs bar where I'll be playing and assures me the vocal P.A. by the side of the makeshift wooden pallet stage will be enough. As they have problems with the neighbours they can't switch it up loud anyway. While I'm soundchecking, members of the club nip outside to hear how loud it is from the street, then come back in and edge the volume down.

But it sounds fine in this small room after the noise terror yesterday and I'm quite looking forward to a more acoustic gig. Everyone here is friendly and helpful and there's already a nice atmosphere. I'm shown around the two upstairs floors of the building. The collective bought the house a few years back and have been doing it up since then. They now have a good living space, with bedrooms, offices, kitchen and of course the bar, which finances the rest of the work. I'll be sleeping in the bedroom of someone who is away travelling for a while, a small corner room almost entirely filled by a raised wooden platform with a mattress on it, surrounded by books.

We sit in the kitchen while the house cook prepares a salad and a pizza which I don't dare eat because it's too near gig time. They promise to save me some for later. Then Henne and I go for a walk along the Weser. People are still stretched out on the banks soaking up the last of the sun, including quite a few punky types who will presumably be coming to the gig tonight.

It's comfortably full by the time I go on, a nice, receptive audience, and the sound is fine. The stage lets me down a bit when the pallets start to move apart as I'm playing, but I hop off between numbers and kick them back into place.

After it's over I sit on the stage, pack up my gear and people gather round and chat to me. I explain about the sound problems with the neighbours and apologise for the set being a bit shorter than usual tonight.

'But TV, you played for two hours and fifty minutes...'

Oops, I did it again, again.

17th May

The last day. Berlin—and if past experience is anything to go by that means long, hot, and late.

After a convivial breakfast with all the members of the house, Henne takes me to Bremen station in the notorious camper van, still with the red and black Toten Hosen flag defiantly hanging in the back window.

The train is pretty full and I have to blunder up and down the carriages with my guitar and bags for quite a while before I spot an empty seat by a smartly dressed woman who only reluctantly admits there's no one sitting there. Well, would *you* want a punk rocker dressed in bleached jeans and an 'Only One Flavour' jacket, reeking of beer and tobacco and looking like he might fall asleep at any moment and dribble on your shoulder, sitting next to you?

I change at Osnabruck and the connection to Berlin is crammed, not a spare seat, people sitting on their luggage in the corridors and toilets. For my £40 I get to spend the next couple of hours crammed against a door trying to stop my guitar and bag getting trampled on as people negotiate the crush and push their way up and down the train futilely trying to find a seat.

My friend Viola is waiting at Berlin Ostbahnhof to pick me up, and we head straight for the Kirche Von Unten. Everything's relaxed there and there's still a bit of setting up to do before they'll be ready for soundcheck. It's a warm evening, and a bank holiday weekend for Ascension starting tomorrow so there's a distinct feeling we're not going to get the usual Berlin crowd tonight, and no one's in much of a hurry. A support has been booked—an old punk band from East Germany—but they're stuck in traffic and won't be here for a while. I see the night getting late.

I sit in the dressing room and try to get my bags in some sort of order for tomorrow. Find my air ticket...9:45 from Schönefeld. Working backwards, that means check in 8:45...that means, leave Viola's place 7:45...that means wake up 7:00, time for a coffee before leaving. It's 8:30 in the evening now...the support band plays at around 10:30...I could be on by 11:30...probably be a long one for the last night, say I play for around two and a half hours...offstage 2:00...an hour and a half to wind down and pack up, 3:30...give it a half hour back to Viola's, that's 4:00... If all goes smoothly I could get three hours sleep.

By eleven the place is packed and like a furnace. I play for three hours, forty three songs, my longest ever gig.

Tomorrow I'll be going home for less than twenty-four hours before the next one.

PART 3: IRELAND

18th May

I get in at around one in the afternoon, unpack my bags and put a load of washing in the machine, ready to re-pack for the Holidays In The Sun punk festival in Ireland tomorrow. I open my post and find a letter from the organisers telling me that I'm due to play at 3:45 in the afternoon and should be there two hours before stage time—which will be tricky, as my plane gets into Dublin airport at 3:10. I phone them up. It turns out that as they hadn't heard from me they thought that I wouldn't be coming so they cancelled my hotel room. They'll book me another one though, there's bound to be a room available somewhere. I explain the problems with the timing, and they tell me not to worry, they'll send someone to pick me up from the airport. If the plane's delayed they can shift my set to later.

The phone rings and it's a woman from Big Issue magazine. 'Is this a good time to have a chat with you?' she asks.

'Not really,' I say. 'Can we do it on Monday?'

'The piece has to be in by tonight.'

'What's it about?'

'We're asking people's thoughts on the Jubilee.'

I don't have any thoughts on the Jubilee. I've been on tour in Europe for four weeks, travelling thousands of miles, sleeping on mattresses on the floor, playing hours every night, and little Britain and its quaint customs seem to belong to another planet. 'I don't think I can help and I'm really in a hurry right now.'

'Just tell me—what were you doing on the day of the Silver Jubilee?'

'I've absolutely no idea.'

'I see. Well, what will you be doing this Jubilee day?'

'I've absolutely no idea. Look I just don't have any interest in the Jubilee whatsoever...and I really am in a hurry...'

What I don't tell her is that I am in a hurry because I have just run a bath, my first in my own home since the end of April, and am speaking to her with no clothes on.

19th May

The plane gets in on time but there's no one at the airport to pick me up. I waste twenty minutes hanging around in case someone arrives, and every now and then try the phone number for the promoter. The number worked yesterday from England but now all I get is a message telling me I am being 'transferred to the Nevada Phone Company,' which then gives me the engaged signal and relieves my Visa card of one and a half euros.

Eventually I get on the airport link bus which goes into town and ask the driver if he stops anywhere near St. Thomas Street.

'We're going to Heuston station,' he says. 'I'll drop you off on the way. You'll just be a few minutes from it.'

When we get into what looks like the city centre I go back to the driver and ask if this is my stop.

'Sit tight now,' he says. 'I can get you a bit nearer.'

At Heuston station I go up to him again. He claps his hand to his head. 'Ach! I completely forgot! I'll drop you on the way back, we'll be leaving in ten minutes.' He sees me struggling with my guitar case as all the other airport passengers jostle past with their bags. 'Here, give me that,' he says, and props it up behind his seat in the cab. Then we chat for a while. He ask me what time I'll be playing and I tell him I should be on stage now.

'Oh no!' He checks his board. 'I reckon we could leave…'

He starts up the engine and drives off, then makes an unscheduled stop in town to let me off. He points me the way over the Liffey and up the hill to St. Thomas Street, waving at me as I cross the road like an old friend.

I jog my way to the venue and arrive out of breath. John, the promoter, is sitting in the ticket office as I arrive. 'TV! Boy am I glad you're here!' He's put Splodgenessabounds, who were supposed to be playing after me, on now and they're just about getting to the end of their set. If I hurry to the stage I'll be able to start straight away and the festival will be back running on time.

It's good to see this concern that things run to schedule when so often the organisation at festivals is completely chaotic. Of course, little details can occasionally be overlooked, like picking up the *artiste* from the airport for example.

It's a sparse afternoon crowd in the hall, most of the large audience who were reportedly here last night still suffering hangovers and not venturing out until this evening. Splodge are already off, so I get straight on the stage and rush through my allotted forty minutes. It goes down well, but it all seems a bit strange after the last few weeks, and now it's still only late afternoon and—for me—the gig is over.

I sit in the area behind the stage for a bit with Matt from Splodgenessabounds and their tour manager Stretch, both of whom are old friends. They had a pretty good gig despite the fact their saxophone player and drummer missed their flights.

'Actually, it went better than when they turn up,' says Matt.

Splodge are going to play an after-show set in a pub called Eammon Doran's in the town when everything's finished here, so I decide to drop off my bags and guitar in the hotel now and come back later. I go back to the office but they—er—haven't actually booked me a room yet. Some phone calls are made and a place is found. John draws me a complicated map to the hotel, but just as he completes it Frank, the minibus driver who failed to pick me up from the airport, walks in.

'Frank, TV Smith needs a lift to his hotel.'

'Tell him to fuck off.'

'Tell him yourself, he's sitting right behind you.'

We have a laugh about it. Frank drives me up to the hotel, then pedantically goes over the directions back to the venue even though I've been following the route on the map all the way. Eventually he tails off. 'Basically, exactly the way we've just come.'

'But in the other direction.'

'That's correct.'

The receptionist at the hotel thinks I'm supposed to pay for the room so I have to explain that the festival is paying and give her John's phone number so he can authorise it on his credit card. She doesn't get through, peers at the piece of paper I've given her and puts her finger on another telephone number at the bottom of the page. 'Would it be worth me trying this one?'

'That's your number,' I point out.

I promise to get John to ring up and sort it out when I get back to the venue, and the receptionist hands me the key to room 210.

'I'll just explain where the room is. You go up the steps over there and you'll see a sign saying, Rooms 201—206. Ignore that. It's further down the same corridor.'

It's a small room with no windows. Hot water comes out of the cold tap and cold water comes out of the hot tap. I've been cleaning my teeth for a while before I realise this.

It takes me half an hour to walk back to the venue, through throngs of people peacefully wandering from pub to pub in Temple Bar. When I get there Matt tells me that the gig has been cancelled, but everyone's going to meet up afterwards at Eammon Doran's anyway for an after show party.

I hang around for a while, watching snatches of bands who don't really interest me, then when the festival finishes I wander off towards Temple Bar, not exactly sure where Eammon Doran's is, but pretty confident I'll find it.

A couple of passing skinheads spot me and tell me they enjoyed the gig. They point out the direction to Eammon Doran's, but say they've just been there and nothing's going on. All the same, I go to check if there's anyone I know around. I don't recognise anyone, but some Scottish punks get chatting to me. One of them tells me he runs a goth shop in Edinburgh, and before I know it I've agreed to an afternoon acoustic gig there next time I'm in the area.

Nothing much to do here, so I might as well head back. I walk through the streets in a light rain to the hotel, where I ask the guy behind the night desk about where I can get the airport bus in the morning. He tells me in great detail, in fact *unnecessary* detail, then looks a bit sheepish.

'Ah—now I've given you all this information I wonder if you'd do something for me...' With a forlorn expression he shows me his packet of cigarettes with just one left in it. 'I've got this terrible nicotine addiction, you see...I shouldn't really ask you, but...I can't leave the desk. Could you just pop down the road to the all-night shop and get me twenty Majors.' He has the right money ready.

20th May

Walking back to the arrivals hall at Gatwick, an elderly Irishman in worn trainers just behind me is barking out a few incomprehensible words to no one in a thick accent.

'Bach...yarr...!'

He may have had a few drinks on the plane.

'Ye no...be bach!'

He staggers up alongside and I realise he is talking to me.

'So...yaill nobby back?'

'What?'

He nods. 'Yer back.'

'Eh?'

'So yaill no' be coming back? To Ireland? On the back o' yer jacket—it says "Only One Flyover."'

'Er, no, that's Only One *Flavour*...'

I meet up with Matt and Stretch again on the Gatwick Express and they tell me about what a great party it was in the basement of Eammon Doran's last night.

The basement?

Good God, Plan A accidentally worked.

5. TV SMITH DISCOVERS AMERICA (2002)

3rd July

I'm leaving on the 14:00 flight for my first-ever tour of the U.S.A.—ten days on the East Coast, many of them in New York, where I'll be staying with promoter Bryan. Arriving on a different flight is ranting punk poet Attila the Stockbroker who'll be making up the other half of the line-up for the shows.

Not that I'll be playing any shows of course! (I didn't get a work permit and right now, with everyone paranoid after the 9/11 terrorist attacks, the chances are I'm going to be given a hard time getting into the country.)

The flight is six hours, but goes pretty fast. I'm surprised to see they have 'Gary Gilmore's Eyes' on one of the onboard music channels. The plane gets in at 16:40 local time and I join the queue for immigration. The woman at the desk studies my passport for a very long time, then gives me a look.

'What's this?' she snaps, jabbing her finger at the back page. It's the expiry date for the passport, September 2011—or, as it's abbreviated here—9/11. Oh good grief.

She finally lets me through. I pick up my guitar, which has been going around the baggage belt for some time, and head outside.

Bam! The heat hits me the moment I walk out of the air-conditioned airport building. I queue for a yellow cab, and manage to squeeze my guitar and bag—and knees—into the cramped space behind the driver. I tell him the address I'm going to, Bryan's apartment in Court Street, Brooklyn, and he asks which end. I tell him I have no idea. 'I'm English,' I explain.

'You've never been here before?' he says.

'No.'

'*Never?*' He shakes his head. 'You gotta to be kidding!' He simply can't believe it.

On the way into the city I see an elevated sign showing the temperature—early evening and still 100 degrees Fahrenheit, 38°C. Attila and his wife Robina are already at Bryan's place, where the sun streams straight into the fourth floor room with its large West-facing window, turning it into a furnace. Bryan apologises for the lack of air-conditioning—there is just a large fan, which moves the sticky air around a little. He points out that through the window you can just about see the Statue Of Liberty across the bay, all you have to do is stand on the couch, crane sideways and look between the two buildings opposite.

Bryan's wife Alyssa gets back from work and we head across the road for a Mexican meal, then next door to Sparky's bar where the boss, a friendly Irish guy called Jerry wants to know all about me and Attila and the punk era in London. We try a couple of the local ales and discuss plans for the rest of the evening. Considering the time-change, it's late for us, but we're going to take a trip into Manhattan because Attila needs a mandolin for his gigs, and Bryan has arranged to borrow one from a group called World/Inferno Friendship Society who are playing in town tonight.

What with the heat, fatigue and the strangeness of being in New York city for the first time, I feel quite overwhelmed as Bryan drives us into Manhattan. We get to the venue just as the band are preparing to go on stage, but sax player Dan takes time out to show Attila the mandolin. Then we watch some of their concert, but the heat in the packed club gets the better of me and after half an hour I go outside and sit in the quiet until Bryan and Attila are ready to leave.

Back in the apartment, Attila and Robina get the spare bed in Bryan's office. I get the couch in the superheated living room where, despite the fatigue, I lie awake bathed in sweat, the fan swooshing warm air back and forth over me. At around four in the morning, the cats get skittish, and so does my cat allergy.

4th July

I finally give up on sleep when it starts to get light and instead leaf through yesterday's New York Times, lead story: 'The first heat wave of summer has closed its firm and sweaty grip on the city.' A copy of Village Voice is plugging tonight's gig: 'Smith still has the ragged, pretty, nasal voice-to-die-for he brought to the Adverts a quarter-century ago.'

Pretty? *A quarter-century?!*

After a few hours the rest of the apartment wakes up. Everyone looks disgustingly refreshed. Normally Alyssa would be out to work in Manhattan by now, but as it's the July 4th holiday she and Bryan cook up breakfast for us all, home fries for me and an extremely large sausage for the carnivores. The sun hasn't come round to this side of the apartment yet, so we sit round the table in the relative cool discussing the day's plans.

The first gig of the tour is tonight in a poetry club in the Bowery, right opposite CBGBs. Usually this is a venue for open mic poetry slots, but tonight there'll be a lot of bands on, each doing short sets, then Attila and I at around ten in the evening—just about the same time the July 4th fireworks are going off. I do wonder if July 4th is a good time to play a gig in New York, but we'll see. To avoid the inevitable holiday traffic, Bryan's going to drive us to the venue early in the afternoon.

I take a walk around the neighbourhood for the rest of the morning. It's a vibrant area, full of shops and cafés, the streets wide enough to give a feeling of space. At the top end of the street, Brooklyn Heights looms up with its high rise shops and apartments; at the more downbeat end where we are you hear the constant rush of noise from the elevated freeway that funnels traffic down to the nearby Battery tunnel leading over to Manhattan. The heat is already building, and despite just wearing shorts and a T-shirt I'm breaking out in a sweat after just a few minutes of walking. I might have to wear shorts on stage tonight, which would be a first.

At about two, Bryan, Attila, Robina and I squeeze into Bryan's little Honda with all our gear and head for the Bowery. There are a lot of police units getting into position, and almost as many T.V. crews. To allay fears about terrorist attacks on this significant day, armed cops stand at checkpoint duty at the entrances to bridges, and the scrubland area beneath them has been cordoned off.

We park just round the corner from the Bowery Poetry Club and as we walk over to it Bryan points out the building where the Ramones took the cover shot for their first album. Inside the venue, a couple of bands have played already. There's one called Yidcore on at the moment. The male guitarist is dressed up as an old Jewish woman with headscarf and long skirt. The singer has dreadlocks, workman's boots and has tied a rubber chicken to the microphone stand.

The venue itself is a long, narrow room with a bar to one side near the entrance, then an area in front of the stage laid out with tables and chairs. There's the capacity for perhaps two hundred people here at a squeeze; at the moment I'd estimate about thirty people are in. Not quite what I expected for my first gig in New York, but at least it's air-conditioned and they sell coffee. The coffee machine has a sign on it: 'DO NOT USE STEAM WHILE POETS ARE READING.' Bless their sensitive, poetic hearts.

Actually, that air-conditioning is a bit strong and I'm rather regretting the decision to wear shorts. I step back outside to a reassuring wall of heat and take in the New York vibe. At the moment, there is no New York vibe. What with the holiday and the paranoia about a possible July 4th terrorist attack, seems like everyone's left the city. I sit in a storefront in the sun, and barely a soul passes me, just the occasional car rumbling past.

Bryan continues the rock'n'roll tour by walking me over to CBGBs where he knows a couple of bands playing in a punk festival there today. I'm still not quite sure why he didn't put me on here, but I guess he reckons that Attila is 'poetry' and I'm 'singer/songwriter' so a gig in a poetry club would be better. He tells me that the line-up of bands in CBGBs is going to be 'seriously hardcore.'

CBGBs is as deserted as the poetry club, but it's interesting to look around. As soon as I walk in I bump into a girl called Adi who plays with a band called the New York Rel-X. Coincidentally, two weeks after Bryan offered to find me some gigs, Adi emailed me to ask me if she could book me a tour and I had to say no. You wait a quarter-century for a U.S. tour then two come along at once.

Further down in the club I meet a band called the Midnight Creeps who know all my stuff and play 'Safety In Numbers' in their set. They're thrilled to meet me and I have to sign autographs and get photos taken. Seems like I'm definitely playing in the wrong club: over the road no one knows who I am, here I'm a celebrity.

Back at the other venue, the manager won't let us use the dressing room, so all the musicians have dumped their gear on the floor in front of the stage. By mid-evening there is still only a sparse amount of people in but I've come a long way for this and I intend to enjoy myself. I get on stage and introduce myself:

'After twenty-five years it's great to finally play a gig in...short trousers.' Good, got them laughing.

It's a nice, intimate little show and I'm happy with the genuine response I'm getting. At the end, Attila comes up and joins me for a couple of songs on violin, just as we used to do when we toured Germany together a couple of years ago, and I mark this one down as a good start, although I really hope we're going to get some bigger audiences for the rest of the tour.

Back at the bar, as Attila takes the stage for his set, a couple of guys are waving around a video camera. 'Brilliant!' they say, '...and we got the whole thing on tape! We'll give you a copy! We make films! Can we make a film about you?!'

'What kind of films do you make?' I ask.

'Porno films.'

Outside the night is still warm as Bryan drives us over to New Jersey to hip radio station WFMU to play a live session. Attila and I are both extremely fatigued now and sit in a kind of daze in the reception area waiting to start. It's past one in the morning, New

York time, now—that's ooh, who knows—very late indeed in Britain. We get a great welcome from resident expert punk rock DJs Dianne and Pat, and pull off a couple of good short performances, then Bryan takes us out through the steamy night and the sluggish holiday traffic leaving the fireworks display, over the river back to Brooklyn where I lie awake on the couch, bathed in sweat until the light comes in the window and I start to catnap. Which is more than the cats are doing.

5th July

Alyssa apologises for having to go through the room when she gets up for work at 7:00 but I can't sleep in this heat anyway, and when she puts on a pot of coffee there's no reason to carry on trying.

Attila and I are both going to be rehearsing with local bands today. The one I'll be working with is called 'Last Burning Embers' and is led by an old friend, Jack Rabid, who I first met fifteen years ago in London when he interviewed me for his fanzine, 'Big Takeover.' Attila will be rehearsing with a folk/punk band called The Spunk Lads. We'll play a couple of gigs with them starting tomorrow, but after these rehearsals Attila and I will meet up at the Bowery Poetry Club tonight for another solo gig there.

I manage my first trip on the subway fairly well but everything takes longer than I expect and I'm running late by the time I find my way to the rehearsal room just off Sixth Avenue. Luckily, Last Burning Embers have done a great job of learning the songs and we only need to go through them a couple of times.

Jack walks me back through the bustling super-heated streets to the subway. I'm back at the Bowery Poetry Club an hour before I need to be, so I wander around the Lower East Side for a while. My eye is drawn to a little old-fashioned Jewish café called Yonah Schimmels, where a sign in the window proudly announces that they bake and serve their own knishes. I go in and order one, just because I've never eaten a knish before. I still couldn't tell you what it is.

I meet up with Attila and Bryan again at the Poetry Club. Tonight there will just be the two of us playing, no support acts, and Bryan has been having strong words with the club manager to get the dressing room behind the stage opened. There are even a couple of free drinks in there. The manager looks extremely pissed off about it all until soundcheck, when a step leading to the stage slips while Attila is standing on it, sending him tumbling to the floor, groaning and clutching his calf. Suddenly the manager is a picture of friendliness and sympathy. You can almost see the word 'Lawsuit!' lit up on his forehead.

It's a similar low turn-out to yesterday but they're an enthusiastic bunch, and there are quite a few people back for the second time. I'm surprised to see my friend Mariann from Switzerland in the audience. Her best friend Janine has been living here for a year so she's come over to visit. Janine lives in Brooklyn Heights, just up the other end of Court Street. The world just got smaller again.

After the show Attila and Robina are both tired and head back to Brooklyn. Before we do the same, Bryan and Alyssa and I get something to eat in a very popular Middle Eastern fast food place. Great food and huge portions. New Yorkers really know how to eat.

A meal like that ought to knock me out, but back at the apartment I can only doze fitfully, tossing and turning on the couch, the fan blasting back and forth over me. It's difficult to know which keeps me awake more: the noise of the fan when it's on or the heat when it's off.

6th July

Tonight I'll be playing at Arlene's Grocery—that's a venue, not a shop—here in New York, so I have the day free. Attila and Robina take a trip into Manhattan, but I decide to hang around Brooklyn and take it easy before the gig.

We're early at Arlene's, hoping to give ourselves enough time to soundcheck as this is the first of the two gigs we'll be playing with backing bands. However, there's no soundman here yet, and everyone working for the venue is ignoring us. It turns out that there are a lot of bands on the bill, each gets allotted a strict one hour slot, including changeover and soundcheck. As people come in they have to tick off who they came to see on a list at the door which determines who gets paid what at the end of the evening. Once again, it's not exactly the Big New York Gig we'd been expecting.

Oh well. I stand outside in the warm evening with Jack Rabid and we get into a conversation about the Rutles. Jack does just about every funny line in the film and pretty soon has me cracking up.

Despite the unwelcoming venue, the gig is good. I do twenty minutes solo, then get Last Burning Embers up and they're very tight, sound like they've been backing me for years. Attila enjoys himself too. He does a similar format, starting off with some solo songs and poetry, then finishes off with the Spunk Lads. But the club is far from full, we walk out of there having been paid virtually nothing, and Attila and I are both starting to feel that although we're enjoying the experience of being in New York, as far as the gigs are concerned so far it's been pretty much a waste of time. Worryingly, next week we'll be out of town and not only will we presumably attract even less of an audience once we leave the city, we're not even sure yet how we're going to travel.

We discuss it over a beer back at Jerry's bar. There is a chance Bryan might be able to come to the gigs, but he has a job as a social worker to keep up, and anyway the car would be so crowded with the four of us and all our bags and instruments that the journeys would be very uncomfortable—and some of those trips will be long. A guy called Rick—punky-looking, with biker jacket, chains and piercings—who Bryan has suggested we hire as a roadie, says he'd like to help out…but he can't drive. A roadie is really at the bottom of the list of things we need right now anyway. Being able to actually get to the gigs would be number one.

7th July
Second gig with the band tonight, this time at Maxwell's, over the river in New Jersey.

Soon after midday, 'Handsome' Dick Manitoba—singer of the Dictators, one of the first punk-sounding bands in the mid-seventies—rings up. He owns a bar in Manhattan where Attila and I will be playing tomorrow and has called to check up on some details about the gig, although it seems he has more important things on his mind. 'Check out Channel 22, Bryan!' he yells down the phone. 'They're running an old episode of The Twilight Zone. It's Robert Duvall! With HAIR!!'

Attila and Robina decide to go on a rock'n'roll trip to Rockaway Beach as a tribute to the Ramones, while I stay in Brooklyn and go on a long walk around the neighbourhood with Bryan and Alyssa, neither of whom have to work as it's Sunday. In sparkling warm sunshine we wander up to the Heights and down to Brooklyn bridge where a wooden-decked area gives a great view across to Manhattan. Alyssa points out the gap in the horizon where the twin towers used to stand, and the building where she works, just a couple of blocks away. When the first plane hit, she fled the building and found herself among hundreds of others running across Brooklyn Bridge, ash and debris drifting down around her like snow. People were falling to their knees weeping, not understanding what was happening. As she tried to calm people and help them along she noticed that on balcony of the Seventh Day Adventist building, which looms above us now on our side of the river, the members stood placidly watching the apocalyptic scenes below, doing nothing.

We have an ice cream.

When we're all back at the apartment, Attila and Robina explain that their trip wasn't quite what they were expecting. They asked for subway directions to Rockaway from two guys working on the elevator of Bryan's apartment block and got sent—presumably as some kind of joke—not to the bubblegum beach paradise namechecked by the Ramones, but instead to the Rockaways housing projects, one of the most threatening and dangerous places in New York State. They wandered around for a bit, rather aware that they were the only white faces around and that everyone was looking at them, then they took the subway back.

Bryan drives us over to New Jersey where Last Burning Embers and The Spunk Lads are loading in their gear. Yesterday Tony Barber, bass player with the Buzzcocks and long-time Adverts fan, told me that he wants to come and guest on guitar for tonight's gig but there's no sign of him yet. When I asked him which songs he knew he said, 'All of them.'

Soundcheck is with one of the most unhelpful soundmen imaginable. One of his other talents is that he has absolutely no sense of humour. He gestures at my guitar, which clearly has a pickup in the sound hole and grunts, 'You have a microphone for that thing?'

I reply, 'I'm sorry, no, I'm English.'

He doesn't even crack a smile, but does manage to make the guitar sound terrible.

It's going to be an early gig as it's been hijacked by a band no one has heard of but who have just signed to Sony and demanded the headline slot. Consequently there aren't many people in the room by the time Attila starts, but he gets an enthusiastic response. Tony arrives with about half an hour to spare and by the time he and Last Burning Embers get up on stage with me there are about fifty people—not many, but the best turnout on the tour so far. All in all it's been quite a good evening for Attila and me, and the band with the big record deal flop satisfyingly when they go on at the end, and quite a few of the audience leave.

That's the last one of the tour with Last Burning Embers so we say our goodbyes for now, although I'll be seeing Jack again in a couple of days when he interviews me in his other role as editor for Big Takeover fanzine.

We take the tunnel over to Manhattan and join the stream of holiday traffic crawling its way back into the city. Looks like New York is filling up again ready for the working week.

8th July

I'm looking forward to tonight's gig in Manitoba's. Not only will Handsome Dick himself be there, but another New York punk legend, Jayne (ex-Wayne) County will be DJ.

Before Attila and I set out for our daily tourist outings we sit with Bryan and have another discussion about what we're going to do for the out-of-town gigs which start in a couple of days time. Bryan's definitely not going to be able to get to the first of them. Attila seems willing to drive, but I don't want anything to do with it—I'm still fading in and out of jet lag, and the idea of having to deal with the routing, parking, finding the venues, figuring out what to do if we have an accident...*forgeddaboudit*. Mind you, the thought of being driven around America by a similarly tired and disorientated ranting punk poet who only passed his test a year ago is also somewhat worrying.

We leave it with Bryan, who promises to get on the computer and work out how much it would cost to go by train, which seems a far more sensible idea.

I take the subway in to Manhattan, intending to walk around Central Park and visit the Metropolitan museum, but New York takes much longer to get around than I'm used to in London and when I eventually get to the Metropolitan and see how vast it is I give up on the idea and go to the nearby Guggenheim instead.

Back at Bryan's, Attila and Robina arrive excited by their trip to the Coney Island aquarium. Attila is something of an aficionado of marine life—when he's not dragging it out of the water on the end of a hook—but what impressed him most was the size of the walrus's genitalia.

'We were just watching it swim past and thought, what is *that*...?'

'It was enormous,' agrees Robina.

'I am the walrus. Coo-coo-ca-*joo*' says Attila.

Manitoba's is a small bar with walls covered with photos of bands, particularly those from the New York punk scene. The place screams rock'n'roll. I'll probably have to do some screaming myself later—the P.A. is atrocious, two domestic hi-fi speakers run by a little mixing desk and amp that seems to have blown some important component. But as the people come in and the atmosphere builds, it's soon clear that this is going to be a great gig. Jayne swishes in wearing very big clothes and comes over to say hello. We haven't seen each other since the Roxy club, when she was a he. It turns out I'm standing in front of an old photo of Wayne County. 'Oooh, lookee there at that little thang,' pouts Jayne, prodding a finger towards the bulge on his '77 era crotch.

I take a few minutes to walk around the block and clear my head ready for the gig. New York is swooning in the heat. In a park around the corner the fireflies dart and swoop, tiny streaks of light like shooting stars. There's a sign outside a nearby bar: 'It's fucking hot! Step inside!'

Jack Rabid is outside Manitoba's when I get back. 'I hear you have a few problems,' he grins.

'Eh?'

'Two words:—who's—driving—?' Word travels fast round these parts.

Attila starts his set and soon gives up on the P.A. and delivers his poems standing on the bar, to big applause. He can't resist throwing in some references to the aquarium and its star turn. Then I'm on. I keep the P.A. switched down low so as not to distort too much and belt it out as best I can and the set goes down a storm with the audience who are now packing the place out, crowded right up to within inches of me. Towards the end Jayne gets a little over-excited and starts shouting over her microphone and playing snatches of 'One Chord Wonders' and 'Gary Gilmore' while I'm between songs. It's all a lot of fun.

9th July

Just a short set tonight at the Sidewalk Café, where gigs are organised by a musician called Lach who has started the 'Anti-Folk' movement to try and reinvigorate the singer/songwriter scene. No soundcheck required, so I have the day free. There's a quick discussion about travel arrangements for tomorrow and we all agree on the bus and train option for the first part of the tour, then Bryan will drive down to Washington and take us around by car for the last couple of dates.

I arrange to meet up with Mariann and take a trip out to Coney Island. On the way to the subway, on the pavement right outside Bryan's apartment, I notice a full size coffin thrown out with the rest of the garbage so I nip back in to get my guitar for a few photos.

Coney Island is bathed in warm summer sunshine. We resist the temptation to see the walrus's genitalia and instead have a quick spin on the Cyclone, a rickety seventy-five year old wooden roller coaster, then walk up the beach and into the Russian area where we take refreshment in a charming old-fashioned tea room. After that I get on the subway back into Manhattan to meet with Jack Rabid for the interview.

The gig at the Sidewalk is a fairly sedate affair. There's a nice vibe in there, low lighting, tables and chairs laid out around the stage, candles on the tables, but not many people on the chairs. Rick the roadie has turned up again but there's absolutely nothing for him to do except sit there and look scary to all the folky types in the room. Attila and I both play well and make a few new friends, but it's a bit of a comedown after last night, and the only fee is a bucket collection, which barely gives us enough for the taxi back to Brooklyn.

We console ourselves with a drink in Jerry's. Rick tells me that after he left us the other night he trod on a rat on his way home. It ran right at him as he was walking along and the next thing he knew—*crunch!*—and he was having to wipe rat brain off his boots.

10th July

Attila, Robina and I take the subway to the New York Port Authority Bus Terminal. We buy our tickets for Worcester and there's still time to get a coffee in a pizza place. Never missing an opportunity to cash in on 9/11, the paper napkins have a picture of the American flag with 'United We Stand' written above it, and below: 'Our thoughts and prayers are with the victims, their families and the people of America.' It's illegal to burn the American flag here, but wiping your greasy pizza-mouth on it is okay.

A few hours later the bus pulls into Worcester and Brian Goslow is there to meet us. Brian is a music fan and independent local promoter trying to get things going in the Worcester music scene; not easy. Many years ago he stayed a couple of days with Gaye and me in London, and when he heard that I was coming to the U.S. he insisted on booking me and Attila into his local club. He's also booked us into an embarrassingly good hotel, which he takes us over to now, and which must have cost a fortune. But, oh boy, I'm glad he did. Tonight I will sleep in a bed again at last instead of on a couch!

Come soundcheck time, Brian walks us over to the gig. Worcester seems to be an enormous concrete multi-storey car park wrapped around a small town centre which it is impossible to get to. We circle the car park for some time then arrive on a street with a couple of fast food places and bars, one of which—the Lucky Dog Music Hall—is the venue for tonight.

Inside there's a decent stage and P.A., but the schedule is somewhat alarming. As usual on the nights Brian organises there are about twenty local bands playing. Usually no one except other band members and friends turn up, and the bands do about ten minutes each. Attila and I will play short sets before they start. It's kind of depressing playing to a bunch of other musicians who aren't really interested and just want to get on with their own gigs but, hey, there's a hotel afterwards. Also there's a very tasty cranberry beer brewed in the pub's micro-brewery. The beer keeps us there for a while and we catch some of the other bands. At one point I look round and see Brian sitting at the back of the bar with an enormous pair of headphones on. His tinnitus is so bad that he can't actually listen to any of the bands he books.

Damn, forgot to eat, and all the food places are shut. When I get back to the hotel it's a choice between ordering something expensive or getting straight to sleep. I go for the sleep option. I can eat tomorrow—knowing how tired we are, Brian has told us not to bother getting up early for the hotel breakfast, he'll come by later and take us out to a diner for a typical all-American brunch.

It's the most comfortable bed in the world, and my first good night's sleep for a week.

11th July

The phone rings at nine in the morning, and it's Bryan calling from Brooklyn to check how everything is. A considerate question, but timing is everything. I shout at him and slam the phone down, then I'm so angry that I can't sleep any more.

I've calmed down a bit by the time Brian Goslow arrives at midday and walks us through the ring of concrete into the town centre to look for something to eat. Pretty hard to find a diner open, it turns out, but we eventually come across one and get some hash browns, toast and eggs. Brian tells us his wife is going to drive us over to tonight's gig in Providence later, which is good news—the bus goes the long way and takes about three hours, a car will get us there in forty minutes. That gives us time to look round the local museum, which is…well, don't plan your holiday around it.

The venue in Providence looks promising, a good-sized club and bar with an arty feel to it. While we're waiting for soundcheck, which no one seems in any particular hurry to get started, we hear about problems brewing for tomorrow's gig in Boston. Someone Attila knows on a local radio station tells him that she phoned the venue and got told they knew nothing about the gig and it definitely wasn't happening. Seems the venue is some kind of art gallery having an opening for a show and the promoter Bryan has been dealing with has nothing to do with the venue, isn't authorised to put the gig on, and now isn't answering the phone. Bryan's advice: pull the gig and come back to New York tomorrow. Attila isn't having it—he's got fans waiting to see him play in Boston and he's going to take things into his own hands and find an alternative venue. He storms off outside with the club's cordless phone and starts ringing around. The girl at the radio station gives him the phone number of some people who put on gigs in the cellar of their house and would be willing to have us. They call it Hardcore House. To go back to New York and have an evening off, or to play in someone's cellar—it's a dilemma. But Attila reckons we can all stay at his friend and fellow-musician David Rovics' sister's place, so what have we got to lose?

As we finally settle on playing the gig tomorrow, tonight's support band start. They have been described to us as 'experimental,' but it is actually so painful to listen to that I can't go into the club. When it's finally over, Attila and I play our gigs. It's not bad, but there's virtually nobody there and it's a relief to go back to the motel and get this day over with.

July 12th

Attila, Robina and I take the train from Providence to Boston and then a cab up to Mission Hill, to the Hardcore House. I have a bad feeling about this. It's a large, wooden clapboard two-storey house on a normal residential street in the suburbs. The band who played last night have just roused from the sofas and floor in the front room and are carrying their gear out to the van. Attila and I have a quick look in the cellar where we'll be playing and I immediately regret deciding to try to save the gig. A tiny room, ankle deep in dust, no stage of course, and thick wooden posts every few feet supporting the floor above. The water from the shower upstairs is running straight down one of the side walls into the floor.

But it's a beautiful sunny day outside, and we have the whole afternoon to look around Boston. Better make something of this trip now we're here. Attila, Robina and I take the subway into the centre and walk over to the waterfront, then go our separate ways, agreeing to meet up back at the house at around five to see if a soundcheck is possible.

I have a pleasant afternoon wandering around the harbour in the warm sunny weather, getting a bite to eat in the market and checking out a couple of bookstores. Everywhere there are 'Cheers' bars, with absolutely nothing in common with the television programme except the logo. Heading for the site of the Boston Tea Party I pass countless millionaire's boats, swanky restaurants and soaring glass-flanked office buildings oozing wealth. The Boston Tea Party Experience turns out to be a tacky tourist trap, mercifully shut.

I sit out in the park for a while sipping an iced coffee then take the subway back to Hardcore House, where nothing is happening. Attila's not back yet. I don't know anyone here or what's going on, so I fetch my guitar from the cellar, sit out on the front steps in the last rays of the sun and set about changing my strings, feeling very tired and depressed about the prospect of tonight's gig. A photographer called John turns up and chats to me for a bit then explains that he's doing a book about punk and asks if I'd mind doing some portrait shots. I tell him I'm not exactly in the best of moods for getting my photo taken but he can go ahead if he wants, so he snaps away discreetly over the next hour or so while the evening unfolds.

Soon Attila returns, his friend David Rovics and sister Bonny arrive, a couple of people who have heard about the gig start to gather, a case of beer gets opened. The band who were originally booked to play set up their drum kit and amps in the cellar and the available space is already half full. Eventually I get to plug in my guitar and try a run-through. Awful. Cables all over the place trailing between the posts, a muddy, distorted sound, a cheap microphone, just a couple of dim lights washing over the area where we'll play—the rest of the cellar in darkness. I give up and go back upstairs to sit on the steps again in the fresh air.

A few more people start turning up, very friendly and interested in the gig. Among them are a couple of the Midnight Creeps, who I first met in CBGB's a couple of nights ago. They walk me over to the nearest liquor store where everyone is buying their booze for the evening as there's no bar in the house. Actually, it's a nice evening outside, and I walk back slowly with my new friends chatting about this and that, my mood improving. When I get back the band are playing and there are a few people in the cellar, but I can't stay in there too long because of the noise and heat and the rising dust.

By the time I go back down to play, the room is packed out with about forty people and there's suddenly a great atmosphere. The sound is terrible, but it doesn't seem to matter. The audience are right up close, totally into it, and it's the best gig of the tour so far. Attila also has a great set and at the end David Rovics comes on and plays one of his songs, which the small crowd laps up.

Then we pile in the car and drive back to Bonny's place. There's no bedroom for me, but Bonny is a holistic therapist and masseuse, and the room I'm allotted has her massage table in it so I have a go sleeping on that. It's quite comfortable for about half an hour but after that becomes torture. I get off and try the floor but it's no better, so I hoist myself back onto the massage table and lie awake the rest of the night.

13th July

It's more than five hours by train from Boston to Washington so we have to clear out of the house pretty early to make sure we catch it. Bryan has pre-booked our tickets, but we have to join the queue in the travel centre in the station to pick them up. It's a bit of a shock to find that the guy behind the counter refuses to let us have them until he sees our passports, due to new security regulations bought in after 9/11 and the ensuing paranoia over terrorism. My passport is in my bag in Bryan's apartment in New York.

Time for the train to leave is fast approaching and it looks like Attila and Robina are going to have to go without me. I show my driver's licence, my Visa card, explain that the ticket is booked on the credit card of a U.S. resident whose address is on file and that I have to get to Washington to play a gig tonight, but still it does no good. It's the law, and this guy is not giving me my ticket. Eventually one of the other workers at the counter takes pity on me, draws me aside and explains that I can simply collect the ticket from the machine outside, no identification needed. So that's my tip for terrorists: get your ticket from the machine.

The journey is long but comfortable, and it's quite pleasant to watch America slip by for a few hours, read a bit and relax.

We take a cab to the hotel the promoter has booked for us in Washington, and Bryan turns up in his car a few hours later. He takes us over to the venue, which looks promising. It's the smaller of two rooms in a club called the Black Cat, but still bigger than a lot of places I play. It's only when we're soundchecking that we realise that there is a heavy rock band playing upstairs in the larger room and they're clearly audible from down here—not great when you're playing solo. Attila and I jiggle our times around so that he gets on before the loud band for his poetry set, then I'll bash out a few songs acoustically and play some more with my sequencer backing band when the noise starts upstairs.

We sit in the cafe next door for a while, where we get served a free but tasteless veggie burger which is just enough to stave off the hunger. Back in the venue it's the same story of this whole tour—only about twenty or thirty people in. We have a good gig, and they all enjoy it, but really it's a long way to come for so few people.

July 14th

Last night of the tour in Philadelphia, and there's some kind of parade going on, the streets lined with flags, and—after violence in previous years—police everywhere. There's no sense of any trouble today though, the city is bustling with smiling people wandering around in the warm summer evening. In fact the only place where there's a bit of space is the Pontiac Grille, the club where Attila and I are playing, where predictably very few have turned up. Even the promoter hasn't turned up. Consequently the keys to the dressing room aren't available and Attila, Robina and I have to dump our bags and instruments in the upstairs bar and hope they'll be alright.

First on is a local solo singer/songwriter who tries to do a crazed Tom Waits thing, but it doesn't work in front of this small crowd. I'm happy with my gig though. The sound on stage is very good, and there are a few pockets of fans in the audience who cheer me along. Attila plays his set, then we pose around for pictures with the group of fans and suddenly it's all over. We load our bags and squeeze into Bryan's Honda and head back to New York where my flight leaves tomorrow evening.

15th July

At the airport, the security guy stops me and points at the design on my Die Toten Hosen shoulder bag—a black skeleton of an eagle with the letters DTH below it.

'Is this supposed to be the American eagle?' he asks grimly.

'Er...no...' God, just let me out of this paranoid country.

'And this...' he stabs his finger at the lettering. 'Death To America?'

Oh yes. Absolutely. I always spell America with an 'H.'

6. EAT! (2002)

25th October

There's an expensively-dressed couple in front of me arguing with the woman behind the check-in desk. They're upset because the flight is fully booked and they've arrived too late to get adjacent seats. It's difficult to feel sorry for them as they arrogantly shout and gesticulate and demand to be upgraded to Business Class. Eventually, unsuccessful, they dump their designer luggage on the belt and storm off in tight-lipped fury. I see them again at the café in the departure lounge, where I take the next table. She has her nose buried in a magazine, he is typing feverishly away on his laptop, and for the next twenty minutes not one word passes between them.

Austria Airlines actually have my vegetarian meal on board: it's a small unbuttered bread roll with some grilled courgettes in it. A bit dry, but quite nice. For dessert, the meat eaters get a rather tasty looking square of chocolate cake; I get seven grapes in a dish.

I'm going to Vienna because my friend Max is getting married tomorrow and wants me to play a song at the wedding ceremony, then a gig at the club he's booked for the reception in the evening. The night after that I'll be taking the opportunity to play the Chelsea, one of my favourite clubs, and just a couple of weeks ago I got an email from a fan called Martin asking me if I'd play in his local club tonight as I was going to be in the area anyway. It's about half an hour from Vienna in a place I wasn't able to find on my map: Perchtoldsdorf.

Max picks me up from the airport and explains the arrangements for the wedding day as we crawl through the afternoon rush hour traffic to the hotel. By the time we get there Martin and a mate of his with the unlikely name of Cheese are already waiting in Reception so I swap cars and leave Max to get on with the organisation for tomorrow while I head off for the gig.

On the way to Perchtoldsdorf, Martin tells me about the last time he tried to see me play, a year or so ago in the Czech Republic. Even though he didn't know the address of the club, he set out with his wife first thing in the morning for the long drive. They got held up at the border, then hit heavy traffic and took another five hours to reach the town, getting there by early evening. They drove around for a bit but couldn't find the club. Eventually they saw a bunch of punks hanging around outside the train station and asked them where the gig was. That's when they found out the venue had burned down during the night. I was playing a replacement gig 500 kilometers away.

So he's organised his own gig instead! It's a small venue called 'Hyrtlhaus' run by a bunch of enthusiastic kids who usually can't afford to invite anyone other than local bands. Normally they'd have someone like, for example, Martin and Cheese's band the Sonic Bastards. 'You wouldn't like us,' they assure me.

The Sonic Bastards would have played tonight but everything was arranged at the last minute and the evening had already been booked by another band, Yellow Page, who have graciously agreed to be bumped down to the support slot. I don't know what sort of music they play, but as we near the club they ring up Martin panicking because they are having technical problems in soundcheck and can't get their in-ear monitoring to work. I bet the Sonic Bastards don't use in-ear monitoring.

The Hyrtlhaus is a nice little club that could hold a couple of hundred people at a squeeze. I settle into the dressing room across the courtyard while Martin attempts to sort out some problems with the P.A. system. Soon he joins me, lugging a speaker box which he proceeds to take apart with a screwdriver. We are still waiting for some other equipment to arrive before I can try a soundcheck. The gig opens in half an hour.

Once we have everything working, soundcheck goes very quickly. Martin is at the mixing desk, and everything sounds fine. Back in the dressing room, I say 'So, you book the gigs, pick up the artists from Vienna, fix the equipment, and mix the sound?'

'Yes, and strangely I don't get paid for any of it.'

He points out a cardboard box full of bread, cheese and fruit. 'I've been reading your tour diaries on the internet,' he says, 'and seen how you never get to eat at gigs. So, eat!'

I explain that I don't like to eat just before I go onstage, but I will afterwards.

While Yellow Page play their set, a few people in the audience chat to me, clearly impressed that I've come to their little club, and I sign an autograph on someone's leg. Then I'm up on the six inch high stage and playing to an excitable crowd who are out to make tonight a gig Perchtoldsdorf won't forget. While I go through my paces, waves of people jump up beside me and dive off into the audience, then go surfing off over their shoulders. Great fun. Even more satisfying, they stop and listen when I play the slower numbers and I get a lot of enthusiastic applause which encourages me to play for well over two hours.

I sit in the dressing room with Martin, Cheese and some of the other people who run the club. We're all really happy with how it went. Martin insists again that I eat some of the stuff they've bought for me, so we move the empty beer bottles out of the way and spread the food out on the table for everyone to share. After they've gone to so much trouble it seems impolite to point out that my adrenaline is still too high for me to feel hungry, so I force a bit down. They take a photo of me with a piece of bread to prove that I eat.

It's nearly two in the morning and I should be rushing back to Vienna now so I can get an early start for the wedding in the morning, but it's very pleasant hanging around in this candle-lit dressing room with a beer or two, meeting new people. By the time I leave, I'm finally starting to feel a bit peckish, and slip a hunk of bread and a tub of cream cheese in my bag. I'm given a present: an Advent Calendar with a little block of chocolate hidden behind each window. The box has had the lettering on the front changed from 'Adventkalendar' to 'Advertkalendar.'

It's three in the morning and I'm finally back in my hotel room and able to unpack my bags. Must say, I'm really getting hungry now. Good job I brought that food back with me, but unfortunately there is no knife.

Have you ever tried making a cream cheese sandwich with a bottle opener?

26th October

Most of the bands who play in Vienna stay in this hotel, the Fürstenhof, for one very good reason: they do breakfast until midday.

I'm in the breakfast room at eleven to give myself a few hours to wake up properly before the wedding ceremony. PamP and Andi from Garden Gang walk in shortly after me—they arrived last night and will also be playing the gig this evening. They join me at the table and PamP tells me the gruesome details of his recent burst appendix. Suddenly I'm not that hungry any more.

It's a bright and windy day in Vienna, warm in the sun but icy cold in the church. I'm led up to the organ loft, where I'll play. From here I can look down over the vast baroque interior, all soaring pillars and stained glass. It's difficult to believe that without amplification anyone will be able to hear me in this huge space, but the people who built these places knew what they were doing: I try a quick chord on the guitar and it comes ringing back at me with a beautiful natural reverb that no effects box or computer software could ever replicate.

Outside the wind is blowing the Autumn leaves around. Max is standing on the steps in a smart dress coat and new patent Doctor Martens he ordered from London specially for the day.

Just before three, the church fills up and I get back up to the organ loft. I don't know anything about the Austrian wedding ceremony so I am slightly concerned that I'll interrupt the priest and start playing at the wrong moment. One of the other guests up on the balcony promises to cue me in.

Ten minutes into the service, I'm on. I blast into 'Lion And The Lamb' and my voice sounds satisfyingly powerful as it soars around the church. Then there's a whole load more religious stuff.

Outside the church René and Mariann have arrived from Switzerland, just too late for the wedding. While they say hello to the newly weds, PamP and I wander back to the hotel, past a spectacularly crashed BMW, to get our gear together for the gig tonight.

I meet the new Garden Gang drummer Michael, who apart from being a nice bloke also owns a small minibus. There's just enough room for me to squeeze in with the rest of the band and get a lift to the Werbeknecht, a restaurant and large cellar bar where the wedding party and gig will be held. It's right across the street from the the Chelsea club, where I'll be playing tomorrow.

PamP can't lift anything heavy in case he breaks his stitches, so I give a hand to unload the band's equipment, hauling amps and speaker cabinets past all the guests waiting for the buffet, down into the long brick-vaulted cellar.

After soundcheck I notice a programme of events lying on one of the tables: There are two other bands and a transvestite show scheduled, then Garden Gang are down to start at eleven, I'm on at midnight. That leaves six hours with nothing to do but sit around in the bar. I'm contemplating this and wondering what state I'll be in by the time I get onstage when I realise that I don't have the slightest desire to drink any alcohol and instead go for a delicous glass of orange juice and lemonade.

Michael shows me a jolly cartoon of a *weberknecht* spider on the restaurant menu and asks if we have them in England.

I study it carefully. 'No, I don't think so,' I say. 'Do they all wear sunglasses?'

I catch the end of the transvestite show, which is proving to be very popular, but after that the bands are less well-attended—too loud for most of the guests, who spend much of the time upstairs in the restaurant.

Things are already running late; it's past midnight and no sign of Garden Gang being able to get on yet. I open my first beer and apologize to Max that I didn't drink during his entire wedding day, but now I'm ready. He looks around in a panic and grabs the nearest bottle so we can clink a toast.

I take a breath of air outside. It's mild and windy, the clouds scudding across the sky. The soundman wanders out of the club to give his ears a rest between bands and stands next to me. We watch the clouds racing by for a while in agreeable silence.

'Think it must be a full moon,' I say.

He shakes his head. 'No, full moon was a few days ago. But you're right, it does feel like a full moon.'

Nice to know he knew what I meant.

By the time I get onstage at two in the morning there's just the hardcore left in the audience, but they're all looking forward to the set and there's a very special atmosphere. I play until nearly four.

At five, Max is ordering a last round of Jägermeister for us all upstairs, and the bar staff look like they're ready to go home. I realise that I'm pretty hungry now, not having eaten anything except a slice of wedding cake since the end of the afternoon, so I sneak a knife from the restaurant into my bag on the way out. Inside the mini-bar in my hotel room I still have a small hunk of bread and some cheese stashed away. We cram into taxis and all head back to the Fürstenhof, where I slip off speedily to my room in case the party re-starts.

The bread is pretty dry after a day in the mini-bar, but I manage some kind of rough slicing with the disappointingly blunt stolen knife and layer on some of the cream cheese. I'm still hungry, but it's past six—I should sleep. Want to be fit for the Chelsea gig.

27th October

I drag myself awake at ten thirty with the intention of having a shower and a leisurely breakfast then meeting up with René and Mariann for a look round Vienna at midday. I'm rather disappointed when I get to the breakfast room to find out that the clocks went back last night for the end of summer time and I could have had an extra hour in bed. A few of Garden Gang have also made the same mistake.

Always good to be back at the Chelsea, and there are even a few improvements this time. The tiny stuffy dressing room upstairs behind the bar now has a window! I sit up there for a while after soundcheck trying to find some energy. I'm so tired I'm shaking.

Max arrives and looks like he's just about clinging on. He explains that he won't be able to stay for the whole set tonight and his new wife Barbara is already in bed asleep.

The good news is that although we'd all been doubtful if there'd be much of an audience on a Sunday night, by the time I get onstage at ten there's a healthy crowd in, probably my best ever turnout at the Chelsea.

I don't know why, but I always feel relaxed onstage here, and tonight is no exception; the gig goes like a dream and the crowd is with me all the way. There is a slight hiccup after a couple of hours when I break my second string of the evening and find that both spare sets I have on stage with me have the vital one missing. I have to apologise to the audience and dive through them, out to the front of the club and upstairs to the dressing room where I hunt through my bags for the only other set I have with me, which to my bewilderment also lacks the one string I need.

I fight the urge to run away into the night and never come back, and instead make my way back through the crowd and explain that I'm going to have to attempt to put on the wrong string and hope it'll hold. The first one breaks just as I've nearly got it tightened to the right note and there's a collective groan from the audience. I ask them to all cross their fingers for me and I try again with another string. It holds. An almighty cheer goes up and I'm off again, another half hour through the pain barrier and beyond, bolstered by a couple of whiskies someone sends up to the stage.

Upstairs, club manager Othmar sits down with me, delighted by the gig. He taps his watch in disbelief, 'Two hours and ten minutes...' He's been on my side, regularly booking me into the Chelsea through the ups and downs of the last few years, and happy to see it all paying off tonight. As expected, Max had to leave after an hour because he was dropping with exhaustion, but René and Mariann are still here and come up to visit. I reach for a beer, and Othmar says to René, 'He never eats, you know. Every time he plays here I offer him a meal before the gig and he never takes it. Except the first time when we went out to a restaurant and he just had this little plate with a starter on it. All the bands that come here—they all want to eat, it's all they seem to care about. But he never eats...'

I interrupt him. 'It's a question of priorities, Othmar. Of course I eat. I love to eat. But when I'm on tour it messes up the gig. You can't play like I do if you've just eaten. And the whole reason I'm here is to play, not to eat.'

When I get back to the hotel much later the chilled final crust of bread in the minibar falls to crumbs when I try and cut it into two with the stolen knife, and the last scrapings from the cream cheese tub cannot bring it back together.

28th October

On the plane, I show my boarding pass to the stewardess. 'This can't be right, seat 3A?' Right at the front of Business Class.

She checks the ticket and shrugs. 'It's a full flight…'

So without telling me, they've given me an upgrade. How nice to be able to spend the hour waiting for a replacement brake temperature indicator light to be fitted, sitting in a wide seat with a glass of sparkling wine. And when we're finally in the air—ravioli stuffed with vegetables in a cream and herb sauce with a caraway seed roll, followed by a peach and apricot layered sponge cake and belgian chocolates. Linen napkins, metal cutlery—except the knife, which is plastic in case I'm a terrorist. Mind you, those serrated plastic knives are sharper than the metal ones. I certainly wouldn't like to have one of those held to my throat. And if I was going to be a terrorist, I would definitely travel Business Class: you get your Grüner Veltliner in a real wine glass, not plastic, so it wouldn't take much to smash that and…

Down below, the thin clouds part and the landscape blazes gold in the late afternoon Autumn sun. The Danube, the Rhine, like burnished ribbons.

7. THE EMERGENCY SANDWICH (2002)

<u>14th November</u>
Congratulation, Czech Airlines, for the most unappetising vegetarian meal I've ever eaten! The side salad is a little dish of minced white cabbage that has seen better days, mixed with a very few kernels of pallid sweetcorn. The main meal is *exactly the same* salad in a bigger dish. The only way to render it edible is to put it in the miniature bread roll, which then makes the individual pot of apricot jam redundant as there's nothing to spread it on, except the 'refreshing towel,' which—on second thoughts—might have been tastier. It could have been worse: the meat eaters are having an intriguing combination of sliced ham with crabsticks.

I've learned from past experience that eating vegetarian in the Czech Republic can be difficult, and I have the comforting thought that in my bag down in the hold—at least, I hope my bag is in the hold—there is an emergency cheese sandwich, just in case I get really hungry over the next few days.

Petr is waiting in the Arrivals hall and we hurry out to his van. Timing is going to be tight—I'm on stage in a club on the other side of Prague at 10:00 and it's now, ooh, 9:15. Petr speaks very little English and I speak no Czech so our conversation during the journey is somewhat stilted.

'Good weather. Nothing snow,' he says. 'Last week, half meter. Then hot rain, all gone.'

'Good—we have long journey soon!' I say. We will be communicating like this for the next four days.

The support band are just finishing as we pull up to the club. Without the benefit of a soundcheck I launch straight into my set. There are about seventy people in the audience and as far as I can tell from their attempts to chat with me afterwards, they enjoy it.

It's a couple of hours drive back to Petr's club in Teplice, where I'll be sleeping, and already it's past midnight. We head through the suburbs of Prague, where the multinational businesses have established a strong foothold since the revolution. There are futuristic office complexes, hotels, home improvement stores...a giant Tesco sits floodlit in a deserted car park as big as an airport. The only place to eat is a drive-thru McDonald's which I would never normally go near, but a man cannot live on minced cabbage alone so I reluctantly eat the only vegetarian thing they can offer—a salad and a toasted muffin with cheese in it.

The Velvet Club has been having a 'pop night' but there's little sign of it by the time we get there—apart from a few solitary drinkers at the bar everone has gone home. Petr heads home too and I go up to the bands' dressing room on the first floor. Actually, I'm still hungry and very aware of the emergency sandwich in my bag, but it's early days and will probably get worse, so I place the tupperware box in the fridge for more desperate times, then climb one more flight of steep stairs to the sleeping room in the attic, which is warm and has a choice of seven beds. It's great being solo.

15th November

I get up late and there's no one downstairs apart from Petr's helper Jyrki, who lives in the club and doesn't speak any English. But I know how to work the coffee machine.

I've been bored here before, so this time I've brought a good book and sit upstairs reading. The idea of the emergency sandwich is tempting me but I resist it, and after a couple of hours Petr arrives and sorts out breakfast—some bread rolls, cheese and marmalade. It's going to be a long day before tonight's punk festival here, at which I will be the English punk legend, playing after four young local bands. I read a bit more, then go for a walk around the town.

It's a murky, grey, depressing kind of afternoon and Teplice is for the most part a depressing kind of town. Behind the club sits a massive factory with scary red and white striped chimneys. Most of the buildings on the way into the centre are faceless Soviet bloc-style mass-housing interspersed with crumbling older buildings that have a lot of character but are so dilapidated they seem on the point of collapse. Everywhere thick steel pipes from a factory complex snake across the ground and bridge over the roads, leaking steam. In the town centre are a couple of modern supermarkets. I spend the few coins I have on a vitamin drink and a bag of some kind of snack which looks quite tasty from the picture on the front but turns out to be little dry biscuits that taste of rosemary and turn to powder in the mouth.

By the time I've trudged back to the club it's dusk, but there's still no sign of anything happening. There are a few people drinking in the bar but I can't communicate with them so I get another coffee and go upstairs and read some more, my stomach gnawing. An hour later, Petr unexpectedly turns up with a meal he's prepared for me in the kitchen downstairs. It's a pretty heavy affair—deep fried cheese with chips and some canned vegetables—and sits in the stomach like a lead weight, but very welcome all the same.

I wander down into the club. A few of the bands have arrived and someone is wiring up the P.A. system, which looks very rudimentary. Seems like nothing much is going to be happening here in a hurry. I leave them to it, go back upstairs and check my phone, which I'd left in my bag during the afternoon. One missed call. Funny—who'd ring? Two text messages... I check the first and see it's from Gaye back at home.

'We have been burgled.'

Oh shit. Check the time of the call—two hours ago. I check the second message, sent an hour later. 'Burgled. No front door. Can't get through to anyone. Who are insurers?' Oh shit, oh shit. I try and call back, but can't—on my English pay-as-you-go sim card the phone will only let me send text messages. So I send, 'Call me.'

Ten minutes later Gaye rings back and tells me what's happened: she was at work when she got a call from the police telling her someone had been seen breaking into our flat. She rushed back, found the front door hanging off where it had been kicked it in and...

The phone goes dead.

What? I try and send a text back but it won't go through. I check my balance—for the luxury of having someone call me from England for a few minutes, the fifteen pounds credit I had has dropped to fourteen pence, not enough to receive any further calls, not even enough to send a text message. Petr's not around so I can't use his phone, there's no payphone in the club and no one here speaks English.

So I sit there, helpless. Aware that the show must go on and there's nothing I can do about the situation at home for the moment I go down to the stage, and try and sort out the equipment for the gig using sign language with the P.A. guy. I don't know if he understands me. There's obviously not going to be a soundcheck. From now on I am in the land of whatever happens, happens.

Petr's back and I use the office phone for a quick call home, where Gaye is sitting with her hands covered in ink because the police have taken her fingerprints to exclude them from those of the burglar. She is waiting for the insurers to send someone round to fix up the door. I feel bad about being out here unable to help.

It's still chaos on the stage. The singer of one of the other bands called, aptly enough, K.O.S. speaks reasonable English and tells me how much he's looking forward to seeing me play, but I'm finding it hard to get involved. My head's in London. The first few punk rockers and skinheads are in the club and the atmosphere is somehow edgy. Around ten, K.O.S. kick off and I watch some of their set, trying to drown my worries with a beer. It's a hardcore punk audience, crazy dancing and mock fighting in front of the stage. Oh God, I really don't feel like this tonight. Second band comes on...more heavy punk, some ska, more crazy dancing...it's already near midnight.

Still two bands to go, but Petr tells me I should go on next, let the other bands play afterwards. I plug in the guitar and it doesn't work. Takes another ten minutes to track down the problem. I'm in a strange mood, and try to focus by playing a mean high energy set, which seems to suit the evening. Somehow it works and I find myself getting locked in to what I'm doing. As I get into my second encore I'm aware of some kind of fight breaking out over to the left of the club and I make it my last song. Glad it's over, really, but feel a bit better having got it out of my system.

I dry off upstairs then come down and get a beer. The singer from K.O.S is looking pretty disconsolate—seems it was him in the fight. He'd been confronting some Nazi skinheads in between songs during his set and after the gig they decided to see him about it. After five of them had laid into him he called the police who arrived and basically said, nothing to do with us, and went away again. I talk to Petr about it, but he's not that sympathetic.

'Big problem here in Czech, Nazi skinheads, stupid kids. But he singer make website, say, you come club our gig, big trouble...' He taps his head. 'No...what?...no *dialogue*...just say, you come, we fight...stupid...'

Two more bands play, it's all too loud, too aggressive. There's a bad feeling lingering from the violence, but as the night goes on things calm down and the atmosphere improves.

Around five in the morning I go upstairs and fall asleep in seconds.

<u>16th November</u>

I get up at eleven. Downstairs in the bar Petr and Jyrki are making a number plate for the van because the original got stolen 'by gypsies' in the night. This could cause a problem when we cross the border into Slovakia tomorrow.

While Jyrki fixes on the home-made number plate, Petr goes up the road to buy some bread and cheese for breakfast, then he disappears again for a few hours and I'm back with my book and coffee until around four in the afternoon. When he returns I make a call from the office to see how things are at home, then we head off for the four hour drive south to Ostrava, where I'll be playing at a festival, due on stage at around 11:30.

Fog. The four hour drive is going to be a five hour drive. Once we get past Prague and have a couple of hours of road behind us we take a break at a motorway service station to get a meal, but they've stopped cooking and so we make do with a sandwich. I feel lucky—it's the first time I've ever seen a vegetarian sandwich on sale in the Czech Republic. It's a bread roll with a filling of cheese and sliced egg. Oh, and the odd bit of eggshell for added calcium.

On and on down the motorway, through Moravia, and finally at eleven we reach the outskirts of Ostrava, where we're guided straight to the venue by the promoter on his mobile phone. It's a big hall on the first floor of a culture and arts centre. Quite a few people greet me as I hurry in, including a bunch who have come over from Poland to see me play for the first time.

I've arrived late, but things here are running later, and the band on before me are only just taking the stage. They play a kind of experimental rock, but they're too organised, too good at what they do to have any air of danger or excitement about their set. Their shoes are too clean. And they play a long time, despite my new little fan club continually shouting out my name between numbers.

The band finally get offstage and I hurry on and I have a very nice gig, the fans with me all the way. Afterwards they promise to find me some gigs in Poland.

It's two in the morning as I pack away my guitar and change out of my sweat-soaked T-shirt, exchanging a few words with the last stragglers who are desperate to invite me to a nearby bar. But I'm tired, hungry, and desperate to find out where I'm sleeping tonight. Petr and I go outside to wait by the van for the promoter, who has promised to take us to the hostel. He turns up after twenty minutes, then wanders off with Petr, presumably to sort out the money—I have no idea what's going on.

I hang around waiting. It's still mild for November, but there's a strong wind blowing. Three in the morning. Brown, dead leaves from the silver birches are spiralling around and clattering across the car park in great drifts. In the distance, the thrum of music from some unseen club. The wind catches the door of the P.A. truck parked up by the entrance to the hall ready for loading and swings it shut with a mighty clang.

Petr's back. He shrugs his shoulders and says we have to wait a bit longer. He plugs in a portable television to the cigarette lighter and the ghostly light of a fuzzy black and white Czech soap opera fills the van. I get out and walk around, away from the drone of the television, the wind whistling around me, the stars crystal clear overhead, the Plough pointing tail down. At around three-thirty the last of the P.A. system is packed away into the truck and the promoter reappears to lead us out of town and into the hills of the surrounding countryside to the hostel. We pull up in a dark lane in the middle of nowhere and a vicious-looking German Shepherd barks and lunges at us, straining on its long leash, as we ring the bell. A sleepy figure shuffles out of the house, tucking in his shirt, and shows us up to two spartan rooms on the first floor, points out a filthy toilet and shower room on the opposite side of the hallway, then disappears without even giving me a key.

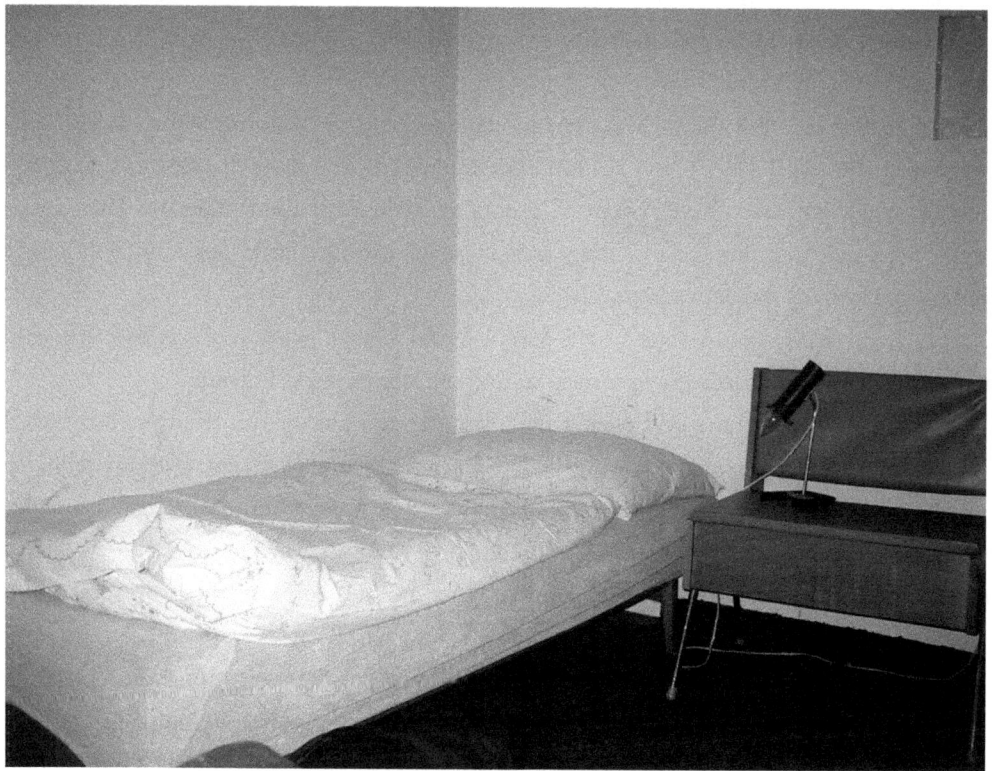

The hotel room with everything...

...even coat hooks

There are two narrow beds in the room. I choose the one next to the radiator, and sit down to start unpacking but it turns out that the springs squeak every time I move, so I switch to the other one. There is a battered wardrobe with nails hammered into the side as makeshift coathooks, and a sheet of faded typewritten paper taped to the wall which itemises everything in the room, right down to the number of pillows (3), table lamps (1), and coat hangers (10). There is nothing here you would ever want to steal, it all looks like it has been accidentally diverted on its final journey between boot sale and skip.

It's now past four in the morning. My stomach is groaning with hunger, and I realise that all I have eaten today is two bread rolls. The only good thing in my world at the moment is that I know that at the bottom of my bag I will find a tupperware box.

Oh, emergency sandwich—your hour has come at last.

17th November

I'm hungry. I'm thirsty. I would have had a drink from the tap but I was halfway through brushing my teeth this morning when I noticed that the water had a suspicious brown tinge to it. Too late to stop when you've got a mouth full of toothpaste. I risk a shower, even though the bathroom contains the soap dish from hell.

At midday we're out of there. We have no idea where we are, but head back towards Ostrava in the hope we can get our bearings and find the road to Slovakia.

Got to eat. Sunday, and all the restaurants are closed. The only place open is a huge Tesco. Petr reckons they will have some kind of Pizzeria and I'm on my knees with hunger by the time we've parked up. All the food concessions at the front of the supermarket are shut, so we head off through the shopping aisles and right at the back find a counter, behind which there are seventy-two chickens spit roasting...and one small square of vegetarian pizza. I queue up anxiously, hoping no one else orders it before me.

Sanitized background music wafts through the supermarket—Tina Turner's 'Simply The Best.' Everyone responsible for this record should have their skin removed with rusty razor blades. I'm volunteering. We stand at a high table in this free market shopping dream world on the anniversary of the Czech revolution and I down the pizza in three bites.

Out past the anonymous concrete housing along the Polish border and south over bumpy roads to the border with Slovakia, where the police give us a hard time about the number plate but let us through. Dusk falls, and the neat cemeteries along the roadside dance with light from the hundreds of candles placed by the graves. Forested, misshapen hills bristle in silhouette against the moonlit sky. Then, finally, we're back on to a motorway and after four hours reach the outskirts of Bratislava, the Slovak capital city.

Seems we don't exactly know where the club is. We drive around endless tower blocks hoping we'll come across it. 'Must find someone who look like punk rocker and ask,' says Petr. But no one looks like punk rocker. After twenty minutes we eventually see a likely candidate so Petr winds down the window and asks directions to the club. There it is, of course—ten metres in front of us.

Support band Zona A arrive moments later. Bratislava is their home town, and Petr and I will be staying tonight at the flat of guitarist Cupe and his girlfriend Eva. We start loading into the club and it's soon obvious why it's called 'Labyrinte'—there's a maze of rooms, each snaking into the next, until you reach the final one, which has the stage in it. It's intimate and low-ceilinged and has all the potential for a good gig.

The place is packed by the time Zona A are ready to start, but word is out that there are some Nazi skinheads in the club and the band don't want to play until they leave. Some negotiation is going on but I can't quite follow it, I'm too tired and the language problems are too difficult. Eventually Zona A get on stage, and the home crowd goes wild, singing along and punching their arms in the air. I wander out into the labyrinth after a few songs and get invited to sit down in one of the adjacent bars with a couple who tell me they have nearly all my solo records. I am impressed—I had no idea anyone in Slovakia would know me.

Back in the music bar it looks like there has been some kind of trouble; the band have left their gear on the stage and gone, and there's a line of security people standing at the front. Kristyna, the singer's girlfriend, says, 'I'm so sorry about this, TV...'

Uh—sorry for what? I don't even know what's going on here but the atmosphere is pretty tense. I grab my guitar and tune up, but there's no soundman around.

One of Zona A comes up to me. 'Sorry about this, TV.' *Sorry for what?!* 'The manager would like for you to start playing as soon as possible.'

'I'm ready,' I say. 'But the soundman's gone...'

Petr comes over to side stage. 'Tim, you'd better start...'

'I CAN'T START, THERE'S NO SOUNDMAN!' Oops, I'm shouting.

Boy, I'm wired up by the time the soundman appears. The place is a sauna of heaving bodies and I give it everything I have for the next ninety minutes, then collapse in a pool of sweat after two encores.

I get into a dry T-shirt and go up to the the bar with Zona A and some of their friends. Everyone's having fun but I feel myself drifting every time the conversation shifts into Slovak or Czech. Cupa spots I'm in trouble and searches out Petr, who jumps up and grabs my guitar, then we're in the van and heading back to the flat, where Eva—a vegetarian—has made tofu soup and a spinach pie. This is more like it!

Eva speaks good German, which means I'm back in the conversation, although with four of us in the room it all gets a bit complicated about who understands who and we keep accidentally launching into the wrong language to the wrong person. There is Czech, Slovak, English and German going on here and it can get confusing. Finally we call it a night. I'm shown to my own room. The cats are shooed out and the fishtank is unplugged so the noise of the filter won't disturb me. Luxury.

18th November

I need to be in Prague for my flight at 5:45 this afternoon so Petr reckons we should leave at around, ooh 10, 11, 12…it's a straight 300 kilometre run up the motorway so shouldn't be any problem. I'm up soon after ten and get a quick shower, and by the time I'm out Eva has coffee brewing. I hadn't realised that Cupe had to get up to go to work in his newspaper shop at seven—after just two hours sleep—but when he pops back for a quick breakfast with us he's looking pretty fit despite the late night.

We're giving Kristyna a lift back to Prague—she turns up shortly before midday and we say our goodbyes and hit the road. We're held up briefly at the border by some police who aren't too bothered about the number plate but seem amused that the documents for the van say it is green when in fact it is blue. Then we're through, and back into the Czech Republic. Petr decides to stop off at a bank in Brno to change up some money into sterling.

'But first we have to get petrol' he says as we pull off the motorway. At that very moment the engine cuts out and we cruise to a stop at the lights. He slaps the wheel. There's still hope though, a fuel station in sight just down the road. Frantically he turns the key a few times and miraculously the engine starts up. We pull across the junction, the van bucks and cuts out again…and we roll the last fifty meters to the petrol pump.

We win!

Through traffic into Brno, the bank, then we stop off at a Makro store so Petr can buy some supplies of toilet roll for his club. While he's in there Kristyna asks me when my flight is, and I say, I think around five forty-five.

But it starts something turning in my mind. When we're back on the motorway I check my ticket. Oh dear, the plane gets in to England at 5:45, leaves at 4:55 local time. Petr shrugs, no problem—still three hours to go and only a couple of hundred kilometres. He puts his foot down.

There are a few road works and police radars about, and I'm getting worried as check-in time passes and we still have 35 kilometres to go. I do not want to miss this flight. We drop Kristyna off by the side of the motorway on the outskirts of Prague and crawl along among increasing traffic round the orbital route. Thirty-five minutes to go and we can see the airport ahead but still have to drive round to the terminal building.

'4:45 or 4:55?' asks Petr.

'4:55.'

'We can do it. As long as you are there ten minutes before fly.'

'You think so?'

'I know. They will shout but will be okay.'

Twenty minutes to go as I drag my guitar and bag out of the back of the van, scattering multi-packs of Makro toilet roll across the road, and give Petr the briefest of handshakes before running into the terminal building, where the screen says check-in has closed.

But there's no queue at the desk so I charge across to it and start pleading. The woman there has to phone up the gate to see if the plane can take my baggage, and talks to them in Czech with an infuriating lack of urgency. She breaks off to point at the guitar case and ask me, 'What kind of instrument is that?'

'It's a guitar.'

'You're going to check it in?'

'I don't mind, whatever's easiest—just as long as I get on the flight.'

'Let me see your other bag. Hmm. It's too big for hand luggage.'

'I'll check it in. I don't care what happens with the baggage. JUST AS LONG AS I GET ON THE FLIGHT!' Oops, I'm shouting again.

She relays the information to the gate, then there's a pause which lasts forever while she waits for a call back to let her know if she's going to be allowed to check me in. The phone rings. She picks it up in slow motion.

It's a yes.

I'm through customs and running down to the gate…where I find the flight has been delayed ten minutes, which stretches into twenty, then thirty. Everyone is complaining about it except me—every extra minute increases the chances of my baggage being on the same plane as me.

By the time we board I've got my breath back and I'm in the mood for a nice glass of wine and some minced cabbage.

8. BACK IN THE U.S.A. (2003)

19th March

I'm leaving at 14:00 for my second-ever tour of the U.S.A.—ten days on the East Coast, many of them in New York, where I'll be staying again with promoter Bryan. The last trip was a bit of a washout, very stressful conditions and low attendances, but I had so many emails afterwards asking me to come back that I've decided to give it just one more try. For most of these dates I'll be supporting New York band World/Inferno Friendship Society, so at least there should be more people at the gigs.

Not that I'll be playing any gigs of course! I couldn't afford a work permit and am hoping that with the second Gulf War looking like it will start any day now the immigration authorities will have more important things to worry about than a guy with a guitar.

On the way to the tube station I notice a strange smell rising up from my shoulder bag. A closer inspection reveals a curious shiny coating on the inside of the front flap. Then I remember—the last time I used the bag was for a gig in Ipswich a couple of weeks ago. Afterwards as I was walking back to where I was staying the night a boy racer roared past in a turbo-charged sporty car and threw an egg at me, scoring a direct hit. I cleaned it up as best I could but didn't notice that it had crept up inside the bag. Heading off for a tour of the U.S. with old egg stinking up your luggage—it's not ideal.

Despite the paranoia over the impending war—last week there were tanks on the streets outside Heathrow—I get through airport security faster than I ever have before and have time to kill before my flight. I wander around the shops and buy a set of high-tech earplugs. Let's hope I don't need them.

There are plenty of things to occupy the mind on a six hour flight. While idly reading through the customs form, I notice a clause stating that I have to declare if I am 'carrying into the country any cell cultures or snails.' Well, let me just check.

To my surprise I'm waved straight through immigration. Clearly I don't look like the kind of guy who's going to be smuggling snails, but the dried egg might have raised a few questions on the cell culture front. Bryan is at Arrivals to meet me and we wander out to his car and drive along the bay, sparkling in the cool Spring sunshine, back to his place in Brooklyn. We switch on the TV and see that U.S. led forces have just launched the first air strikes against Iraq. It's wall-to-wall war on all channels.

When Alyssa gets back from work, the three of us go for a good Mexican meal across the road, then it's back to Bryan's, where I'll be sleeping in the office. The cats have the knack of hiding under the bed just out of reach, but I soon discover the knack of gently sweeping them out with an umbrella until they realise the game's up and stalk out of the room in a huff.

20th March

Wake up early after a dream that I have to play a gig but all my plectrums are broken.

As I check my emails on Bryan's computer, he sheepishly points out a small piece of tinted window shade from the World Trade Centre that sits next to the monitor. 'I suppose it's a bit tasteless, but—well, it just floated in the window. I had to keep it.'

The first gig of the tour is at Maxwell's over in New Jersey and on the way we stop off at WFMU for a live session on Dianne's afternoon show. When we come out the rain is hammering down, which gets me worrying about whether anyone will brave the elements to come out to the gig. We drive the couple of miles over to Maxwell's and find World/Inferno Friendship Society waiting to soundcheck. The band are a nine-piece with members from New York, Israel and Turkey. There are six guys and three women, and the instruments include a horn section, percussion and accordion as well as the usual guitar, bass and drums. At least with a set-up like that you don't have to worry about earning a living from music. It's impossible.

I have a good gig, then World/Inferno play a blinder to a full house of their New York fans. After hanging around for a while after the show drinking with some of the audience and getting quuite a lot of beer spilled on me by the more enthusiastic of them, Bryan takes me back to Brooklyn, where we watch some of the twenty-four hour war coverage on the television with increasing despondency until we can't take it anymore. Bryan dozes on the couch and I slip off to the bedroom, sweep the cats out and hit the sack.

21st March

Bryan's exhausted from spending the night on the couch, whereas I've had a good night's sleep and I'm starting to feel like I'm finally recovering from the flight. Mind you, this jet lag's a funny thing: one minute you're feeling top of the world, the next your head is full of lead and you're slumped over the side of the chair thinking, I would do *anything* to go to sleep for twelve hours *right now*...

Before we leave for Boston I walk up the road to the local music shop and buy lots of plectrums. Always respect your dreams.

With just Bryan and me on the road, there's plenty of room in the Honda—good job too as this is going to be a five hour drive. We hit traffic straight away leaving New York, but it's fairly interesting as Bryan points out the sights as we crawl along. Ooh, look—Rikers Island. Not to be confused with Coney Island.

Flags of all sizes have sprouted by the roadside and from buildings along the way to support the servicemen in Iraq. Sometimes this support takes unusual forms: a fast food place we pass near Providence has a twenty-foot high buck-toothed yellow rabbit outside, and planted on its chest is a banner saying 'Pray For Our Troops.'

The venue is an odd one. It's called the International Community Church, has an open door policy to people of all religions, and occasionally put on bands particularly aimed at young people. The gigs run early and are non-drinking and non-smoking events. They also appear to be non-P.A. system events: I walk in to the plain assembly-room style hall in the basement of the church to see a guy struggling with a tiny mixing desk and a couple of shoe-box size speakers nowhere near big enough for this room. All that's coming out of them is the sound of feedback. About ten young bands are hanging around waiting to play. World/Inferno phoned Bryan up a while back to say they weren't going to bother with a soundcheck—now I see why.

We're invited into the church kitchen in the next room and are delighted to see there's some food there for us. Even better, it's vegan—although closer inspection reveals a rather disturbing slab of imitation duck, made of seitan. Pronounced 'Satan.' Interesting choice of food for a church.

Jack, the singer of World/Inferno, wanders in and reveals a bottle of red wine from inside his jacket which he proffers in my direction, but is spotted by one of the gig organisers who rushes over in a panic.

'No, no! You can't have wine in here! What would happen if the police came...!'

Possibly the police have better things to do than search church kitchens looking for private citizens drinking wine, but who knows? This is America.

A photographer called John who's been emailing me about taking some portrait shots since I met him last time I was in Boston walks into the kitchen just as I'm toying with the last of the strange duck. He tells me he's found a great location for the shoot, and takes me up some stairs to the balcony of the church. We are stopped on the way by one of the gig organisers who asks what we're doing. He lets us pass when we say that we just want to get some photos, but explains that he doesn't usually let people up here because they have homeless members of the congregation sleeping in the room on the opposite side of the balcony, and also the dog is usually loose so we should be careful where we tread. Indeed, the unseen pooch has left a few offerings in amongst the pews.

As we start to take the first photos, a woman comes into the church below us and kneels briefly at the altar, glancing nervously over her shoulder to see what we're up to in the balcony. Then she breaks into a bout of free-form wailing which fills the church. At the end of every passage she stops for a moment. The last note reverberates around, then the room settles gradually into silence, at which point she suddenly starts up again. Meanwhile, the thrashing of drums and electric guitars in the background suggests that the gig in the basement has begun.

'Just try and look natural,' says John.

As he snaps away, I point out to him that this is one of the most surreal experiences I've had. John tells me about one that beats it: last year he went to photograph an ex-member of a punk band who now lives in an extreme religious community on Cape Cod. The church there was having what they call a 'Hell House,' a series of walk-through tableaux set up under canvas inside a church, designed to warn of the perils of Godlessness. John was asked if he'd like to go into the Hell House, and found himself being led in complete darkness through the most bloodthirsty scenes imaginable, all acted out by members of the church in full costume. It included one where Christians were being questioned about their religious beliefs by military police, then dragged outside their homes and shot when they refused to deny Christ. The final tableau consisted of screaming children covered in blood gnawing on the legs of the devil. When John came out of the Hell House a terrible storm was raging so he was offered a bed for the night by the church, but he was so shaken up he drove for hours through the storm home to Boston, where he lay awake the rest of the night.

Bryan comes up to tell me that I'll be on in half an hour so we hurriedly wind up the photo session. Downstairs the hall is packed with young people and there's a good atmosphere. World/Inferno greet me as I hurry into the kitchen, and a number of bottles of wine appear. They tell me that while I was upstairs some of the local bands played, but the P.A. system was really bad. I get straight out into the venue and plug the guitar in. The sound is truly appalling, and none of the controls on the mixing desk make any difference. The sound man just shrugs his shoulder and looks apologetically at me. I sigh and put down the guitar. 'I'll be back in a moment.'

I go into the kitchen and tell World/Inferno the news: 'It's the worst P.A. system I have ever heard.' Then I go out and play the gig.

Luckily it's a great audience. They're thrilled when I unplug after the first number and play acoustically, even though hardly anyone can hear me once they start clapping along. There's no stage, so the front few rows gather around campfire-style while those at the back stand on chairs and sit on shoulders to see what's going on. Meanwhile, behind me, a couple of the guys from World/Inferno are plugging my guitar and vocal microphone into one of their amps, and while it's hardly hi-fi it's good enough to get me through the next 40 minutes.

The crowd go even wilder for World/Inferno. The room is a sweat box, and people are being passed over the heads of the audience. Some have come dressed up for the evening; at one point I see Spiderman go by.

Then there's the little matter of where to stay tonight. World/Inferno are spreading themselves among friends in the area, Bryan and I are considering whether to head back to New York or stay at a place just outside Boston owned by relations of his who are away at the moment. In the end, the idea of driving for five hours is just too daunting so we decide to take the local option.

Good choice—as soon as we get out of the city the fog is so thick that it's impossible to read the street names from the car. Despite this, we eventually find our way to where we are staying, a large house out in the woods. It's chilly here, thick snow still lying in drifts on the ground. Bryan has instructions on how to get in by pressing a security code into a keypad, but we have a nasty moment when we can't find the keypad.

Eventually we're in. It's a great relief to be in the warm; kitchen, shower and bedrooms at our disposal. Oh, and rather a good selection of wine. A note says we're welcome to help ourselves to whatever we want. Well, that Merlot looks promising...

Bryan checks out the news on the computer. 'Oh my God,' he shouts from the other room. 'We just accidentally bombed Iran instead of Iraq with a Tomahawk!' Smart bombs, just one letter out with the spelling.

Bryan, guitar, car

<u>22nd March</u>

We have to phone up Bryan's relations to find out how to get the automatic garage door shut, but then we're off back to New York. Although we're out of the house by ten it's soon clear we're not going to make it to the city in time for the peace march being held this afternoon, but Alyssa is there and we get reports from her on the mobile. When we get back to Brooklyn there's just time to get a quick bite to eat and change guitar strings before getting on the subway for tonight's gig at the Tribeca.

Bryan asks for directions at the subway from a cop, who sends us in the wrong direction and we go so far that we end up having to get a cab back to the venue. By the time we finally walk in, World/Inferno and Dianne from WFMU are already there and soundcheck is underway.

This is a good-looking club, a nice size and a decent P.A., but the management have a rather unfriendly attitude to the bands. When I finish my soundcheck I see all nine members of World/Inferno being led into a side room in the backstage area downstairs by the boss of the place and the door shuts behind them. Some time later they come out looking pale, and tell me that the manager stood in front of the door and told them: 'I hear you sometimes use pyrotechnics in your act. I'm telling you now, there's going to be no FUNNY STUFF tonight. Any FUNNY STUFF and you are going to be in big trouble...'

Bryan introduces me to Mojo, who is the biggest black guy you ever did see, about the size of a house. Mojo helps Bryan at some of his gigs, mainly doing DJ sets, but he's also useful to have around to help with security. You would have to be suicidal to try anything on with a guy this size. As with many big people, he has an extremely sweet and funny nature. He's an ex-Vietnam vet and has had to kill people in combat while he was over there. He is very dismissive of some of the people who cause trouble at gigs: 'They just have no idea what life is worth...'

Bryan, Mojo, Dianne and me decide to get out of the club for a while. We squeeze past the line of people waiting to get in, and can't help noticing what a young audience World/Inferno attracts. In the bar, Mojo says, 'When ah was walkin' outta that club ah felt like a CHALD molesta'! Summa these kids is no bigger'n ma HEAD! Ah'm tellin' ya, ah've eaten DINNAHS bigger'n most a these kids!'

Back at Tribeca the place is packed out. I have a really good feeling about this one, and sure enough, it's a fantastic gig. I'm particularly pleased that the new anti-war song 'Not In My Name' is going down so well. I had a feeling I might be lynched for playing this over here but the audiences so far have reacted really well to it, and tonight they're even singing along.

Once again, World/Inferno are playing to a home crowd and go down a storm, although I sense a certain bad mood in the air after the way they've been treated by the management. Also, they've not been given any complimentary drinks by the club—probably because it might lead to FUNNY STUFF—so there are a lot of pointed references from the stage by Jack to the fact he is drinking delicious water tonight. I, on the other hand, am drinking delicious beer: a fan in the audience came up to me at the bar wanting to talk to me about songwriting and after I answered his questions he turned to the woman serving and said, 'Whatever this guy wants, all night, on my tab.' Way, hey!

The night gets late and security is shunting us out. As we leave I notice that a rather amateurish painting of a shipwreck in the dressing room has been defaced. One of the drowning victims now has a speech bubble saying, 'This club! This club!' Another is saying, 'Eight Bucks for a drink...?' I wonder who could have written that?

Doll

While looking for a cab, Bryan points out the corner where the shot for the back cover of the first New York Dolls album was taken. The building is covered in scaffolding so it doesn't look much like I remember it, but I nip over there for a photo anyway. You have to.

23rd March

A short set tonight to help launch a weekly protest song night promoted by Lach at the Sidewalk Café. They don't have soundchecks there so I won't need to arrive until just before I play, and as it's a beautiful Spring day I head off mid-morning for a long walk. I stop off at Brooklyn Heights for a bagel and an energy drink to set me up for the day. An inspection of the label of the energy drink reveals that it contains not only the expected ginseng and ginkgo, but is also 'boosted with eleutherococcus senticosus,' and advises me to strap on my seat belt before it 'kicks in.' Heaven knows what I'm drinking.

Over Brooklyn Bridge I stroll, into Manhattan, then down past the gawping tourists and army guard outside the hole in the ground that used to be the World Trade Centre, and on to Battery Park where I notice a small area of patchy grass cordoned off with a sign in front of it: 'Lawn Closed—Do Not Enter.'

I sit on a bench for a while, taking in the warm sunshine and looking across the sparkling waters of the bay. Then, with the sun sinking below the horizon, I make my way back along the waterfront past the old piers, many of which have been turned into characterless tourist shopping centres. Starting to worry about how late it's getting, I take the subway across to Brooklyn but can't get the connection I need so jog back down Court Street to Bryan's, where there's just enough time for me to change strings on the guitar before we have to get back on the subway for the Sidewalk Café.

Not many people in the venue, but it's only a small room so it's cosy enough, and my set goes well. Then there's a list of people up to do a few songs each for the rest of the night. I don't really want to listen to any more music, and the upstairs bar is filled with the noise of the Oscar ceremonies on television, so Bryan and I walk the block to Manitoba's, where I'll be playing tomorrow, for a nightcap, then take a cab back to Brooklyn.

24th March

I'm looking forward to tonight—back at Manitoba's nine months after my first appearance there, Jayne County on the decks again. The sound was terrible last time I played, so as soon as we arrive I get straight down to fiddling with the faders and EQ on the mixing desk, keeping up a running commentary into the microphone the whole time to hear if things are improving. 'I'll just plug into channel two here and roll some of the mid off. YEAH! TWO, TWO! ONE, TWO! Yep, that's not bad...don't want any of that reverb, though, unless there's a shorter one, let's try a fifty millisecond delay...delay...'

Manitoba leans over from the bar and addresses the room. 'What language is that guy speaking?'

with Handsome Dick, Mojo...

Plenty of familiar faces in the audience, and another very enjoyable gig, lots of people singing along. Jayne starts spinning records straight after I've finished and then it seems half the audience want to get a photo of me and her together, or me and Manitoba, or all three of us. There's no backstage, so nowhere to escape for even a minute, and the sweat hasn't dried before I'm being dragged back and forth across the room by people with cameras. There are also many Adverts and TV Smith records to sign. While I'm doing my meet and greet, Bryan—in his secondary role as bartender—keeps a steady supply of drinks heading in my direction.

...Jayne County & Leee

I'm surprised to bump into the legendary New York photographer Leee Black Childers, who I haven't seen since he photographed the Adverts back in 1977. Leee is thrilled to hear that I still live with Gaye and delighted that I am still playing. 'We liked a lot of the London punks—the Clash and the Pistols—but you know, we always thought that the Adverts were the nice guys,' he tells me. He wants me to meet the latest young band he is helping out and insists on holding my hand and taking me over to them. 'Don't worry,' he whispers as he leads me through the crowd, 'it's nothing *homosexual.*'

Bryan and I go out to a restaurant with Dianne and Bobby, the ex-drummer from Bad Religion, and by the time we get back to the apartment it's past five and already light. I lie in bed aware of the sounds of morning starting up outside, and although it's not *that* disturbing and probably won't stop me from sleeping, it occurs to me that this is a good time to try out the high-tech earplugs I bought at Heathrow. I get out of bed and rummage through my bag until I find them, but there's a dilemma. There are two types of noise: the chattering of birds in the trees outside the apartment, and the low rumble of early traffic coming in on the elevated freeway at the end of the street. So do I use the high frequency filters or the low frequency filters? I decide that the bird noise is more annoying than the traffic so I check the instructions and see that to cut out the high frequencies I have to plug in the purple end pieces into the earplugs. But afterwards I can still hear the birds quite clearly so I decide to try the low filter instead, get out of bed again and remove the purple filters—not that easy to get out actually—and push in the blue ones.

Well, I'm damned if I can tell the difference. In fact, I can still hear everything as if I wasn't wearing earplugs at all. The only noticeable change is that the stiff plastic stalk containing the filter feels like it's going to plunge down into my eardrum every time I turn over. Isn't it a design fault if a pair of earplugs punctures your eardrum? I get so worried about it I remove them and pull the blanket over my head.

But after all that I can't get to sleep for ages.

25th March

Although I was late in bed last night, the time change is still playing tricks on me and I wake up after a few hours and go through my emails. Apart from meeting with Jack Rabid at lunchtime I have the day free, so I'm going to take it easy. If I can't sleep, at least I can relax. Late in the morning, after quite a few attempts to phone him, I finally hear back from Jack, and take the subway in to his office in an old tenement block on the Lower East Side where he puts together 'Big Takeover' magazine.

'Hi TV,' he says, 'didn't think you'd be in a hurry for lunch, heard you were having breakfast at five this morning...'

Blimey, word travels fast round these parts. It turns out that Bobby from Bad Religion is staying at the office at the moment and told Jack about last night as they passed on the stairs. Bobby was rushing out in the hope of meeting his hero Ringo Starr who's doing a book signing up the road. Jack and I wander out for lunch. We discuss music, the world and the war, then Jack goes back to work on the magazine and I go for a walk around East Village, over to Washington Square and on up to Times Square, then get a subway back to Bryan's place.

In the evening we meet up with Bobby again outside the Bowery Ballroom, a nicely shabby mid-sized music venue. Bobby is in rather a bad mood. He'd bought along an old

Beatles poster to the bookstore for Ringo to sign, but had to queue for three hours before he could even reach the great man. Even worse, it turned out Ringo would only sign copies of his book and nothing else. When Bobby finally got to him, Ringo glanced at the poster, signalled to his personal bouncer with a shake of his head, and Bobby was hustled away without even getting to say a word.

We bump into Manitoba and his wife up in the balcony. The venue is full, but the band are dull, and after playing 'spot the riff' for a while, Bryan, Bobby and me slip out to find somewhere to eat. We decide on Chinese as New York is famous for the quality of its Chinese food, and end up being presented with one of the most bizarre menus I've ever seen. Neither Bryan or Bobby are vegetarian but even they are surprised to find items such as 'Chicken and Frog,' a pairing rarely seen together in the wild, let alone on a plate. We get out of there and go to a place that serves an omelette. We're just round the corner from Manitoba's again, so it's back there for a nightcap.

As we sit around the table with a tequila, Bobby shows me how to fold up a dollar bill so it looks like the twin towers in flames. Handsome Dick tells me his dentist is called James Brown. Take it to the bridge!

It's late but mercifully not light when we get back to Bryan's and after the last few nights I'm not going to have any trouble sleeping. One thing's for sure, I'm not bothering with the earplugs.

26th March

Another day off, time for another look around the city.

Walking up 5th Avenue a dishevelled-looking guy falls into step beside me, gesticulating and speaking loudly in a very angry tone of voice. I'm not sure if he's dangerous or just a bit strange. 'You're no bigger'n a molecule to me!' he shouts suddenly, and I speed up to get away, but he keeps up pretty well and he's soon back by my side. 'The ego on these guys is *unbelievable*,' he rants, brushing against me. 'They think they're bigger'n Proxima Centauri!'

I'm getting a bit alarmed now, but when I almost walk out into the street while the 'Don't Walk' sign is still showing, the guy gently raises a hand in front of me and drops his voice. 'Hey, careful buddy...'

On towards Central Park and the Metropolitan. I pass an area bristling with news reporters, cameras and police and realise it's the Iraqi embassy, which was mentioned in a news report yesterday as being 'probably the safest place in New York.' I give up on my plan to look around the Metropolitan today when I realise there's not enough time left, but have a quick wander around the entrance hall—more than I managed last year, at least.

Outside it has started to rain, and it's got pretty cold, so I head back and spend the evening with Alyssa and Bryan. I'm enjoying myself and feeling pretty relaxed after a couple of days off but looking forward to getting back to playing. Tomorrow Bryan and I will drive down to Philadelphia for the first out-of-town date of the tour.

27th March

Things have improved at the Pontiac Grille in Philadelphia since last time I was here in July. This time they're letting me use the dressing room! Mind you, because I'm supporting the nine-piece World/Inferno Friendship Society, there's still nowhere to sit. It's a narrow cubby hole up on the top floor of the club, every inch of floor space covered with instruments and bags, every inch of wall space covered with graffiti. 'Nirvana are there somewhere,' says the promoter.

Nirvana are there somewhere

Bryan wants to check out a couple of the local independent record stores so we take a walk around the area. The second store we go into, the guy behind the counter is in the middle of a phone call and breaks off for a minute when he sees me.

'Say, is your name Tim?'

'Yes...'

'TV Smith?'

'Yes.'

He puts the phone back to his mouth. 'He's just walked in. You wanna speak to him...?' He hands the phone over to me.

It's one of the U.S. fans who's been emailing me, and who just happened to be phoning the store to find details of tickets for tonight. We chat for a while. I've never actually met him.

Then the store owner brings out some copies of the newly-released Adverts Anthology for me to sign. I'm pretty surprised to see it; I didn't know it was out yet and don't even own a finished copy myself. I sign the gig poster hanging behind the counter—so *that's* how he knew who I was—and we get some photos taken together for the shop wall.

Back at the club, my set goes well. It's not an all-ages show so a lot of World/Inferno's audience can't get in, but I recognise quite a few people from last time I was here. When I play Lord's Prayer I notice the guy selling tickets at the door jumping up joyously with his fists in the air. As I head for the dressing room after the set he grabs me and asks who he should contact because he wants to do a trip-hop cover version of the song. He says it will be very different from mine. 'See, I do a sort of Jamaican Dance Hall mixed with Harry Connick Junior.'

We have a motel booked on the outskirts of town. One of the bridges on the way is shut for repairs, so we have to take a different route and suddenly the map doesn't work any more. We are miles up the road on the freeway, take a U-turn and head back into Philadelphia only to become completely lost again. We don't know where we are or how to get where we are going. It's past three in the morning, there's no one around to ask. We will never find the motel. We will never sleep. We will drive around Philadelphia until we die.

28th March

When we eventually found the motel last night we were greeted by the slowest receptionist in the world who took another half hour to fill out the forms, just what you need at four in the morning. Consequently, our first priority when we reach Washington today is to find the damn motel and check in. It's another Motel 6—cheap and not very cheerful, way out of the centre in what looks, according to Bryan, like a former housing projects building. Bryan should know; he had to visit the projects all the time in his previous job as a social worker before he turned full time music agent earlier this year.

So we're in, and there's the time to shower and air a few clothes before we need to go to the gig. At five we meet up in Reception with Bryan's brother Eric, who lives nearby, and he drives us to the subway in his posh company Mercedes. He has no intention of parking it outside the gig, he tells us. Although Washington is home to the White House, the Pentagon, and numerous billion-dollar industries, it also has rampant poverty, violence and high unemployment, and tonight's venue is in one of the rougher areas. In the subway Eric studies the map and considers our options. He points at one of the stations, 'We could get off here and walk the rest of the way. There *are* three of us…'

The Velvet Lounge is a venue in miniature, a compact stage in a small room with a really good sound system. It's on the first floor, with the bar downstairs. The place has a good atmosphere, and it's so small it shouldn't be too hard to fill—good news after my last appearance in Washington at the Black Cat, where virtually no one turned up.

As soundcheck approaches a discussion starts about the running order. There's a local band on the bill as well as World/Inferno and me, and they insist they have to go on second, bumping me into the bottom slot. Their advertising promotes them as being authentic punk rock and I feel like telling them that there wouldn't be any punk rock if me and a few other bands hadn't started it twenty five years ago, but I really haven't got the energy to argue. I tell them to pick whatever slot they like on the bill, I don't care. In a bad mood, I go and hang around outside, where waves of police cars drive by and sirens wail in the distance. A guy comes up and talks to me for a while then starts trying to tap me for money, not menacingly but fairly insistently, until one of the door staff chases him off.

My gig is good. A lot of the World/Inferno fans who follow them around have tuned into me now and know the songs. The gig by the authentic punk band is satisfyingly boring, then World/Inferno come on and go down a storm.

Have forgotten to eat but it's too late now. Cab to the motel. Sleep.

29th March

Breakfast is a priority, so it's a bit of a shock to find that Washington is almost completely closed at weekends. Bryan and I drive around for ages, getting increasingly tetchy, parking up and trying one door after another to no avail until we finally come across a couple of expensive designer coffee and snack bars right in the centre of town. Revived with coffee and something to eat, we get back in the car and head off for the last gig of the tour in Richmond, Virginia.

Down here the freeways are clearer, flanked with long stretches of forest, hardly a big town to be seen along the way. We head straight for the motel, which proves to be some way out of Richmond, right on the edge of the local airport.

Driving into town, the sky is turning a thunderous shade of grey, a ghost of a rainbow settling over the downtown tower blocks. Our map to the venue doesn't show the one way streets so we have to drive in the wrong direction for a while through some rundown areas—'Mmm, yes, this is definitely the 'hood,' says Bryan at one point—and try to circle our way back.

Fittingly for the last gig of the tour, this is also the last gig for the 929 Café, a long-running Richmond alternative music venue whose owners are now closing it down. The promoter has managed to re-book all her scheduled gigs into other venues in town, but it won't be the same. On the bright side, all the drink she's bought for future shows has to be used up tonight because she doesn't have any way to move it. We'll do our best!

Tonight has that elegiac quality of all good last nights. I've become good friends with World/Inferno Friendship Society and the fans who travel around with them over the last two weeks. While a local support band play, we hang around outside in the steamy air watching the lightning flash over the rooftops, taking a few photos of each other and reminiscing about the tour, until the security guy for the venue comes out and grumbles at us for drinking outdoors.

Right after my set the storm breaks. I stand by the back door watching a blanket of rain drop out of the sky. It's really something. Within a couple of minutes the water level rises, up over the threshold of the door and...uh oh, the corridor from the back door slopes down into the venue and soon the water is flooding into the club like a river. The promoter is trying to mop it away and the security guy is out there in the downpour trying to unplug the drain, but the rainwater is already settling in great pools around the toilets at the back of the club. Still, makes a change from what usually lies in pools on the floors of toilets at clubs.

When the rain has slackened off and the worst of the flood has been mopped up I take the opportunity to visit the loo, and notice that on the wall in front of me someone has written 'TV Smith is better than all of you.' Nice to know people are thinking of me at that special moment at the urinal.

World/Inferno play, then we all end up in the bar next to the venue. After saying our goodbyes Bryan drives me back to the motel. Oh the irony: it's now the early hours of Sunday morning, the tour is over and I'm standing on the balcony looking out over an airport runway but it will be Monday night before my flight leaves from New York, Tuesday morning before I get home. Suddenly the word 'hijack' springs into my head.

30th March

So much for Spring, it's snowing, and there's a seven hour drive through the blizzards and traffic to New York ahead of us. When we finally get there it seems to take nearly as long to find somewhere to park. There is a handy spot near the apartment down a dead-end road by a sign marked *End* but Bryan refuses to park there because, he says, for a number of junkies and gang members it literally has been the end.

Still another day to go before I get out of here.

31st March

The snow has stopped but there's a freezing wind howling over Brooklyn. Bryan drives me to the airport late afternoon before the traffic builds. We go the longer but more scenic route, along the bay, the coastal flats etched out against the water in the crisp cold air. The world has never been in sharper focus.

So, tomorrow morning I'll be home and after only four or five days I'll be over the jet lag and functioning more or less normally and able to carry on with my life. And will I come back to America? Last year's trip was pretty much a disaster; this time a lot better. I'm building a small fanbase on the East Coast now, but is it enough to sustain another visit? Have I got the time when there's so much to do in Europe? In America I don't have any records released, I'm not officially allowed to play gigs without a work permit, could knock myself out touring and still not get anywhere. But the people who come to the shows enjoy them and keep asking when I'll be coming back…

Will I? Won't I?

THE END

9. FIESTA! (2003)

24th April

Well, this is going to be a nice change—a few gigs in sunny Catalonia, set up for me by Jonathan, the bass player in a Spanish band called Suzy & Los Quattro. The idea came up more than a year ago in a 'wouldn't it be nice if...' kind of way, and finally it's happening. TV Smith mania is not exactly sweeping through Spain but Jonathan managed to find three gigs. I'll be lucky to get much more than the cost of my flight back, but it's the chance to play in a new country, and Suzy & Los Quattro are recording a single with a couple of my songs on it so I'm going to sing on that while I'm here. Who knows, it could be the start of something.

Jonathan has taken a lot of trouble to make sure everything runs smoothly. He's making sure I get a bed every night, has promised to find me vegetarian food and has planned all the gigs and the recording session down to the finest detail. He even emailed me a few Spanish phrases that he thought I might find useful:

'Jonathan, cállate de una puta vez.' *Jonathan, won't you please shut the fuck up?*

'Jonathan, el bacon NO es un vegetal.' *Jonathan, bacon is NOT a vegetable.*

Suzy and Jonathan are at Barcelona airport to meet me, along with their friend Uri, who helps out with the driving. It's early evening so we head straight off to Tarragona for tonight's gig. I'll be playing a solo show at this one, then for the next two nights Suzy and band will be supporting me and we'll play a few songs together.

Despite the detailed plans, we still can't find the club. I sit in the back of the car and gaze appreciatively at Tarragona's tree-lined streets, fountains and Roman amphitheatre as we drive around, while Jonathan and Uri try to make sense of the map. Increasingly frustrated and with soundcheck fast approaching, we stop on a high bluff overlooking the town to study the map in more detail. I get out to stretch my legs, and spot a building in a street far below us with shutters down and a large coloured sign above it.

'Er, Jonathan, what's the name of the club...?'

'Zero.'

'It's right there.'

He gives me a you-bastard-how-did-you-do-that look, but I've been finding clubs I've never been to for years—I can almost smell them. Sometimes I actually can smell them.

The club is locked up. For a moment I wonder if they really know I'm playing tonight, but then I spot a poster—which claims I am 'T.V. Smiths from the U.S.A'—and we eventually find our way in through a back door.

Let us in, it's T.V. Smiths

After soundcheck we are left with a lot of time to kill before the gig so we take a walk through the steep streets to a local café. Jonathan helps me out with finding some vegetarian options on the menu and recommends I try the local speciality of bread smeared with olive oil and tomato. I ask him what it's called.

'Well, outside Catalonia it's called "Catalan Bread."'

'And in Catalonia?'

'In Catalonia we call it "Bread."'

We go back to the venue, where there are only twenty people in so far. It seems a long way to come for this result, and I feel myself going into a bit of a slump. To make it worse, my throat is burning and I'm getting the distinct feeling that I'm going down with something. But it's my first time here so I play for two hours. By the end there are eighty people in and they seem to be enjoying it. In fact, when I finish they applaud so much I have to come back on stage for a five song encore. The promoter congratulates me and seems very happy. Jonathan tells me that my first gig in Spain was a success!

It's just a short drive back to Calafell where we arrive in the early hours at Jonathan's parents' beach front apartment, which they've kindly vacated for us to take over and drink wine, eat pizza, listen to music and stay up late in traditional rock'n'roll fashion.

25th April

From the living room window you can look out onto a vast sweep of white sands and sparkling blue sea. Beneath the balcony, a few people are taking their morning walks. The tourist season isn't upon us yet, and the owners of the beach-front cafés and shops are lazily opening the shutters and pulling tables and chairs out onto the paved promenade. I've woken up in worse places on tour.

I take a long walk up the beach, enjoying the sun, but anxious about my throat, which is still sore. I suppose this would all be too pleasant if there wasn't something to worry about.

I've woken up to worse views

Back at the apartment, Jonathan wants to cook me a traditional tortilla before we go to today's gig in Barcelona. We wander through the narrow backstreets to some little shops where we buy potatoes, onions and manchega cheese, then head back to the apartment where Jonathan gets slicing. Finally the potatoes hit the pan and the artistry starts. Jonathan is looking tense. Wouldn't it be embarrassing to cook the national dish for an Englishman if it all went horribly wrong?

It will either be a triumph or a disaster

'There comes a moment when cooking a tortilla,' he says anxiously as he gives the pan another stir, 'when it will either be a victory or a disaster.'

It's a victory! We sit at the table with Uri and Suzy eating slices of tortilla and chunks of manchega, a gentle sea breeze drifting through the balcony window. Jonathan breaks out the beers, but I stick to water, still worried about my throat. I learn that the brand of this bottled water, 'Veri,' is the Catalan word for 'poison.'

Shame we have to spoil all this by going to a gig really, but mid-afternoon we cram into the car and leave for Barcelona, stopping on the way to fuel up at a petrol station which proudly announces its name 'ARS' on a giant sign above of the forecourt. How one longs to shin up the pole with the 'E.'

We park in an underground car park near the cathedral and hurry on foot through the packed streets to the venue in Plaza Real, loaded down with guitars and various bits of musical gear. Last time I came here I was on holiday, meandering around looking at the architecture; now I'm barging through the tourists wishing they would get out of my way.

I get my soundcheck done and then sit outside one of the cafés on Plaza Real with Jonathan and Uri to wait for the rest of Suzy & Los Quattro to turn up. They've phoned to say they're stuck in traffic, and with the club's opening time fast-approaching it's doubtful if they'll get here for soundcheck. It's nerve-wracking for me because we haven't had a chance to try out the songs we'll be playing together, and Jonathan is looking worried too. Months of planning can disappear in one traffic jam. He orders a beer, and I opt for an expresso in a desperate attempt to find some energy. I'm trying not to admit it to myself or anyone else, but my throat's killing me and I'm not sure if I'm going to get through this evening. And anyway, has anyone in Barcelona heard of me? Will anyone turn up? I even catch myself thinking: maybe the van won't arrive in time and we'll have to cancel the gig and I can stop worrying and have an extra day to recover and…

Twenty minutes before the club is due to open the mini bus sweeps into the square, scattering the street entertainers in its path, then it's all hands to get the gear unloaded and onto the stage. There's a lightning soundcheck for Suzy & Los Quattro, then I join them and there's just time to run through the beginnings and endings of the songs we'll be playing together.

Now we have a couple of hours before the gig starts so we go across the square to a falafel place. While we're there, Johnny Quattro shows me a scar on his hand that almost stopped him playing guitar a while ago. It's a nasty looking deep wound, running from the base of the thumb right across the palm. He explains how it happened: his girlfriend works for a sanctuary that rescues abused chimps from the tourist industry. One of the chimps was particularly sociable and when Johnny visited the sanctuary to see his girlfriend he would always spend some time in the enclosure with the chimp and they'd play together. Over time they became firm friends. Then the boss of the sanctuary banned any outsiders from having contact with the animals. For weeks when he visited his girlfriend, Johnny had to ignore the chimp's gestures to come and play with him.

Eventually the boss started allowing visitors back into the enclosures, and when Johnny went in to see the chimp again it grabbed his hand and bit it.

'He was just letting me know he was upset because he thought I'd been ignoring him,' says Johnny. 'If he'd wanted to, he could have bitten it clean off.'

After this incident the chimp was filled with remorse. When Johnny plucked up courage to get back into the enclosure with him, the chimp gently stroked the scar and made 'sorry' noises. Now they are best friends again.

Backstage we get a few photos of me and Suzy for the cover of the single, then it's time for the band to get going. First time I've seen them and I enjoy it, very entertaining feel-good pop punk. I even start to feel good myself.

The band finish and I go backstage to congratulate them. 'That was the worst gig we have ever played,' says Jonathan. Now the performance is over the pressure of the day is really catching up with him. I hurry on stage for the solo part of my set, which goes fine. The sore throat disappears as soon as I start singing and my voice feels strong. Not a bad start for my first time in Barcelona. Then the band join me for the songs at the end, the audience starts dancing, and immediately it feels as if we've been playing together all our lives.

Outside it has started raining. We carry the gear out to the van, which is parked a few streets away, then Uri, Jonathan and I walk back to the car. It's late, we're tired, and we're looking forward to getting the drive over with, relaxing with a quick drink back at the apartment and getting some sleep. This plan goes wrong when we're pulled over by the Guardia Civil on a roadblock on the outskirts of Calafell. 'This *never* happens,' groans Jonathan as he gets out of the car to speak to them. I stay slouched in the back, pinned down by my guitar case, while they meticulously search the front of the car. They hardly glance at me. As we drive off Jonathan tells me that they seemed a bit nervous of me and asked him if I play 'Post Rock.'

Hey, I just intimidated some of Franco's former elite security force. How cool is that?

26th April

We make an early start because we have a long drive ahead of us to Castellon and want to get to the studio and record my vocals before the gig.

The studio was built by Coky—one of the guitarists with Suzy & Los Quattro—and has everything you need except a toilet, for which you have to go to the café across the road. We go there anyway to bring back some food to keep us going. You have to try the local speciality of course, in this case a kind of stuffed pastry. The vegetarian option is filled with mushroom and spinach—and also, as I discover after the first few bites, some sausage slices, giving me my first Spanish U.M.M. (Unexpected Meat Moment.) I discreetly put the rest to one side so as not to offend my hosts but Jonathan spots it. 'It had to happen,' he apologises. 'This is Spain.'

The recording goes well. It's soon done, and we're able to get over to the venue, stopping at my hotel on the way so I can check in.

I have a good feeling about the Ricoamor club as soon as I walk in. The stage is so small that most of the band have to stand in front of it, but it doesn't matter. We're all on top form and soundcheck feels as exciting as an actual gig.

To pass some time before we go on stage, we take a walk to a nearby café with Javi, who'll be releasing our single on his label. I point out a building opposite and Javi tells me it's a Bingo hall, very popular in this part of the country. 'Do you have Bingo in England?' he asks.

The club is full, the gig is a big success and on its own makes my trip here worthwhile. On the last note of the last encore Jonathan throws down his bass and it smashes in half. Rock'n'roll! We take photos.

Even better, Jonathan tells me that a journalist from Ruta 66, one of Spain's best music magazines was here and loved the show. A good review in there could really help set things up for another tour. We're all in a good mood and after we've loaded up the gear into the van we start looking at the options of where to go to celebrate our last night. We've been invited to a party at a bar in town so we head for that, ditching my bag and guitar at the hotel along the way.

It turns out we're at someone's stag night—fancy dress recommended—and pretty soon the place is filling up with nuns and bandits. The groom arrives covered from head to toe in bandages, followed a moment later by the bride, dressed up as a nurse. At the bar there's a guy waving around a toy rifle and shouting 'Don't mess with Texas!' in a George Bush voice.

'That's the journalist,' says Jonathan.

Something catches his attention. I follow his gaze to see Uri, who usually doesn't drink, with a glass of rum in his hand. Jonathan nudges me. 'Uri turns into a crazy person when he drinks rum.'

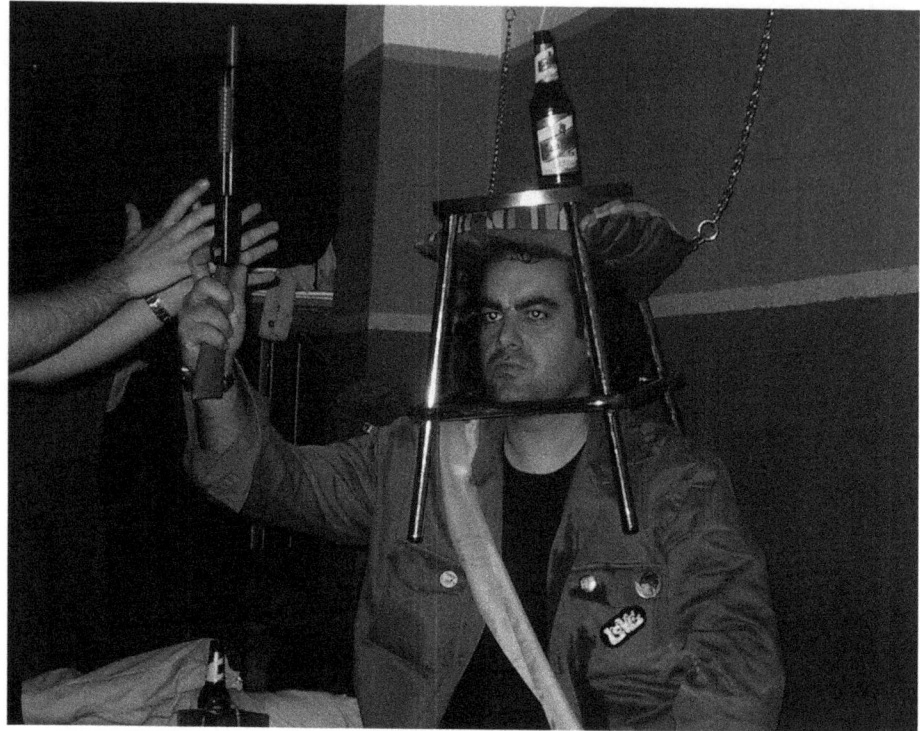
Uri's anti-missile shield

Half an hour later Uri has a metal stool on his head and is telling everyone that it's his anti-missile shield. The music is blasting out and the nuns and bandits are dancing. The journalist puts the toy rifle to Uri's head and shouts 'Don't mess with Texas!' while Suzy shimmies around them.

Fiesta! This is what I came to Spain for!

27th April
We go for coffee to the same café where I had the U.M.M yesterday and all have a good laugh about last night, although Uri groans when I show him the photos. I am an absolute menace now I carry around this digital camera. Mind you, even then I didn't get a snap of his 'Totem To Those Who See Beyond,' an elaborate sculpture which he constructed from various bits and pieces he found around the club and then attached to the wall. It was very late.

Time to say goodbye to the band, then Uri—sober and dependable again—drives me back to Barcelona airport. The last few days have been a good experience. No professional tour agent would have risked bringing me to Spain, but thanks to the hard work of a few fans I now have the beginnings of something here, and I'm looking forward to coming back and building on it.

On the plane the stewardess offers me the tray and looks as if she would like to kill me when I ask for the vegetarian meal I pre-booked. But she manages to find it somewhere in her mysterious trolley, and instead of the dull tuna sandwich the carnivores are being served, I get a delightful little dish of artichokes and asparagus with a wedge of tortilla, as well as a tiny pack of crackers called 'Crack,' which have among their listed ingredients 'dust from milk.'

I will have two days at home, then I go to Germany for a month of gigs.

10. HOW TO FEEL HUMAN (2003)

21st July

My first gigs for two years in Finland, where in Summer the sun never sets and the mosquito never sleeps. Why wait? I got bitten at home in London last night and now there is a swelling the size of a small plum on my thigh.

Today's a travel day, no concert. Jukka meets me at Helsinki airport to drive me to Tampere, where I'll be spending the night at his place. I was originally invited over for a big open air punk festival, but I've taken the opportunity to come a few days early to play a private gig for him and some of his friends and family at a summer cottage in the countryside.

'When I asked you, I never thought you would actually come,' says Jukka as we get into the car.

During the drive, he talks a little about the Finnish tradition of getting away from it all in the country. Many Finns have summer cabins, some going every weekend, some just for a few days when the weather is good. Away from work and worries, relaxing in the idyllic setting of a lakeside surrounded by forests, the chance to sauna and swim and, of course, drink. 'At times like these, you can feel like a human being,' sighs Jukka.

He goes on to tell me about a German friend of his, married to a Finnish woman and living in Berlin. The couple had often dreamed of owning a summer cottage in Finland and recently heard of one being sold for the paltry sum of 3,500 euros. It seemed too good to be true, and in a state of excitement they flew straight over to have a look at the property. Unfortunately it was too good to be true: the cottage itself wasn't too bad but it was situated miles from civilisation in the middle of a swamp.

'Talking of which,' says Jukka, 'have you heard of the great Finnish sport of swamp football?' Two teams gather together in a swamp that goes up over their knees, and attempt to kick a ball about.

We stop off at a small observation tower by the roadside on the crest of a low hill. It's ten in the evening and the sun is still just above the horizon. The recent heatwave has brought daytime temperatures of 30 degrees and is sparking off localised storms that we can see sweeping across the forests in the distance, the occasional lightning bolt flashing down to the tree tops. Jukka stretches his arms out expansively. 'Ah, what a view! Forests, fields, lakes—well, actually you see all that wherever you are in Finland...'

When we get back to Tampere we sit out on Jukka's balcony and crack open a beer. I tell him I am a bit worried about mosquitoes after they nearly ate me alive last time I came here in the Summer and he is moved to tell me of another Finnish sport, which involves fifty men standing in a large tent full of mosquitoes. Whoever has the most feeding on him at the end wins.

Finally, one sport I could be good at.

22nd July

My Finnish pre-pay SIM card with quite a lot of credit left on it doesn't work any more, so before we head off to the forest I drop into a phone shop in Tampere to find out why. They tell me that because I haven't used the card for two years it's been taken out of service. The credit is gone forever, but for eight euros they could reactivate my phone number and sell me some more. I can't think of any other business that has the legal right to take back something I've already paid for just because I haven't used it.

Another forest, another festival

A couple of hours drive out past Lahti and on to...well, who knows? The villages thin out, the roads thin out. Suddenly there is a home-made wooden sign *To The Festival Area* pointing up a dirt track and we are pulling into a small glade in the middle of the forest, a couple of wooden cabins around it. Jukka's family and friends are already here—children are running about while mums and dads sit on the wooden veranda picking over the wild strawberries and blueberries they've gathered this afternoon.

The live music will take place in the evening, but until then there's work to be done to prepare for it. Jukka, along with Hessu and Tommi—two long-standing members of the Helsinki Crew fan club—set about erecting a canvas canopy over the amplifier and mixing desk, while I sit in the sun and put new strings on the guitar, first taking care to layer on some roll-on mosquito repellent I've brought with me from England. Then we hustle down to the lakeside sauna cabin—men only on this trip, to spare my blushes.

Where to feel human

It's a beautiful warm day, a light breeze, the sky blue. Hessu loads some logs into the sauna and lights it, and while it heats up the plan is to take a swim in the lake, which laps right up to the edge of the cabin. I express my doubts to Jukka about how cold it's going to be, but he lifts out a thermometer hanging on a string from the wooden jetty and assures me that the water temperature is twenty three degrees.

It's like swimming in the Mediterranean. The sun is up so long during the day that it can warm even deep water lakes like this one. Hessu swims up and explains that there are two sorts of lakes in Finland: brown and clear. This is a brown lake—and indeed, although the water is translucent it does have a brownish tint to it. 'It's called Lake Swede,' he says with some distaste. Finns aren't big fans of the Swedish. This is because they are their neighbours, they are richer, and they have a comical sing-song language.

By now the sauna has heated up. The routine is to sit in there until the sweat pours off you, then go out for another dip, repeating the process until you reach a state of zen-like calm, at which point you open a beer. Jukka stretches out on the jetty, bathed in the dappled sun beaming down through the forest canopy, and takes another sip. 'Finally...' he says, '*Now* I feel like a human being.'

Hessu and the right kind of wood

I head up the hill for a soundcheck. The P.A. is pretty basic but there are enough bits and pieces of equipment to get everything working. Soon the rest of the men come back from the sauna and the women take their turn. Hessu sets about lighting the barbecue. 'I'll just move these first,' he says, carrying a few pine logs away from the side of the grill.

'Why?' I ask.

'This is the wrong type of wood,' he explains. 'It sends up these...well...what do you call that kind of pocket of gas that rises up then ignites in the air and causes forest fires?'

Strangely, there is no word for that in English.

The women are back, the barbecue is lit, and I realise it's time to put on some more mosquito repellent. I tell someone that I am a bit worried about all the mosquitoes and she says, 'Actually I'm more worried about the snakes.'

Snakes?

Jukka starts cooking up some vegetables on a flat pan over the flames. Meanwhile some musicians from a nearby cabin arrive and set up their gear in the glade. The drum kit is homemade, and consists of a large cardboard box and various beaten out pans and milk churns fixed to a frame of wooden planks. The drumsticks are two bundles of twigs. About thirty people have gathered for the performance, and sit around on the swing bench and on folding chairs as the band start to play.

Next up, it's the Helsinki Crew's band 'UJO' doing their hilarious Abba routine that I first saw a few years ago in a festival in Lapland. Basically, three guys (their fourth singer couldn't make it today)—each wearing a T-shirt bearing a photo of the head of a member of Abba—sing Abba songs to cheesy karaoke-style backing tracks, with the lyrics translated back from English into Abba's native Swedish, and attempt the dance moves from the videos.

Then UJO move into part two of their short set and surprise me by doing the same technique to my own song 'Cast Of Thousands'—belting out the vocals, complete with harmonies and counter melodies *in Swedish*, while the music they have recorded for this one-off performance plinky-plonks along behind them. I am speechless.

UJO sing ABBA

And just as I thought there couldn't be any more surprises, UJO step down to enthusiastic applause and Jukka steps up. 'Now I am going to do something not many people have heard me do…sing!' he announces, and launches into an acappella version of 'Adverts Blues,' a song recorded in the late seventies by a Finnish punk group in tribute to my old band.

If I didn't feel welcome before, I do now. I plug in and begin to play, taking requests and making up the rest of the setlist as I go along. The only thing bothering me is that the mosquitoes seem to have realised this is their big moment. While I'm busy playing guitar and unable to swat them, they stealthily descend. I can feel them moving around on my back. People are probably noticing that at the end of every number I am frantically twitching and slapping myself. Damn, I'm trying to sing and there's one on my chin. My nose! They are taking the piss. During one of my more gentle ballads one lands on the back of my left hand and between strums I manage to whip my right hand over and give it a smack without breaking rhythm, after which I sing the rest of the song with the bloodied corpse—MY BLOOD!—clinging to my hand. 'Normally I'm an animal lover,' I wail before starting the next song.

Kick out the mosquitos

It's only when I finish two hours later and dash back into the cabin to grab the repellent, that I realise the roll-on is in fact empty, and presumably has been for some time.

Hmm, what else is there? Up on a high shelf I find something that looks extremely toxic called 'OFF!' I would be tempted to add another word before that.

Jukka wanders into the cabin with a big smile on his face. 'You know, sometimes I almost have the illusion of being happy,' he says. 'And you have been responsible for, well, quite a few of those times.'

Then, no blushes spared—we all know each other well enough now—everyone heads back down to the lake for mixed sauna and swimming.

It's as dark as it gets now, not a breath of wind, the surface of the water mirroring the light charcoal of the sky and the glittering moon. Jukka pulls up the thermometer and declares the water is still twenty three degrees. As I float there in the total silence gazing up at the stars it occurs to me that I almost feel human.

23rd July

I'm looking at one of the mosquito bites in the middle of my chest and it's slowly dawning on me that it is in fact a third nipple. Then I wake up.

Down at the neighbour's cabin by the lake, breakfast for everyone is being cooked on a roaring barbecue made of a circle of bricks filled with logs. Before breakfast, though, a morning dip. Feels quite a bit cooler this morning, but Jukka checks the thermometer and says, 'it's twenty—er, let's see—three degrees.' I reckon Jukka could come down here in midwinter, chip a hole in the ice with an axe, draw up the thermometer and still claim it was twenty three degrees.

Back at our cabin, Hessu shows me what looks like a small tennis racquet but turns out to be a battery-run mosquito zap bat. Simply press a button on the side of the handle and the wire 'strings' of the racquet charge up with 3,000 volts. Waft it over the mosquito and suddenly—no more mosquito. 'I even tried it with a big wasp once,' says Hessu. 'It took three goes, but killed it. You can have this one, I've got a spare. You have to be careful, though, it really does give out quite a charge. Look...' He presses the button and jabs his finger lightly at the wires. 'OW! Ooooh! AAAGH!!'

Maybe I will take the batteries out before packing it into my bag.

The weather is deteriorating and it's time to leave. I get in the car with Jukka and family and as we head for Tampere the sky blackens, lightning forks around the towering forests on either side and the rain sheets down. When the storm passes over we pull off the road into a little village for a coffee in a pretty old wooden café next to a church. Jukka has a quick look up the road to see if there is anything of interest to do or see in the village, but there isn't. I point out a poster on the wall of the café showing what seems to be a local attraction and ask him to translate.

'It's a sort of stamp museum,' Jukka tells me, reading through the description. 'Well, actually, it's just someone letting people in to his house to see his stamp collection.'

Alas, we don't have time as I have to rehearse with Punk Lurex in Tampere this evening. 'You can see my stamp collection when we get back,' Jukka says brightly.

In Tampere, Jukka gives me the key to his place as he reckons he'll be too tired to come out for a beer later. It takes it out of you, all this feeling like a human being. I grab my guitar and meet up with Punk Lurex in the rehearsal room, where we do an interview for 'Finland's second biggest-selling newspaper,' as the journalist describes it to me. Then we run through the songs for our festival performance together in two days. It all goes smoothly despite the fact we haven't played together for two years, and leaves us looking forward to the show. But first one more gig on my own tomorrow. I should start concentrating on that.

So why am I still sitting here in this karaoke bar, surrounded by framed photos of elderly bewigged Finnish crooners, while Tiina and Ritta go to fetch yet another round of beers? How many beers must a man get down before you can call him a man?

But I still find my way back to Jukka's place.

24th July

Over a late breakfast Jukka shows me the second biggest-selling newspaper in Finland, which has a good article and photo in it. Another newspaper—presumably *the* biggest-selling in Finland—has a front page story about a group of Finnish friends who brought back some very cheap brandy from Estonia which turned out to be mixed with ethanol and killed three of them. They thought something was a bit odd when they added water to it and it turned green...*but they drank it anyway.*

I spend a few hours on Jukka's computer going through my emails, then at five I walk down to the Tulliklubbi for soundcheck. Tonight is the official warm up show for Puntalarock, which starts tomorrow, featuring five of the punk bands from the festival and me. Soundcheck is quick and there are still hours before gig time so I go for a walk round the town, getting back as the club opens at nine. Mikko, the organiser of the festival, runs through the schedule with me. I'm supposed to be on stage tonight at 12:30, then after the gig he will drive me out to a hotel in the countryside, somewhere near to the festival site.

There aren't many people in the club as the first band goes on but an early arrival is Robert, who I know from previous gigs, and who invites me over to the table where he's sitting with a couple of friends. Onstage the band are playing very fast and very loud. Robert leans over and tells me that earlier in the year he worked on the door of a hardcore punk festival.

'It was horrible. I was searching the people coming in for alcohol so I had to listen to every single band. Except for Anal Thunder. Then I was eating.'

I have a chat with Tommi and Annastina who've travelled up from Helsinki. Tommi tells me about an early gig by a band Jukka was in some years ago. The drummer started the set with two frozen liver sausages instead of sticks. As he played, the sausages gradually thawed and disintegrated. When they had turned into mush and were splattered all over the drums it was the end of the gig.

I wander outside to give my ears a break from the noise. It's peaceful out here. The sun is low on the horizon, and over on the other side of Tampere the onion-shaped domes on the Russian cathedral are glowing gold as the light strikes them from below.

It's nearly one in the morning before I get to play. I overrun a little, but people start shouting for requests towards the end of my allotted time and it would be rude to refuse. I retire to the bar afterwards to chat with people before packing my stuff away. Mikko and his girlfriend come up and stand nearby. I ask if they're in a hurry to leave, and Mikko vaguely shakes his head. His girlfriend says, 'There is no hurry to go. But please—hurry.'

So an hour later I'm in a hotel where there is no one around and the bar isn't open. The room is basic but okay. There is even a television, but it shows only one channel which consists of a bored-looking girl replying to mobile phone text messages that scroll down one side of the screen, all in Finnish, of course, so I can't understand a word.

Also in my room: a Tampere guide from 1999, a gardening catalogue and a half-eaten bar of milk chocolate which someone has rewrapped and placed in the bedside cabinet. Let the party begin!

25th July

The music doesn't start until five so I spend the day walking by the canal in the blazing sunshine, up to a large lake and then back for a wander around Lempäälä, the nearest town. At 4:30, Mikko picks me up and we drive over to the festival.

The site is a large grassy area on a slope below a forest. Further down the slope there is, of course, a lake. The large main stage is at one end of the grassy area, and hidden in among the trees further up the hill is a cute little second stage, with a cleared area of stubbly tree stumps and a few small wooden cabins in front of it.

First band of the day in the forest

I meet up with Tiina and Riitta from Punk Lurex and we bump into Hilu, a presenter on a Helsinki radio station who interviewed us a couple of years ago. The sun is fierce, so we step into a tiny patch of shade behind the mixing desk while we chat. Hilu says the weather was similar to this when she was at Puntalla last year. She made the mistake of wearing fishnet tights for the first day and when she took them off that night her legs 'looked like a ham.'

In order to avoid having to listen to hours of hardcore bands before we play, Riitta suggests we go and visit her aunt who lives in Lempäläa. This will be convenient because Tiina has promised to pick up Howie, an English friend who works at the same university as her, from Lempäälää station and give him a lift to the gig. He has difficulty getting about at the moment because of a back injury. Riitta winces as another band starts up. A few days ago she was playing accordion in a folk festival in the north of Finland—now this.

'I hate this music,' she says. 'We must go.'

Riitta's aunt and uncle don't seem too surprised to find a middle-aged English punk rocker in bleach-streaked jeans, and a mohican-haired university lecturer on crutches arrive at their place. They offer us a beer and we sit outside in the sweltering heat. As evening descends I start to worry about the mosquito problem and ask if anyone has any repellent. They seem surprised I should ask.

'Still getting used to the Finnish mosquitoes, eh?'

The uncle fetches a couple of battered-looking products out of the cottage, gives one of them a test spray as he comes across the yard and wrinkles his nose in disgust. 'These haven't been used for a while.' he says.

It's the familiar 'OFF!' but in spray format, and 'OFF! Super' in roll-on. I suspect I will need the 'OFF! Super' and roll it lavishly over all my exposed skin, then rapidly become aware that it really does smell very unpleasant indeed. I think the 'OFF!' may be off. Howie is inspecting the label. 'Ah yes,' he says, 'this is the stuff that's now banned in California.' The aunt goes and sits on the other side of the table from me because she can't stand it. A while later she disappears into the cottage and comes back with a plastic bag full of dead fish, which for a horrible moment I think must be a traditional Finnish mosquito repellent, but no—she's off to feed her hedgehog.

Hedgehogs eat fish?

Back at the festival a band is playing and the audience is dancing around in a cloud of dust. I'm beginning to feel quite queasy with the smell of 'OFF!' but there is only cold water in the backstage toilets, and the 'OFF!' won't wash off. Frustratingly, there's hardly a mosquito to be seen.

As the time approaches for Punk Lurex and me to start there are nearly a thousand people in the audience. There's an embarrassing moment backstage when Security don't believe I'm performing and attempt to throw me out, then I hit the stage, first playing a half hour solo set, then a half hour together with the band. We finish five minutes before curfew but can't carry on because we haven't learnt any more numbers together.

Onstage with Punk Lurex OK

Dead on one the bar closes, so us musicians who have been taking it carefully all evening are unable to buy any beer and are left to drink from the dubious bottles of home-brewed wine that many people here carry around with them.

At some point I realise I don't know how I'm supposed to get back to the hotel. The last bus to Lempäälä left half an hour ago and I wasn't on it because I wanted to hang around after the show and assumed someone would be driving me to the hotel. I mention it to Mikko, and he says yes, yes, he could drive me back. The only trouble is, he's a little bit drunk. Ah, right.

But there's always a solution: Punk Lurex are staying in one of the cabins by the second stage, the cabins have two bunk beds in them, and as Riitta has gone back to stay with her aunt I could take the spare bed. I don't have a sleeping bag, toothbrush, towel or anything for an overnight stay but at least there will be a place to sleep.

It's past three and the sky has lightened to a steely aquamarine. After a few more rounds of wine, I mention that I'd like to drop my bags off and at least get a look at where I'm sleeping before we carry on with the festivities. We trudge up the slope, past groups of punks passing round bottles and squatting around campfires—hope they're using the right kind of wood!—and scramble over the tree stumps to the cabin. When we get there, I find the idea of that bed is just too attractive to resist and, ignoring the cries that I have to go back out for more drinking, I haul myself onto the top bunk and let sleep settle over me.

The only trouble is, after the first half hour or so, this adventurous notion of sleeping in a log cabin in the forest doesn't seem quite so romantic any more. No blanket, no pillow and there's a chill in the air now. I climb down past drummer Piise sleeping soundly on the bunk below and lift up the small rug from the floor to put over myself, but it barely covers my torso. Right outside the cabin a large group of punks have settled down around a fire and are playing music and talking loudly. My earplugs are back at the hotel. I toss and turn for a bit, then give up on sleep, and leave the cabin to see if I can find Tiina and Kukka.

No sign of them, but there are plenty of other people staggering around the site in states of extreme drunkenness. I'm feeling really fatigued now, don't want to be awake, can't sleep. I start to fixate about the idea of getting back to the hotel. Wouldn't it be great? A bed...with a duvet and pillow...a shower and toilet...all my *stuff*...! Maybe I could walk it? It's a long way, but how long could it take...20 minutes? A half hour? OK, at worst an hour. Even if it was an hour and a half, I'd be back there by six...

Someone staggers up, an American by the sound of his accent. 'Say, can you drive...?'

'What?' I think about it. Theoretically I can drive, but at the moment I can barely walk.

He ploughs on. 'We've run out of beer and we've got to get to Lempäläa to get some more.'

Interesting!

'We've got a car but we can't drive cos we're too drunk. Can you drive us?'

I could drive them into the ditch. But...they're trying to get to Lempäläa! They've got a car!

'Look, I can't drive you,' I say, 'but if you find anyone who can drive, *let me know!* I want to get to Lempäläa too! I was thinking of trying to walk it so it'd be great if I could get a lift.'

The guy looks at me as if I'm mad. 'God, you'll never walk it. We tried that last year—the same thing happened, we ran out of beer and we couldn't get a lift so we set off on foot. After two hours we still weren't anywhere near so we gave up and walked back.'

He goes crashing off through the forest to look for a sober driver. I feel the chances are slim.

Just then I see the festival organisation's minibus backing out of the backstage area. I run up to it and wave through the driver's window. 'Hey, are you going to Lempäälää? I need a lift!'

The driver looks at me like I am an unpleasant bug that has just squashed on the windscreen, shakes his head in annoyance, then throws the van into first and speeds off up the track. He's lying, I know it. He's lying.

I trudge down past the campsite to the lakeside to ponder the situation. Here there is only silence. The lake is a vast plate of pewter reflecting the forest around its rim. It's beautiful.

Sure would be nice to be in my bed though.

Right. Maybe there's a bus. Why wouldn't there be a bus going from a forest in the middle of nowhere to Lempäälää at five in the morning? I head past the campsite and the main stage, then up the track past the cabins towards the entrance gate. A few other walking wounded stop me on the way and say, 'Nice show!' I say, 'Uh.'

Slight language problem at the site entrance. There are five or six people still on duty there but they speak virtually no English, in fact they seem to think I am Swedish. I try and explain my predicament but receive increasingly baffled looks until I finally hit on a simple sentence that they understand:

'When...is...next...bus...to...Lempäälää?'

They smile at each other. Poor Swedish punk rocker! 'At midday.'

Almost six hours. Right.

'Taxi?'

'You're welcome!'

Right.

I go back to the cabin and toss and turn for another hour, then head to the backstage area where to my amazement Mikko is awake. And sober! 'Yes, I'll take you back now,' he says. 'I'll just be a couple of minutes. My girlfriend is still asleep in the car. There's coffee brewing over there...'

Things are looking up. I grab a coffee, rush back to the cabin to get my bag and I'm gone.

26th July

Thoroughly refreshed after a couple of hours of morning sleep, I look out of my window to see punk band Conflict being interviewed by Hilu on the terrace outside the hotel. As I don't know how I'm going to get back to the festival this afternoon I nip out and have a word with her and establish that, as I suspected, the radio team will be driving back to the site when they've finished the interview and, as I hoped, there's enough room in the van for me.

Although hanging around a punk festival—I'm not even playing today but I couldn't get a flight until tomorrow—is not top of my list of favourite things to do, I have a pretty nice time. The weather is great and there are lots of friendly people around.

Dusk falls and the familiar mosquito worries start to arise—I managed to successfully shower off the 'OFF!' back at the hotel. I get into a discussion with someone about the insect problem.

'In Lapland it's the midges,' he tells me. 'Here it's the mosquitoes and those other things, those biting flies...'

'What, horseflies?'

'No, not a horsefly, but some kind of fly...with coloured wings, not a wasp...that gives a really nasty bite.'

A fly with coloured wings? THAT BITES?

Conflict play and there is much pogoing and slam dancing from the young punks in the dust at the front. It's been a good festival, but now 'The last bus to Lempäälä is LEAVING!' is announced from the stage and the bar shuts, so I'm left to drink from plastic bottles of dubious homemade wine with some friends out on the grassy slope behind the stage and wait while Conflict wind down from their show so I can get a lift with them back to the hotel. While the conversation goes on around me I feel a sudden sharp pain on my wrist and look down to see a peculiar-shaped fly fastened on there. It could have had coloured wings, I don't know—it was a bit of a blur because I swiped it off so quickly.

So I say my goodbyes and then I'm in the van with an English punk band, their German tour manager and a Finnish driver, and we're speeding miles through the forest.

God, I would never have made it if I'd tried to walk last night. I'd have collapsed by the side of the road somewhere and woken up with a mosquito blanket.

Tomorrow morning I'll get picked up from the hotel at eight by Mikko and driven to Tampere for the early train to Helsinki, then I'll bus it to the airport for the flight to London which includes a two hour stopover in Copenhagen. I'll get back by mid-evening, then I'll have almost a month at home, much of which I'll spend organising the next round of gigs. I don't know where I'll be going after this or what will happen when I get there, but doubtless it will involve long journeys, a lot of waiting around, the usual ups and downs, probably a fair amount of sideways too. And—if I'm lucky—every now and then the illusion of happiness.

11. GO WEST. NO VEST (2003)

1st October

Will I? Won't I? Of course I will.

So it's back to the U.S.A. for my third trip, this time starting off on the East Coast where I'll be playing with the Midnight Creeps as my backing band, then over to the West Coast for the first time for some solo shows. Here I am again at JFK airport, feeling like a criminal as I try to sneak into the country without a work permit. There's always the chance I'll be turned back, and this particular immigration official is getting awfully close to home with his questioning:

'What's the purpose of your visit?'

'I'm on holiday.' Please don't attach the lie detector.

'Mr Smith, have you ever been to Nashville?'

What, where they have all those musicians? 'No!'

He looks at me suspiciously. 'Have you ever been to *Glasgow*?'

Ah. 'Well…yes…a couple of weeks ago.' Playing a gig. Don't tell him that.

He taps a few keys on his computer and peers up at me again. 'Have you ever posted anything to America?'

'Um, yeeesss...' A box of CDs to sell at the gigs.

'To what address?'

'The address on the visa waiver form where I'm staying.'

Where Bryan, my tour agent lives. Prepare to be put on the next plane back to England.

He stamps the visa. 'OK, have a good stay.'

I just have time to drop my bags at Bryan's apartment in Brooklyn before we're off to the opening night of a club he's promoting in Manhattan called the Niagara. Although I'm tired after the flight I'm interested to see the venue because I'll be playing there myself in a week. Bryan warns me that it's just a small basement bar, and he's not exaggerating—tonight's band, the Star Spangles, arrive shortly after us and when the drummer has set up his kit on the tiny stage there's no more room on it and the rest of the band have to stand on the floor.

The room is packed by the time the Star Spangles start and I watch some of the set over the heads of the crowd. It seems to be going down well, but I'm feeling the jet lag and after a while retire to the back bar for a quiet beer.

Afterwards I have to wait for Bryan to finish up business at the club and we don't get back to his apartment until 4:00—ten in the morning for me really. I put in the earplugs against the roar of morning traffic coming into the city over the nearby freeway and try to sleep. It's pretty cold. I get up to search through my bags for a vest and realise that I have forgotten to pack any. Just as I'm drifting off, something else pops into my head: I think I also forgot to pack the vests I wear on stage. I'm tempted to get out of bed again to check, but sleep wins.

2nd October

Sure enough, no vests. I fire off an email home asking Gaye if she can post some over—with luck they could reach me by next week.

Leafing through Time Out and Village Voice to see if the gigs have been advertised I'm quite surprised to see that I'm playing at the Southpaw in Brooklyn tonight. In fact Bryan tried to get me a gig there but they wouldn't confirm, so I gave up on it and instead arranged to go to Providence today to rehearse with the Midnight Creeps. I just hope no one turns up to the Southpaw.

North out of New York on the Greyhound bus and nothing to do except read and gaze out of the window. After four hours we pull into an ugly casino centre in the middle of nowhere and a bunch of people smelling of fried food shuffle onto the bus and start talking loudly about television shows and baseball. An hour later we arrive in Providence and as everyone gets off I notice that the woman sitting across the aisle from me has left something behind.

'Excuse me,' I call, 'you forgot your cardigan.'

She glares at me. 'Oh, just *leave* it!' she snaps.

Ah.

I'm met by Heather and Jonas, guitarist and bassist from the Midnight Creeps, and we walk up to their tour van for the short drive over to the house where most of the band live. They've built a rehearsal room in the basement and have been practising the songs we'll be playing together for quite a few months now. The rest of the people living in the house are rather looking forward to finally hearing them with some vocals.

Heather tells me that both Jenny, the singer, and Jeff, the drummer, are sick at the moment and she hopes I'm not going to catch it. I tell her I'm not worried—I've been touring round England for two weeks with a cold which I'm just about getting over now. Jenny is on the front porch of the house as we arrive. She's been making T-shirts all day for the band and as well as being blocked up with the cold is high from the chemicals in the printing ink. The T-shirts bear the message 'I'M A CUNT.'

Upstairs, the normally talkative Jeff says a quick hello then disappears into his bedroom. The rest of the band explain that he's really ill—the cold has infected his throat and he now has an extremely painful 'pus pocket' there. Mmmm! Rather more sociable is Heather's cat, Shithead, who is paying me a lot of attention. I intend to keep an eye on Shithead: her favourite trick, Heather tells me, is to jump on your back when you're not looking, dig in her claws and cling on.

Despite Jeff's pus pocket, the rehearsal goes extremely well. We only have to run through the songs once, then Jeff goes to bed and the rest of us sit around with a couple of beers while other members of the household pass through and say hello. Heather tells me that the Midnight Creeps actually played a gig down here in the basement a couple of weeks ago. It was a big success, two people got taken to hospital!

I'm introduced to someone who goes by the name A.P.A—short for Accident Prone Andy. He was one of those who ended up in hospital after an incident involving a keg of beer and a plank of wood. Best not to ask.

One of the other guys who passes through the basement has a very red, swollen eye. I'm told that he fell off a three storey building a few weeks ago and miraculously wasn't killed because he landed on something soft—his face.

We go upstairs for another beer and I meet Jess, who travels with the Midnight Creeps as their photographer when she can get time off from her regular job as an animal welfare worker. Heather points out that Shithead was recently spayed and is chewing the ends of her stitches all the time—maybe Jess could do something about it? 'Sure,' says Jess. 'But you're going to have to hold her.'

Heather firmly scruffs the struggling animal while Jess goes to work with the scissors. 'There, there, Shithead,' she coos.

Then we're all off to a party in the neighbourhood. I haven't eaten all day so I make short work of the remaining dips.

Eventually, late, I end up back at Jenny's place where I'll be staying the night in her spare room. We listen to some cool Bukowski tapes until I'm full of beautiful words, then I go and sleep.

3rd October

Jenny's partner offers to fetch some urgently required coffee. I'm a bit unenthusiastic when he tells me the only place nearby is a Dunkin' Donuts, but he assures me that they sell a new 'gourmet brand' coffee. He's right—it's good. And it comes in a special purple cup without the Dunkin' Donuts logo on it, which saves embarrassment when drinking it in public.

We gather outside Jeff's at eleven and wait in the cool, clear Autumn sunshine until everyone is ready. The antibiotics are kicking in and Jeff says he's feeling a lot better. We're heading back to New York for the first show, my first-ever at the legendary CBGB's—part of a three day punk festival—and we're all excited about it. First we stop off at the laundry to pick up the 'I'M A CUNT' T-shirts, which had an overnight wash to fix the ink.

Three and a half hours later we're parking up in a handy space right outside CBGB's. The club has recently taken over the neighbouring building which they are calling the CBGB Lounge, so the festival will take place over two stages. Me and the Creeps will be playing in the Lounge rather than on the larger stage in the original club, which is a little disappointing but as we're headlining the night there I can't complain.

We get a short soundcheck and everything sounds good. Then it's a long wait to get on stage. I meet a couple of people who turned up at the Southpaw the other night only to find I wasn't playing. I feel embarrassed about it, but they're just pleased I'm here—they thought maybe I hadn't been allowed into the country and the whole tour was cancelled.

I hang around the merchandising table, which is being manned by a friend of mine from Poulton-le-Fylde, near Blackpool, who I last saw a couple of weeks ago when he organised a gig for me there. Two friends from Scotland, Gerry and Mo, pass by—I last saw them at a gig in Glasgow, a couple of days after I played in Poulton-le-Fylde.

The merchandising stand is at the back of the room near the toilets, which are getting increasingly unpleasant as the night wears on. Someone tells me he just saw a mohican punk rocker throwing up all over the floor in there, and shortly afterwards I notice two of the CBGB's staff going in wearing rubber gloves and armed with long-handled plungers. Just before I'm due on stage I risk going in there myself, only to find a sign pinned up on the door: 'Closed. Full of shit.'

The gig is great, and packed with people. The only trouble is, I am much too hot in my long-sleeve T-shirt and I don't really feel like wearing an 'I'M A CUNT' one. By the end of the gig there is chaos in the room, people spilling over onto the low stage. Gerry jumps up and grabs a microphone and sings along, then when we leave the stage he stays up there, shouting in broad Glaswegian: 'C'mAAAAwn—show yirr appreciaaation!! That wuz BRAAHLLIANT!!'

4th October
I'm leaving the Creeps in New York to play their own set at the festival tonight, while Bryan drives me back to Providence for a solo gig supporting Mission of Burma. Should be a good one.

Mission of Burma only play rarely, partly because their guitarist developed tinnitus a few years ago. They soundcheck with a large plexiglass screen wrapped around the drum kit to muffle the volume, and the guitarist wearing a large pair of sound-baffling headphones. I ask him about it afterwards and he tells me that he wears extra earplugs inside the headphones.

There are about 600 people in by the time I get on stage and I have a good, short and intense set that goes down really well.

Bryan and I are going to be staying over at Jeff's place as he's still in New York. We squeeze Accident Prone Andy and a visiting friend called Kara into the car and drive over there, stopping in Andy's flat downstairs for a quick beer before we call it a night. Andy's flatmate is just heading for bed when we arrive, and meets us with a toothbrush in his mouth, but changes his mind about sleep and joins us instead.

A few beers later, Kara says, 'When I drink, first I can't feel my hands, then I can't feel my feet—then I'm done.'

Well, Bryan and me are both done so we head upstairs.

I've been asleep for a few hours when I feel the call of the beer coming through. Always an interesting moment this, negotiating my way to the bathroom in the dark, in the middle of the night in a house I've never been in before. The worst was after I'd played a gig in Hull: the owner of the club let me stay in a band room above the venue but unfortunately he didn't tell me that the place was alarmed. When I got up in the early hours to use the loo, bells went off all over the house.

Tonight I plod out of the bedroom, feeling my way along the walls, and successfully find my way to the toilet down the hallway. That's when Shithead lands on my back.

5th October

Think some of Shithead's fur must have got in my eye—it's red and swollen, looks like I have fallen off a three-storey building.

No gig tonight but Bryan and I are both keen to get back to New York, so we gather our stuff together and wake up Andy, who asked to get a lift with us.

The nearest Dunkin' Donuts doesn't have the gourmet line coffee, so on the way out of town we stop off at a 7-11, which advertises 1300 varieties. Inside there are four jugs of different types of coffee on the counter, plus a few flavoured syrups which you presumably mix in to get the other 12,996 varieties.

I buy a pair of cheap sunglasses to cover up the hideous eye. Andy buys a pair too. We look pretty cool. I pay at the counter and the girl hands me my change. 'Here's your change,' she says. 'Although you probably already knew that.'

Bryan is at the car filling up the tank and says I looked pretty funny standing under the sign saying '1300 varieties of coffee' in my 'Only One Flavour' jacket.

Back to New York—the third time I've done this journey in three days. Halfway back Bryan gets a call on his cellphone and hands it to me. It's Adi from the New York Rel-X, who's organising the punk festival. One of the bands has had to pull out—would I like to play again?

So there's just time for a shower at Bryan's and it's back out to CBGB's. You wait years to play there and then do it twice in a weekend. Even better, tonight's going to be on the main stage in the original club.

The Midnight Creeps are hanging around the venue already, most of them still hungover. They played a great gig yesterday to a rapturous response and duly celebrated afterwards, little realising they'd be called on to play again today. Jeff says he was thrown out of Central Park by the police at three in the morning for playing on the swings in the children's playground. They told him it would have been alright if he'd had a child with him.

By the time we get onstage mid-evening there are even more people than in the Lounge two nights ago and the place is buzzing. It's also super-hot, which is unfortunate, bearing in mind my T-shirt problem. Towards the end of the set the crowd are grabbing the microphone from me and singing along and at one point I get pulled in and relax for a moment with a bit of crowd surfing as the audience pass me over their heads. As far as I recall it's the first time I have ever done this. I am 47 years old.

The next band on seem a bit embarrassed to have to follow us. They're setting up their stuff on the stage as we're trying to get our things off and one of them says to me, 'I have all your records—it's an honour and a travesty to be playing after you.'

Off to my side Heather says archly, 'Ooh—an honour *and* a travesty...'

And the night wears on.

<u>6th October</u>

A day off before the next two New York gigs. I take a long walk around Manhattan, and along the way buy a sleeveless vest for when I'm onstage and a thicker T-shirt I can wear at night.

In the evening, Bryan and Alyssa and I drop into Sparky's bar, where all eyes are on the television, which is showing a live game from the baseball World Series. 'Normally we never watch it, but this is a big one,' says Bryan, gazing up at the screen. He then attempts to explain the rules to me, which is a mistake.

<u>7th October</u>

My cold, which I thought was going away, seems to be making something of a comeback. Or maybe it's an allergy to the cats. Either way, it's hard to shake these things off when you're on tour. I snuffle my way through the day feeling dizzy and light-headed and rapidly use up the supply of handkerchiefs I brought over from home.

Late in the afternoon Goldblade arrive on a flight from England. Bryan has arranged some gigs for them, and they'll be staying at his apartment for a few days, the three of them sharing couch and floor space in the living room. I am hanging on to the bed in the computer room. Before Bryan and I leave for the gig I have a quick chance to catch up with singer John Robb. Last time I saw him was in Poulton-le-Fylde.

When we get to the Knitting Factory, the Midnight Creeps have already set up and are sitting at the bar, making the most of the Happy Hour 'two-drinks-for-the-price-of-one' policy. I go for two-coffees-for-the-price-of-one to try and clear my stuffed up sinuses.

Singer Jenny is also still heavily blocked up with a cold. The only really fit person is Jeff, who's made such a good recovery from his pus pocket that he's stopped taking the antibiotics.

The venue downstairs looks good, but the sound man is exceedingly unfriendly and tells me off for walking over the stage and checking what kind of microphone is available: 'It's all set up for the support band!' he complains. The support band are a bunch of kids playing their first-ever gig and borrowing most of our gear. By the time they're ready to start there still aren't many people in. The television over the bar is probably a clue as to why: there's another baseball game on, tonight featuring the New York Yankees against somebody or other. But the great thing about your first gig is, it doesn't matter—the band are out to enjoy themselves, audience or not, and give everything. I like that.

Then it's time for the rest of us. The Midnight Creeps roar through their set, take a ten minute break, then they come back on with me. By now the room is much fuller and it feels like a proper gig. It's hot up there and I feel a lot more comfortable in the sleeveless vest. The only annoying thing is that from the stage I can still see the television over the bar broadcasting the game. I make some comments about it in between songs and to my surprise it actually gets switched off.

So, the final score: TV: 1, Television: 0.

8th October

I get my laundry done in the morning and it's dry just before I have to leave the apartment for tonight's gig. Even better, a package from home arrives with two of my stage vests inside.

The last New York date for now—although I'll be flying back for yet another gig in CBGB's for the last date of the tour—and it's down to Niagara, the little club I visited the first night I arrived. I'm glad I checked out the place then—having already heard another band play helps me to adjust the level of the various amps in soundcheck, and after a short run-through everything is sounding pretty good, although only one microphone works so there won't be any backing vocals. Jayne County turns up with her shopping trolley full of vinyl and the evening is ready to kick off.

I step outside the club for some fresh air and find four young guys hanging around out there who haven't been allowed in because it's an over 21's show. Two of them have travelled up from Virginia, a journey of more than four hours. One of them is watching the cars streaming up 1st Avenue with a look of disgust on his face.

'We're not used to the big city,' he says. 'We're used to cows and trees and stuff.'

'Look, there's a tree!' I say encouragingly, pointing to the park across the street.

But he doesn't seem to hear me. His gaze rises sadly up to the sky. 'Wow, you really can't see the stars in the city...' He shakes his head. 'That sucks, man. That really sucks.'

The Midnight Creeps are pretty tired. After a late night they got thrown out of the place they were staying at eight this morning when the cleaning lady arrived, and ended up sleeping a couple more hours in the van, parked up in a Dunkin' Donuts car park. But as soon as they start playing tiredness is forgotten. Then its my turn, and it's really good fun, on the floor and eye to eye with the audience. Adi from the New York Rel-X is there, Bryan and co-promoter Mojo, Jenny from the Creeps, some of the Star Spangles. I share out the lone microphone so they—and everyone else who's crammed down the front—can join in the vocals and it's a great party.

Bryan and I creep back into the apartment past a sleeping Goldblade at four in the morning. Have to get up at nine for a seven hour drive to Pittsburgh.

9th October

Jeff calls to say they're outside so I say my goodbyes to Bryan and Goldblade and head to the van. We get an hour or so down the freeway before the urge for coffee and breakfast becomes too strong to resist. The only place we can find is a Dunkin' Donuts set in a ghastly fake village, comprising a cluster of retail outlets around a pretend bandstand and fountain, like some kind of Stepford Wives nightmare. And they don't do the gourmet coffee.

Hours later we make another attempt, and pull off at a strip of gas stations and restaurants, including a Taco Bell, which at least churns out cheap and decent fast food. We all troop in there, and Jenny disappears into the rest room, reappearing a few minutes later with freshly washed hair. She sits at the table with us, combing it out, then grabs handfuls of paper napkins from the counter and begins to pat it dry. 'Why is everyone in here staring at me?' she asks.

Personally, I am thrilled to find that the cutlery on offer includes a plastic 'spork.' It's a cross between a spoon and a fork. I take a few away with me to show the folks back home.

On either side of the highway the woods are blazing with autumn colour, a patchwork of red, ochre and green. By late afternoon we pull into dreary Pittsburgh and drive through depressing suburbs reeking of urban decay, everything boarded up except for a few liquor stores, until eventually we find the venue, an incongruously pleasant vegetarian café called Quiet Storm.

The band and I are shattered from the drive and collapse into armchairs around the café. I will play an early evening solo gig here before moving on to a club gig with the Creeps at another venue. The café is a good size and there's a decent stage—at the moment covered with children's toys. An hour later the soundman turns up along with promoter Manny, and we clear the toys off the stage and I have a quick soundcheck. The plan is that I'll play a short set in the middle of five other bands, then Manny will take me and the Creeps down to the next venue, which he's also promoting. Meanwhile, we can choose anything off the café menu to eat.

The food looks great but I can't risk eating right now—I'll be on in less than 90 minutes and I know that food will just sap my energy, which is already low thanks to the long journey and the head cold which seems to have got a lot worse over the last couple of hours. I order something to take away for later, then sit at a table outside and drink a Chai tea, worrying about the fact there's hardly anyone in the venue. I notice Manny putting up a poster for the gig on the door. Bit late for that.

The first band starts up, to an audience of about twenty people. They are a two woman outfit, guitar and drums, playing tuneless shouty songs which really grate on my nerves so I stay outside chatting with Heather. She winces at the sounds coming from inside.

'I am just *this* far away from running out into the traffic,' she says.

'I'll race you,' I reply. We are very tired.

Presently the rest of the Creeps join us. Jeff says, 'I think I'm going to have to throw myself under a car.'

I say, 'Get to the back of the queue.'

I order another Chai tea before getting on stage—it's really sorting out my cold and giving me a good burst of energy. Still hardly anyone in when I start, but the show goes as well as can be expected. Most of the audience come over to thank me afterwards and apologise for the low turnout. 'You'll get a lot more people at the next place,' they assure me.

It's already past ten when we get to the 31st Street Pub, but we walk in to find three people in the audience. It's been a long day for this. Now I have to wait for a local support band to play, then the Midnight Creeps to do their set before I finish off for the night.

My heart sinks when I see the first band arrive. The guitarist unpacks a large box of effects pedals and spreads them all over the stage, then the singer, a Japanese girl, sets up a theramin. With ten people in the audience they begin a tortuous experimental set which involves lengthy guitar improvisation while the singer wails over the top.

I go and sit outside, where the evening is still mild. There is no one on the streets. The board advertising forthcoming bands is completely blank—they haven't even bothered to chalk up tonight's gig on it. Presently the owner of the bar comes out and raises his eyebrows at me as he closes the front door firmly against the racket within. 'I'm going to kill myself,' he says.

Get to the back of the queue.

I go back inside to order a beer. The people behind the bar are talking loudly over the band, who are now crouched on the stage chatting to each other while the effects loops do their stuff. Manny comes over and says that the Creeps and me should cut our sets short. Yeah, give the people here more time to hear some guitar effects pedals!

Secretly pleased to get this thing over with, we cut a few songs out of our sets and run the two together. Two hours later we're out of there and at the Motel Six that Bryan's booked for us. Before going to bed I head over to the Creeps' room to spend an hour or so with them and help out with the tray of beer we bought from the club. Finally, suitably bleary, I head back to my room.

Kill the cockroach. Go to sleep.

10th October

We drive out of the motel and straight to a diner so we can get breakfast. It's past midday and the large car park is packed. Obviously the King's Diner is the place to go for lunch if you live in Pittsburgh. Heather is wearing her knee-length boots with 'Cheap Sex' emblazoned up the side of them, Jenny a shorter-than-short pink polka dot mini skirt. 'OK,' she says as she gets out of the van, 'let's go turn some heads.'

We get given a table in the back room and Jenny gets to work drawing on the 'King's' place mat with the crayons provided. It doesn't take me long to lower the tone by adding the necessary 'F' and 'U' on mine.

It's not as easy to leave Pittsburgh as you might think. A series of roadworks funnel us off the wrong way and to our horror we are heading back into the city. Another turning leads us astray yet again and we have to pay a toll to go in the wrong direction for another ten miles until there's finally a slip road where we can turn around. Goodbye Pittsburgh! Forever.

Three and a half hours later we're in Cleveland. The club still isn't open so we go to find tonight's motel and check in. On the way we drive past a gas station with a sign outside: 'GOD BLESS AMERICA!' And in smaller letters underneath: 'Checks cashed—69 cents.'

We decide to rest up for an hour at the motel, and I spend the time washing my sweat-soaked gig T-shirts and a batch of used handkerchiefs in the sink, then hang them up to dry on the coat rack. Hopefully this should be the last handkerchief problem of the tour—today my head has cleared and I'm feeling a lot better.

Back to the venue, the 'Beachland Ballroom.' We hang around for hours to get a soundcheck, then there's another long wait afterwards. There aren't a lot of people in by the time we play, but at least it's better than Pittsburgh.

11th October

My clothes and handkerchiefs still aren't dry so I switch the air-conditioning unit up to 'Full Heat,' open up the folding stand you're supposed to put your suitcase on and set it on the bed so it's in the direct blast of the hot air, then hang my damp things over it. After thirty minutes, everything's dry and the room is like a Turkish bathhouse.

Through some of the most uninteresting countryside known to man on the seven hour drive to Chicago.

Jeff attempts to brighten one of the trips through the toll booths by wearing a set of plastic yokel rotten teeth that he bought in a rest stop. We are all giggling like naughty schoolchildren as we approach. 'Nice teeth!' says the woman in the booth nonchalantly as she takes the money. I guess we're not the first bored travellers to have passed this way.

We hit Chicago at rush hour and crawl along the elevated highway, past miles of post-industrial wasteland, monumental iron structures sending out long shadows in the twilight gloom below. We pull up at the Fireside Bowl right on time, but there's no one there.

A half hour passes, an hour, still no-one turns up. It's getting on for six now, and it looks like there's not going to be enough time before the gig to check into our motel so Jeff rings them and leaves his credit card number so that they'll hold the rooms for us.

Waiting around is bad enough, but after the long journey a few of us are feeling a pressing urge to find a toilet right now. When a guy from the club finally arrives and unlocks the door I head hurriedly for it, but he blocks my way. 'I'm not actually opening up yet,' he says.

Heather pushes past. 'I don't care,' she says. 'My teeth are floatin'!'

TV and Heather Creep go bowling

The Fireside Bowl is a bowling alley, with the lanes blocked off and a stage and gig area set up at the front of the room by the bar. Looks promising.

The venue starts to fill up and we have a terrific gig, probably the best so far. Also, unfortunately, the last one together until the final date of the tour in ten days time when we meet up again in New York.

We load the gear into the van. It's got chilly, there's rain in the air and it's past two in the morning. Now we have to find the motel. We have the usual unreliable computer printout, but hope that maybe Jeremy and Analucia, two friends of the Creeps who live in Chicago, might know the way. Unfortunately they only moved here recently and don't have a clue how to get to the motel. Instead they follow our van in their car, intending to come in for a beer when we finally find the place. We drive around for a half hour until we find the road marked on the map, but there's no sign of the motel. Finally Jeff phones them up. They explain that the motel is on a road with the same name in a completely different part of Chicago. Oh, and another thing—they sold our rooms to someone else.

'Thank you,' says Jeff, 'for WASTING MY TIME!!'

So. It's three in the morning. We're freezing cold and have nowhere to sleep.

There is a quick discussion in the middle of the street, and Jeremy and Analucia say there is couch and floor space at their apartment and we're welcome to stay the night with them. Rescued!

12th October

The Midnight Creeps drop me off at Chicago airport, from where I'll be taking a four and a half hour flight across the country to San Francisco. I'm the lucky one: the band now face a twenty hour drive back to Providence.

The skies are clear. Vast tracts of desert and mountains glide by below with hardly a town in sight for the whole journey. Finally we sweep in over the bay and land at San Francisco airport, about twenty miles south of the city. I put my clock back three hours.

I negotiate the taxi-sharing scheme and fifteen bucks gets me to the door of the hotel Bryan has booked. The routing of the first few gigs mean I'll be here for four nights, which will give me a good base to look around San Francisco, a city I've never been to before and which I'm keen to get to know. The hotel room is small, with a shared toilet and shower up the corridor, but there's a washbasin, refrigerator and microwave, and downstairs they serve breakfast until 9:30. It's clean and comfortable. I'm going to be fine here.

Mid-evening I head off to have a look at the city, down through Chinatown and past the City Lights bookshop, ending up in one of the ubiquitous Mexican *taquerias* where they serve a good cheap vegetarian burrito. I get to bed by midnight—three in the morning, given the time change—and slowly realise that the people refitting the shop on the opposite side of the cul-de-sac from my room really are going to go on all night. As another pane of glass crashes into the back of another lorry, I reach for my earplugs.

13th October

I struggle down to breakfast moments before 9:30 to find a table next to the reception desk with a wicker basket holding one single bagel and next to it a pump vacuum flask of coffee. There are quite a lot of crumbs, suggesting something was going on here earlier. I root around the debris on the table until I find a pat of butter, then take the bagel on the little polystyrene plate provided along with a polystyrene cup of coffee up to my room.

Take me to the bridge

No gig tonight, so I have the whole day to look around. The sun is shining, the sky is blue and it's as warm as a summer's day. I walk up to a lookout point with striking views over the bay and Alcatraz, right across to the Golden Gate Bridge, then make my way down steep flights of stairs until I am at the harbour. I buy a travel pass and take a series of rides on the excellent metro and bus network, rather more randomly than I intended as the numbering system has changed from those shown in my guide book. Soon I have a pretty good take on the layout of the city. Around mid-afternoon I choose a café that looks promising and get a terrific meal of tofu and fresh vegetables, then walk up Haight Street—once home of the hippies, now home of the hippie-related shopping opportunity—and on into the Golden Gate park until the approaching dusk and a chilly wind off the Pacific drives me back to the hotel.

Maybe I did a bit too much walking—there's a large blister on my heel. I check out my shoe and see that the ribbing around the ankle has split and is poking through the inner lining. Luckily the polystyrene bagel plate is still in the waste paper basket so I tear a small piece off and fit it into the heel over the broken ribbing. Works a treat.

Nothing to do this evening so I go to a nearby multiplex cinema and watch a movie on the gigantic Imax screen. When I get back out onto the street at midnight a very different San Francisco awaits: homeless people in doorways and down-and-outs begging for money while municipal workers steam clean every corner, working around the cardboard boxes, to bring the city back to its pristine condition ready for the morning.

On the way back to the hotel I buy a sad little microwaveable pizza-for-one from a 24 hour convenience store and only notice when I get back to the room that I accidentally picked up a meat one. Oh well, it won't do me any harm to go to bed hungry—I almost forgot I was on tour and thought I was on holiday there for a moment.

Outside there is a strident beeping and grinding of gears as a lorry backs up to take another load of debris from the building opposite. Yes, I am on tour. I put in the earplugs.

14th October

Bagels. There's more than one. There's even one with seeds on it. And this time there are packets of cream cheese! And jam! No coffee left, though.

The piece of plate in my shoe kept slipping yesterday evening so I take some blu-tack from my shaver—that's the blu-tack I use to stick down the 'off' switch so it doesn't start shaving away by itself in my bag—and fix the polystyrene back in place. Works a treat.

There's a gig tonight but I don't have to leave until six, so I take a bus out to the Golden Gate Bridge. It's a true icon, and well worth the visit. I walk most of the way across, enjoying the feel of the sun on my face and the wind sweeping in from the Pacific, and take in the view. Then I hop on a bus back towards the city, get off near the bay's edge and follow my map on a long walk back to the harbour. From there, another bus and the subway gets me back to the hotel. In case I don't get to eat tonight at the venue, I buy an emergency 99 cent burrito that I can microwave later if necessary. I double-check that it's a vegetarian one.

Right, back to work. I'll be playing these West Coast dates with a guy called Dr Frank, who is in a band called The Mr T Experience but is playing solo for these shows. He picks me up from the hotel with his driver Bobby, who is also in the band and will be joining him on bass guitar for a few songs.

In an hour we are in San Jose. There's no one at the venue, so we retire to a nearby Mexican restaurant and get to know each other over a beer or two. Frank and I discuss whether or not people are going to turn up at these coming gigs—after all, I've never played here before and Frank doesn't often play solo. Neither of us is particularly confident of a good turnout, and there's the bloody baseball—even here in the restaurant every eye is fixed on the television screen. Anyone would think it was the national game. When we get back to the club we get the impression that despite the friendly welcome, the great ambience, the terrific stage and sound system this is simply a place where no one is going to turn up.

And they don't. But it's still better than Pittsburgh.

By the time Frank and Bobby drop me off at the hotel it's late and I'm pleased that the emergency burrito is in there waiting for me. Unfortunately though, I can't get the microwave to work. The burrito sits there uselessly while the screen flashes promising things such as '2 MINUTES'—but nothing actually starts the cooking process. There will be no *ding!* tonight.

Outside, raised voices and a mighty thump as another section of plasterboard lands in the street. Earplugs.

15th October

I need to get some clothes washed before leaving tomorrow so I bag them up and head up the street to the nearest laundrette, wearing just a T-shirt and shorts. Feel a bit of a fool—the weather's changed and it's unexpectedly chilly out there. All the workers out for lunch from the nearby financial district are wrapped up in long coats and scarves.

Tonight's gig is here in San Francisco. I've arranged to meet Dr. Frank at the Café Du Nord, where we'll both be playing support sets for Penelope Houston, who used to be in local punk band The Avengers in 1978. The venue is a pleasant basement room run by ex-musicians. They give us something to eat and we sit around a table in the bar area chatting as audience members start to arrive, many of them stopping to say hello to Penelope and Frank as they go through.

Penelope is currently playing in an acoustic duo with a guitarist and seems a bit put out that tonight has been written up in the listings as a 'punk night.'

'I hope you're going to be punk, TV.' she says. 'I'm not. Dr. Frank—are you going to be punk?'

In fact, all three of us have completely different styles and the audience enjoys us all.

Frank and Bobby drop me off at the hotel. Just before putting in the earplugs to muffle the noise of the rebuilding works outside I watch a few minutes of the news on television. The main report is of a tragic Palestinian car bombing, with grisly images of mangled wreckage and people being put in ambulances. Running along the bottom of the screen, the tickertape headlines have a quite different story: Russian man puts a litre of gasoline in his washing machine, which explodes.

16th October

So, goodbye San Francisco. I've enjoyed my four nights here and liked the city but now I'm getting restless and ready to move on. Tonight we'll be playing in Sacramento in a small café run by Kevin Seconds, founder of punk band Seven Seconds. Kevin has created a great little venue in the True Love Coffee, and after we arrive early evening I'm quite happy to hang out there, sitting at one of the tables outside in the still-warm air reading a book while baseball plays on the television inside.

I slip back in to the venue when I hear Kevin starting his set. The place isn't full but there's a good atmosphere and the gig goes well. Dr. Frank is more relaxed than on the previous couple of nights, funny and in form, and my set goes well too.

We pack up as soon as possible after the show as we have a long trip tomorrow. Bobby drives us out to his home in a small town about half an hour away, leaving Frank and me the bed and couch while he sleeps in his parents' apartment on the floor below.

17th October

We figure on a minimum seven hour drive to Los Angeles, most of it through boringly flat semi-desert countryside. It's hot outside, but Frank likes the car cool, so Bobby turns the air-conditioning up full and I put on a jacket. Talk turns to some of the differences between the U.S.A. and Britain.

'In Britain nature is really safe,' says Frank. 'Even the spiders don't bite.'

'Really?' says Bobby incredulously.

'You don't get much in the way of dangerous spiders round here, do you?' I ask.

Bobby says, 'Oh, I come across the occasional Black Widow...'

Now he tells me.

I spend some of the journey phoning around to check up on where I'll be sleeping over the coming days. I call Nick, an old friend from England who now lives in Los Angeles with his wife Laura, and make sure that everything's OK for me to stay with them tonight—he says it is. The last time I stayed there was a few years ago when I played my first ever gig in Los Angeles. The only people who turned up then were two brothers, Don and Jack Cheney, and Don's son Max, who all drove up from San Diego. When Don found out I was playing San Diego on this tour he emailed me offering to let me stay at his place after the gig. I ring him up next, and his wife Wendy answers. I've never met Wendy, but Don has told me that she's a big fan of my music and is excited about meeting me. I tell her I'm checking if it's still alright for me to stay. 'Of course,' she says, 'but I should warn you—I might squeal.'

When we arrive at tonight's venue, the Echo Lounge, we're all exhausted after the long drive, and as we didn't have time to stop and eat on the journey I break the no-eating-before-a-gig rule and follow Frank and Bobby to a diner up the road where I get a good veggie BLT and drink many free refills of coffee.

Back at the venue not many people are in. Dr Frank starts his set and struggles getting across to such a large, mostly empty club. His songs and easy-going stage persona are much more suited to the more intimate venue. At the end he says, 'TV Smith will be up in a moment with something—er—more substantial.'

The great thing about a big club like this is that the sound system and the lights are really good; I enjoy playing because I can hear everything well, and the lights in my eyes mean I can't really see the audience so I don't get dispirited that there's so few of them. And of course it's better than Pittsburgh.

After the show I get gratefully into the car with Nick and he drives us to his beautiful house and garden up in the hills above Eagle Rock, where we have a pleasant couple of hours with a few beers talking over old times.

18th October

Wake up to the sun beating through the window. There's a mini heat wave in Los Angeles, and by midday the temperature has climbed to 90 degrees. Frank and Bobby drop by in the afternoon to pick me up and there's enough time to hang around in the garden for a while. Tonight we have separate gigs because the one we were supposed to play together got cancelled a few weeks ago. Now Dr Frank will be playing in a record store and I've been added to the bill of a punk festival being headlined by the Vibrators in a venue called The Showcase Theatre. Frank has played it before and warns me that there's no point in getting there too early. He's right—the place is in the middle of miles of drab retail outlets with nothing else going on. The only sign of life in the area is at the theatre itself which has hundred of young punks hanging around it, mostly with mohicans, body piercings and tattoos. Bobby gives me a hand out with my stuff and I notice he is limping.

'Ah, I think I had the air-conditioning on too high—I can't feel my feet.'

Then the car drives off, and I am standing alone on the pavement with my guitar and bag, suddenly aware that I am the oldest, straightest-looking person in sight.

Inside there are a lot of members of bands hanging around. I manage to get a thirty second soundcheck then climb the steps at the back of the club to a stuffy windowless dressing room on the first floor, where three large, noisy fans swish the air about to try and combat the heat. I sit in there chatting to Knox, singer with The Vibrators. Last time I saw him we were playing a double-bill in London's tiny Twelve Bar Club.

A few large boxes of pizza arrive, but it's too near my gig time to eat. Instead I wander down to the venue and check out some of the bands, at the same time keeping an eye out for Don and Wendy who will be driving me to San Diego after the show.

The gig is great, a surge of young punks up against the stage going wild when I play. Afterwards I can't get back to the dressing room for half an hour because so many of them want to talk to me. Finally escaping the throng I hear a woman's voice beside me:

'EEEEEEE!! Sorry—I squealed.' It's Wendy.

I have a quick word with her and Don, then get my guitar up to the dressing room and pack my things together. I'd like to have seen the Vibrators gig but I want to get the journey over with, so as they take the stage we slip out of the venue and head off, getting into San Diego about an hour and a half later, around midnight.

Don says that he hopes I like dogs because they have three of them. I'm more of a dog person than a cat person for a number of reasons: I'm not allergic to them, and they don't jump on your back in the middle of the night when you visit the loo.

19th October

Two gigs today, but we have a few hours to kill first and decide to visit San Diego Dog Beach. A twenty-minute drive away, it's one of two beaches around the city where dogs are welcome and consequently it seethes with them, running around and making the most of being off the leash. You have to be careful you don't get your feet swept out from under you by a doggie miscalculating its turn on the sand. It's a hot day, but there's a sea mist keeping the sky a heavy grey. We walk for half an hour then settle down and watch the canine chaos around us while the sun tries to burn its way through the thick clouds above.

Back at the house, Max comes over to visit, and we sit around the television to watch one of the family's favourite videos: a tape of a show called 'Armed and Dangerous,' one of those series that uses documentary film of police arrests and spices it up with reconstructions and interviews with the officers involved. This episode features Don's brother Jack and his heavily pregnant wife being followed up the highway towards Los Angeles by twenty cop cars and a helicopter after Jack has been seen 'acting suspiciously outside a Howard Johnston motel in the early hours of the morning.' With speeds never exceeding fifty miles an hour this is the slowest police chase ever. The flotilla of vehicles crawls along the highway for four hours until 'the suspect' pulls up for gas and is surrounded. He gets out of the car and heads for the gas pump, apparently surprised to be suddenly pounced on by a posse of armed police officers. 'Look, there's Jack,' says Don, 'he's pixillated!'

Wendy and Don on dog beach

Even through the pixillation you can make out Jack's big grin as he leans in towards the camera, and it is obvious that he is off his face. In the interview that follows, a well-groomed officer avows that he is pleased that the incident was resolved without anyone getting hurt.

Well, we've seen the family video and now I must be getting along to the first gig of the day in a local record store. After that, there's a club gig which I'm a bit worried about because the original promoter pulled out a couple of weeks ago and the show was only salvaged at the last minute. When we arrive at the record store there's no one around but I see Frank and Bobby's rental car parked outside so I know they're nearby.

There's a lot of waiting around until the gig gets going. People trickle in, including a Mexican couple who are really excited to meet me. When I play they cheer and whoop through the entire set, particularly at the anti-American comments. All thirty people in the room seem to enjoy themselves and it's one of those nice little intimate, impromptu gigs.

It's nearly nine, and I'm not due on at the other club until around midnight. Don and Wendy tell me they are going to pop home for a while, maybe have a nap, and see me later at the club.

A nap? 'Hope you wake up in time!' I say nervously. I'm staying with them again tonight.

Frank, Bobby and me make off in the rental car to the Brick By Brick club where the manager greets us. He was afraid we weren't going to turn up and is so relieved to see us he tells us to order whatever we want to drink. 'Don't pay for anything!' he announces. Things are looking up.

Unfortunately, the problems with the late confirmation of this gig mean it hasn't been well publicised and there aren't many more people here in this big club than there were in the little record store earlier. But those who are here seem to be looking forward to it. Three guys from Anaheim approach me and tell me that they couldn't make it to the Corona gig near their home yesterday because they had to work, so they've travelled all the way down here to San Diego today. 'We were so worried,' one of them says, 'we'd heard you weren't going to turn up!' They didn't know about the record store appearance. Not being able to afford to drink in the club all night, they went out to a liquor store, bought a sixteen pack of beer and sat in the alleyway round the corner working their way through it. Now they are pretty drunk, but delighted the gig is going to happen. 'We're so stoked you're here, man! You don't know what this means to us!'

The Mexican couple arrive. They've never had the chance to see a TV Smith gig before, and now two come along at once.

No sign of Don and Wendy.

Two days off after this, then just one more gig to play back on the East Coast in New York, so tonight I can give one hundred percent without worrying about wrecking my voice for tomorrow. Despite not having a soundcheck, everything sounds great on stage, most of the people in the club come down the front, and when I finish an hour later I'm left wishing I could have gone on longer.

After the show I find Don and Wendy, who tell me their nap turned into a rather deeper sleep than expected. Luckily they'd set an alarm, but for a few moments when it rang they didn't know where they were or what was happening. They made it to the club in time for the second song of the set.

While I'm saying my goodbyes to Dr Frank and Bobby there's a bit of a commotion at the back of the club as two of the Anaheim guys carry their friend into the car park. He is out cold. They come back in and thank me for the gig, and when I express concern for their friend they laugh it off and say he'll be alright when he's slept it off. The only problem is, he was supposed to drive them back tonight. At that moment a mobile phone rings and one of the guys reaches into his pocket and glances at the display. A look of panic comes over his face. 'It's his wife! What am I going to tell her?!'

How about: your husband has drunk too much and is lying unconscious in the car?

"Hello?" he says innocently, and listens to the voice on the other end. He thinks for a moment before answering, his mouth opening and shutting silently as he tries to form proper words. 'He's, er...he's, arrr....he's...*indisposed* right now...' he says finally, while the rest of us fall about with laughter.

20th October

Time for a last couple of hours in the garden before the flight to New York. I'm a little disappointed that I don't hear anything from the parrot next door, who Wendy has warned me usually keeps screeching out the word 'DADDY!'

Don's giant tortoise has lumbered out of its enclosure and wants feeding so Don gathers up a pile of vegetables and holds them up to its mouth. The massive beast munches away methodically for about ten minutes. Don tells me he bought it years ago when it was tiny and called him Colin, which was cute when it was small enough to fit into a cottage cheese pot, but seems rather inappropriate now.

It's goodbye to the dogs, then Don and Wendy drive me out to the airport, via a challengingly fiery lunch in a Thai restaurant, so spicy it temporarily leaves me unable to speak. Then it's more goodbyes, and by mid-afternoon I'm on a flight to New York, getting in just before midnight.

Bryan told me earlier on the phone that Sniffin Glue founder and Alternative TV frontman Mark Perry will be playing on the same bill as me at CBGB's in two days time, and is also staying in the apartment, so when the cab drops me off I steal quietly past the sleeping figure on the couch and into the computer room, where Bryan is still up. It's like coming home!

Then I fold out the bed, persuade the cats out—good grief, I'm already sniffling—put in the earplugs to block out the traffic and drift down to a deep sleep. The last thing I remember is sneezing.

21st October

I say hello to Mark—last time I saw him was at a gig just round the corner from my home in London. He's off soon to rehearse with the band who are going to be backing him tomorrow. Me and The Midnight Creeps don't need any rehearsal after a week on tour together so I don't have much to do today, except go out for a walk around Manhattan. The temperature change is a bit of a shock after California, New York is in the grip of an autumn chill.

In the evening, Bryan, Alyssa and I go up the road to a restaurant, then meet Mark, just back from his rehearsal, at the apartment and all turn in reasonably early, ready for tomorrow's big gig at CBGB's.

22nd October

Mark is sorting through his bags and pulls out a shirt with a skull pattern printed over it. 'You know, I always like to wear a shirt when I'm onstage,' he says. 'I just don't feel right unless there's a collar up around my neck.'

'I'm the opposite,' I say. 'I hate it unless I'm just wearing a sleeveless vest.'

Old punk rockers, eh?

At the club I bump straight into Heather who tells me that the rest of the Creeps are next door in the CBGB Lounge. 'Hey, I got you a present,' she says, reaching into her bag. 'We stopped at a Taco Bell and I thought of you.'

It's a handful of sporks!

I go to say hello to the others. 'Hey,' says Jenny, 'I've got something for you…'

More sporks!

Jenny is wearing a T-shirt with the word 'CUNT' stitched across the front in satin. It looks a really professional job, and I'm thinking about asking her how she made it so I can steal the technique for my stage vests, but she catches my eye before I get the chance.

'TV!' she exclaims in mock outrage, 'Are you looking at my tits?'

'Nooo…' I say, 'I am looking at your "CUNT."'

We're all excited to be playing another gig together again, but as the first band starts there are only about thirty people in the room and they're not giving much of a response. Thankfully, over the next hour or so things improve and by the time we're due on the room is fairly full and there are quite a few familiar faces in—not as packed as the punk festival a couple of weeks ago, but it still looks promising.

We play the tightest of the whole tour, and most of the audience have either seen us before or heard word of the previous CBGB's gigs and are out to enjoy themselves—they go wild from the first song and stay with us all the way. I'm left thinking: I'd like to play with this band more often. If it wasn't for the three thousand miles between New York and London, I probably would.

Anyway, all good things must come to an end, and tomorrow I'll be on a flight home. It's time to leave behind all my friends in America and get back to all my friends in Europe. Not that you ever really leave anything behind—the best travels with you. I'm taking back plenty of happy memories and a bag full of sporks.

12. CULTURE SLUSH (2004)

3rd February
The new Terminal 2 at Tampere airport is somewhat basic. Built to accommodate the cheap flights from companies like Ryanair, it's not much more than a cattle shed set a couple of hundred yards away from its smart big brother Terminal 1, like a guilty secret. We get off the plane and have to queue outside in the sub-zero cold to get to passport control. I guess when they were building the place they had to cut a few corners on costs: 'Hmm, Arrivals Hall…do we *really* need one of them…?'

Although it's convenient being able to get a direct flight here, there wasn't a lot of choice of flight times and I've had to arrive the day before the first gig. It's nine in the evening by the time I get out of the airport. Jukka is there to meet me and we drive in to Tampere. He's already picked up the key to my room at the Iltatähti residential hotel as the staff there leave at five. The Iltatähti is to hotels what Terminal 2 is to Terminal 1, a budget version of the real thing. I've stayed here before and the standard of the rooms varies a lot so I'm relieved that the one I'm in today is fine, there's even a shower and toilet in it. The advertising pamphlet for the hotel is a little short on things to boast about, though: 'Rooms are for rent for one night or longer time—as you wish.'

Wait until the rest of the hotel world hears about this!

Jukka and I go for a beer in nearby O'Connells—the Irish bar I played a gig in a few years ago—and run through the plans for this short trip. My first gig will be here in Tampere tomorrow at the Telakka club, then I'll take the train down to Helsinki for a gig in the Semifinal. Couldn't find a gig for the next night, Friday, so I'll return to Tampere for a day off and spend another night in the Iltatähti, then take a coach on Saturday to the final gig in Lahti. Back to Tampere by coach on Sunday for the evening flight home. It's not much of a tour, but I always like coming to play in Finland and was particularly tempted by the thought of experiencing the extreme cold of a Finnish midwinter for a few days. Unfortunately it looks like I will be thwarted on that one: the weather forecast predicts that the temperature will rise to just above freezing tomorrow.

Jukka heads home and I wander back to my room. Nothing to do except watch late night Finnish television, which is some of the worst in Europe. There are three channels still broadcasting at the moment: two showing mobile phone text messages scrolling up the screen, the other broadcasting a Finnish version of a BBC Italian language tuition course called Italianissimo. I started trying to learn Italian a few years ago and watched these programmes back then so it's disconcerting seeing all the familiar clips of actors going into train stations, ordering coffee, asking the way to the opera, etc., in Italian, with Finnish subtitles and explanations. There are also some lengthy screen shots of verb tables that weren't in the English version. Ideal bedtime viewing.

4th February

No point in getting up early for the hotel breakfast—they don't do one—so I sleep late, shower and then go for a walk around Tampere. Soundcheck isn't until seven, so I have quite a few hours to kill.

Outside the snow is melting and it's a hard trudge through the grit-filled slush on the streets. I feel more like I'm doing a workout than a walk. Mid-afternoon I drop into a supermarket to buy some rolls, cheese and fruit for tomorrow's breakfast and am back in the hotel by four. I've been there an hour and am in the middle of putting a new set of strings on the guitar when there is a knock on the door. The hotel manager is standing outside and says, 'This is not your room. You have to leave.'

I phone Jukka, and he tells me that there's been a misunderstanding—in fact the venue is booking me a different hotel for tonight.

I hurriedly pack together all my stuff, drop my key into Reception where they glower at me because they are waiting to close up, then carry all my stuff up to the Telakka. I ask the woman behind the bar if she knows anything about a hotel for me and she says, 'I think the other band is booking something for you.'

I say, 'I don't think they are.'

She phones the promoter and he tells me that he has arranged a room in the nearby Ramada, one of the best hotels in town. He has got a cheap rate on the room, about sixty euros—but I will have to pay it myself. I tell him that I thought the venue was paying for the hotel and he says, 'Well, let's see.'

That's not quite the 'Yes, they will pay' that I'd liked to have heard, but there's nothing else for it so I carry my bags over to the Ramada. The receptionist can't find a room booked in my name but knows about the cheap deal with the Telakka, signs me in, and asks if she should send the bill to the venue. I agree that this would be a good idea.

So this is how the other half lives! A luxurious double room, complete with its own en suite sauna—a large cabin with two rows of wooden slatted benches, space for seven or eight people. The idea of firing up my own personal sauna is attractive but soundcheck is fast approaching and I only have time to unpack and drop my groceries into the mini bar before heading straight back to the Telakka.

The support band are already setting up their gear when I walk in, and Punk Lurex OK are also here—they'll be playing a few numbers with me at the end of my set. Guitarist Riitta couldn't make it but we wanted to do it anyway as it looks as if it could be the last time we get the chance; bassist Tiina tells me that after their recent tenth anniversary the band have more or less decided to call it a day.

The Telakka is run by artists and attracts an arty crowd. If they don't like the music they tend to tell the bands to shut up. Indeed, the hardcore band who play as support go down rather badly and I'm relieved that my set is well-received. Punk Lurex join me for the finale and it's a bitter-sweet moment.

Although I'm in one of the best hotels in Tampere there are still only three channels broadcasting at 3:30 in the morning. I watch some more Italianissimo. It may not be the most entertaining thing in the world, but if anyone needs any Italian/Finnish translation done, I'm your man.

5th February

No doubt breakfast here would be exceptionally good but I go for the extra sleep instead, wake up late and get the bread, cheese and fruit out of the minibar for my own little buffet.

The train gets me into Helsinki at four in the afternoon. I do a quick interview in the elegant bar above the train station with a local radio DJ, then record a station I.D. for him: 'I'm TV Smith and you are listening to RADIO EXTREME ROCK!!' Get a few curious glances from the other people in the bar.

The temperature is just above zero but there's a fierce wind. Chilled to the bone and hampered by having to carry my bags and guitar everywhere, I ditch any idea of sightseeing and head straight up to where I'll be staying the night—another hotel I've been in a couple of times before; cheap and basic but fairly central and only a ten minute walk from the venue. I switch on the television. They're showing a French soap opera with Finnish subtitles. The next channel I try shows fifty numbered boxes on the screen, with a few lines of Finnish and a phone number. After some considerable time, box number 47 turns around and there is a picture of a horse on it.

Always great to be back at the Semifinal. Everything goes well at soundcheck, then it's a long wait to showtime. At least there is somewhere to hang around now: the notorious Semifinal backstage area—a flight of stairs leading up to a brick wall—has had a kind of wooden platform built over it so there is at least somewhere to sit.

By the time I get onstage there is a good-sized audience and the response is great. I play for over two hours, and by the time I've finished it's almost 12:30 and time for the club to close. Most people have to work tomorrow so the place quickly empties and I'm on my own. I get a couple of bottles of beer from the bar and make my way along the ice-packed pavements to the hotel, where it's time for a little more Italianissimo.

6th February

Breakfast is served in the room as there is no space for a separate breakfast room in the hotel. I idly switch on the TV while I'm eating, and find the Italian film 'Don Camillo' with Finnish subtitles. Actually, I would quite like to see that, but I have to catch the midday Tampere train because I'm going to meet with Jukka and tour agent Harri to go through the contracts for the gigs, and before that I need to pick up my room key for tonight before Reception shuts.

At the Iltatähti I'm given the room next to the one I was in two nights ago. There are subtle differences to the previous room. For a start, there are *two* minibars: one of them, just like next door, is simply an empty unplugged fridge; the second is a plywood casing with the word 'Minibar' on it and nothing whatsoever inside. On a table there is a large chintzy coffee cup decorated in blue and gold, and a coffee percolator and filter papers. But no coffee. Well, I'd love to brew up some delicious hot water right now but there's no time—I have an appointment to keep with Jukka and Harri.

We meet up at a café across town and Jukka tells me about an independent distributor called Sammi who is interested in taking on a few copies of my new record for Finland. Then we discuss how I'm going to find the club in Lahti tomorrow, and Jukka goes off to print off a map. A few minutes later he returns holding a copy of the map, and with someone tagging along beside him. 'Ah, Tim, this is a bit of a coincidence, but…can I present to you, Sammi!' The world just got smaller again.

The contract work is soon done, and I wander back to the hotel and switch on the television to find a film of 'Animal Farm,' original English dialogue with Finnish subtitles. It's a live action version, and is quite watchable until the scene where the animals look through a window and are unable to tell the difference between the humans and the pigs. In Orwell's book this was the final scene. The film makers, however, seem to have decided that it's a bit too depressing and have tacked on a more upbeat ending. Imagine a furry glove tickling a human face—forever.

Tiina's young son Artu is very keen to meet the English person, so she drives over with him in the early evening and takes me back to her flat a few miles out of Tampere. She brews up some coffee, then Artu asks if we can all watch a video together. It's 'Asterix and Cleopatra' dubbed into English from the original French, with Finnish subtitles. Tiina says she also has the Swedish version.

The weather is really getting cold again now. The ice stubbornly refuses to clear from the car windscreen and Tiina drives me back into Tampere, navigating through a tiny clear patch directly above where the heater is blowing.

Shortly before midnight I am back in O'Connells. The place is packed and I'm lucky to get a bar stool. As soon as I've ordered a drink, someone comes over and starts up a conversation.

'Are you from Wales? In the last month I've met a Scottish guy, an Irish guy and an English guy...I was hoping you might be Welsh.'

I tell him that I'm sorry I can't complete the set. He buys me another beer and tells me that he is the guy who sells the doughnuts in the old observation tower in Pynnikki park, which I visited with Jukka the first time I came to Tampere. They are very good doughnuts, he tells me. If I want to go to the tower again while I'm here he'd be only too happy to give me a free one! (Value: one euro and thirty cents.)

By the time I get back to the Iltatähti I can't be bothered to watch Italianissimo.

7th February

The hotel closes at three today but the bus to Lahti doesn't leave until five so on the way to the bus station I step into the warmth of a shopping centre to get a coffee. The place is packed and I have some trouble negotiating my bags and guitar through all the people. When I finally find a free table in a café I notice that there are a large number of chef's hats visible above the heads of the crowd. Some announcements are made through the shopping centre's P.A. system, then the chef's hats start bobbing up and down in a frenzy. Some time later a bell rings, then there is enthusiastic applause. Curious, I finish up the coffee and wander through the crowds to see a line of chefs in front of a table stretching down the mall, a freshly-made sandwich running the entire length of it. At the far end, by the bus station exit, there are news cameras rolling, and a tape measure is being ceremoniously unwound. I have stumbled upon an attempt to make the longest sandwich in the world.

No time to join the festivities, I have a bus to catch. A couple of hours later I arrive in Lahti, and make my way over to the venue, the Torvi club, for soundcheck. Jukka has told me that the Torvi is one of the most respected rock clubs in Finland—a legend actually, as it says on its advertising—but if the truth be told it doesn't look much. It's a fairly dingy room full of tables and chairs, a two inch high stage in one corner. But the manager and sound guy are very friendly and I'm able to get set up straight away and the sound system isn't too bad. The manager tells me he'll now take me over to where I'll be staying the night—as it turns out, an extremely basic hostel just around the corner. An elderly couple run it and it's clean and everything, it's just…the room is tiny, no toilet or shower, and it's situated right next to the reception area where the couple sit and chat and watch television. I feel like an intruder in someone else's home.

It will be fine for a few hours sleep but I really don't want to spend any more time here. I gather together what I need for the gig and head out, stopping on the way to ask if there is breakfast in the morning. The lady points upwards to where the ceiling tiles have been removed exposing a network of pipes. 'As you can see,' she says, 'Gordon should have fixed the plumbing but he hasn't actually done it yet.'

Mmm, right. Not quite sure what this has to do with breakfast but shame on you, Gordon.

I slip away, stopping only to check that the door code I've been given actually works for when I come in later. Wouldn't like to be stranded outside on a numbingly cold night like this.

The manager of the Torvi asks if I'd like something to eat—he also owns a restaurant up the road. 'It's a Greek restaurant,' he says. 'Not *really* Greek, though.' I say that I'd love to get some food, so he takes me over there and explains to the non-English speaking cook that I'm vegetarian. She gives me an expression somewhere between hurt and angry, but comes up with a spring roll.

Back at the club, four guys who came to the Helsinki gig a couple of days ago are already settled at a table in front of the stage. They are keen to tell me about the terrible cheap hotel they have just checked in to. 'We are going to get killed tonight,' one of them says. 'The building looks like the house in Psycho and the landlady looks like a murderess. When we got to the room, we opened the wardrobe and found a rifle in it.'

Tonight is going to go late—I'd hoped to get onstage by eleven, but people are still coming steadily in. When the place is comfortably full I kick off a 38 song set, and the audience stays with me all the way, everyone getting into it. Seems the Torvi deserves that 'legendary' description after all.

I hang around on the stage after the show and chat to people. They seem to have been very inspired by the evening and all say they want me to come back to Lahti. One guy tells me that the local punks have their own club and would like me to become a member. He hands me a homemade tag with a safety pin fastener. On it are the words, 'KAIKKI MUU ON PASKAA PAITSI KUSI.' I pin it on my T-shirt. The guy points at the lettering and says, 'It means something like, The Shit But Not Piss Club.' Finally, a club that wants me for a member.

Back at the hostel there is a bit of a treat: as it's the weekend, BBC World is on TV instead of the usual Italianissimo. Right now at nearly four in the morning they are showing a programme with all the latest travel news and advice. There is a 'don't drink the green tea fingerbowl in Vietnam' item, then a piece about how the travel industry is responding to terrorism. I learn that the authorities are legally allowed to search luggage on US flights, so if you're intending to lock your bags the official advice is— leave a key attached to the padlock.

More great news: the US wants to ban queues for the loos on planes because they are 'a security risk.'

Piss yourself—America rules the world!

8th February

I open the curtains to the evocative view of twelve toilets dumped in the snow outside my window.

I've lost my map, so at reception Gordon—for it is he—gives me directions back to the bus station. We shake hands as I say goodbye and get a good static blast. Gordon tells me that it's because of the weather—outside it's minus 16C.

Back in Tampere, I wait out the hours until my evening flight at Jukka's flat. I tell him about the sandwich event in the shopping centre and he finds the report for me in the local newspaper. The idea was to break the world record by making an 80 metre sandwich in ten minutes. They measured it and it came in at 79.67 metres. A second measuring was demanded and this time the sandwich came in five centimetres over the record. I guess the bread swelled up a bit.

Toilets in the snow

Night falls and we walk to the car to go to the airport. The snow is glinting and sparkling under the streetlights. Jukka points out that you can hear it is getting colder by the way the snow is crunching under our feet.

By mid-evening I am back in the barn, or Terminal 2 as they like to call it. The plane is being hosed down with de-icer by a man on a gantry, sending up billowing clouds of steam into the heavy falling snow. Soon we are up in the air and on our way, the lights of Tampere falling away below and disappearing under the low clouds. In two and a half hours I'll be in Stansted, an hour after that at Liverpool Street, another hour for the tube and the walk up the road, home by midnight.

13. A VEGETARIAN IN SPAIN (2004)

12th May

The tour's off.

Just leaving for Heathrow when I check my bag for my passport only to find it isn't there. I unpack everything and lay it all out on the carpet to sift through, but there's still no sign. I had the bag ready yesterday and left it near the front room window, which was open a crack…someone could have got an arm in…

In a panic I phone up the British embassy and they tell me there is no way I will be able to travel to Spain today without it—if I go in person to the embassy they will be able to supply a replacement but it will take two weeks. With sinking heart I phone up Jonathan in Barcelona, who put together the tour, to tell him that I'm not going to be able to come, but his phone is switched off. In desperation I have one more look around the house, and—good grief—there is the passport: in the section of the bag where I always put it. But a different bag.

There's less than an hour before my flight leaves. In front of me at the tube station someone is buying a travel card, which requires a lot of forms to be filled in. I check the minicab office—twenty minutes to the first available taxi. Back to the ticket window, which is finally free, then I'm on my way to Heathrow. By some miracle the airport is virtually empty, there's no queue at the check-in desk, and I'm through security and at the gate with ten minutes to spare. Two hours ago I truly believed this would not happen. I am rather stressed out, but…the tour's on!

From Barcelona airport I take the train to Sant station where Jonathan meets me. He says he is mightily relieved that he had his phone switched off earlier or he would have completely freaked out. I'm relieved too: if I'd got through to him to tell him that the tour was off I would have stopped looking for the passport and it actually would have been off.

We head over to a hostel near Jonathan's flat, where I'll be staying the night. The place is pretty basic. The view out of the window is of the lift shaft. Just before leaving for soundcheck, we cross the road to a café and sit in the warm sunshine to discuss the plans for the next few days. I send an SMS home and the predictive text on the phone won't let me write 'soundcheck' as one word—then changes 'sound check' to 'sound bleak.'

But in fact everything sounds fine at 'Rosa de Foca,' the little bar putting on tonight's gig. My only worry is, I've never played this club before, and they don't even usually have gigs on Wednesdays. The concert has to start early evening because of complaints about the noise, and with less than an hour to go no one seems to be around.

My worries turn out to be right: by gig time there are only 30 people in. All the same, there's a good atmosphere and it goes fine.

A friend of Jonathan comes up to me and explains that he's always been a big Adverts fan and last year bought the re-release of 'Crossing The Red Sea' with all the lyrics in. That's when he found out that one of the lines in 'No Time To Be 21' is 'no maybes, no guessing'—not what he'd been singing for the last twenty years, 'no babies, no guessing.' He'd been wondering what I had against babies.

It's got quite late despite the early set. Outside, the streets are empty and Barcelona seems to be pretty much closed. Late night, no food: yes, after a bumpy start things are back to normal. But the tour's on!

13th May

The alarm goes off at 6:39. I reach out to switch it off then realize I didn't set an alarm—the walls are so thin it's coming from the next room. Then it's a few more hours of broken sleep as people get up in the rooms around me and leave—I can hear every footstep—and the ancient lift groans up and down the shaft.

I meet up with Jonathan at the same café we went to yesterday. There's no gig today, but I'll be rehearsing with Suzy & Los Quattro in Castellon tonight. Uri will be driving us but has to work late so it looks like we won't get out of Barcelona until nine. It's going to be a midnight rehearsal.

Jonathan invites me over to a restaurant he knows in the neighbourhood for a late breakfast. Everything here is home-cooked, unlike in the tourist places nearer the centre. But it would be difficult to figure out the menu if I was alone as it's all written in Catalan. There are hidden dangers for the unsuspecting vegetarian: Jonathan points out that the Catalan word *truita* means both 'omelette' and 'trout.'

Weighed down with good food I take a metro into town, walk down the Ramblas to the sea front and spend a pleasant few hours there soaking up the sun. I arrive back at six and text Jonathan to tell him I'm going for a coffee. He sends a text back to say he'll come and meet me—will I be at 'the usual?' I've only been in Barcelona one day and already I have a 'usual.'

Half an hour later we're sitting out on the balcony of his top floor apartment watching a storm approaching over the rooftops while we wait for Uri. Jonathan tells me he's a bit disturbed by the way his cat has been behaving lately. He's noticed that it has been catching lizards and—as he puts it—'playing with them to death.' The other day he happened to look over onto his neighbour's balcony and saw that the cat had laid out the lizard corpses there…all in a row.

The guitars and bags for the trip are already sitting ready in the hallway. Jonathan shows me a bag he has packed with extreme care: inside, enfolded in bubble wrap is a bottle of Viña Ardanza rioja. When he came to visit me in London recently he—er—*borrowed* a bottle from his father's wine rack. I thought it was one of the most delicious wines I've ever tasted so I asked him to look for another bottle. He found one from the same year, 1998, in a wine shop in Barcelona and it wasn't too expensive so he snapped it up. We will take it with us and celebrate the end of the tour by opening it on the last day.

By 9:30 Uri, Suzy and Johnny Quattro have arrived—the rest of the band are already in Castellon—and we squeeze into the car and head off. And I mean literally squeeze: every square millimeter of the boot is crammed with luggage, Uri just manages to fit behind the steering wheel, Jonathan is pinned into the passenger seat with my guitar in front of him, and rest of us are pushed awkwardly together in the back. There's a two hour journey ahead of us. We're so tired by the time we get to the rehearsal room that the temptation is to just say 'that'll do' after the first run through, but we're trying out a couple of new songs and force ourselves to iron out the problems.

Jonathan tells me we'll all be sleeping at Tommy Quattro's place, where we stayed last time. Try as I might, I can't remember last time. I remember the petrol station we stop at to buy some food and wine on the way though. We stop here every time we're in Castellon because it's the only place that has anything vegetarian. It's my 'usual.'

As we drive out of town I'm trying to recognize the route. I remember staying at Tommy's parents' flat once, but that was in the centre of town. I lean over to Jonathan and tell him, 'You know I just don't remember this place we're staying at.'

'You will,' he assures me.

But even as we park up outside the large apartment block by the sea and carry our bags into the lobby it's still not ringing any bells. Maybe I'm just tired. As we wait for the lift I say, 'You know, I really don't think I've been here before.'

Jonathan gives me a worried look. 'TV, you are scaring me.'

I'm feeling very confused. We stack the first load of equipment into the lift and Jonathan gets in to go up to the apartment with it, a thoughtful expression on his face. Just as the door starts to close he says suddenly, 'No—you are right! You have never been here before. I was mistaking you with Clive from the Surfin' Lungs!'

As the door clangs shuts I say, 'Jonathan, you are scaring me.'

Upstairs, we gather briefly round a table and open some cheap wine from the petrol station. Uri complains that this is the one night he can drink because he doesn't have to drive any more and we have bought a 'puta' wine. We come very close to uncorking the Ardanza but thanks to extreme fatigue and the fact that the wine is all the way downstairs in the car we manage to control ourselves. Partly to stop it getting too shaken up, but mainly because we are weak and need to put temptation out of reach, we will leave the Ardanza there for the next few days while we continue the tour in a rental van, and pick it up again when we return to Castellon for the last gig.

14th May

We have a few hours free in the morning while Uri goes to pick up the van. I go with Suzy and Jonathan into Castellon, where they want to visit their record label, No Tomorrow. Urgently in need of breakfast, I leave them in the office and head off up the street, shrugging off Jonathan's offer to come with me and help with the language. It's time for me to test the small amount of Spanish I have learned, even though Jonathan tells me that most of the time when I try and speak Spanish it sounds like I'm saying something in Italian.

Things don't go too well. I end up in a sandwich bar that is clearly advertising vegetarian sandwiches so I ask for one of those, *sin carne, sin pesce*—without meat or fish. The woman serving says she has just the thing, but when it arrives it seems to be bulging with what looks suspiciously like some kind of thin-shaven white meat. 'Pero…es carne?' I suggest, taking off the top of the baguette and peering under it. No, no she tells me…it's not meat, try a piece.

I do. It is.

Still insisting it's not meat, she takes away the sandwich and a few minutes later returns with one topped with cheese. Aware that this is almost certainly the same sandwich with the meat-that-is-not-meat removed and replaced with cheese, I pick at it for a moment with rapidly fading appetite then leave the rest on the plate.

Back at No Tomorrow I explain to Jonathan what happened and he says we can get some food on the journey. Meantime we go over the road to a bar for a quick chat with Javi, boss of the label. Time to put my Spanish into action again and order an orange juice. 'Pulpo d'arancia' I say confidently to the waitress and there is a silence.

'TV, you are thinking Italian again,' says Jonathan. 'You have just ordered an orange octopus.'

We're halfway to Madrid before we stop at a service station and finally get the chance to buy some food. Jonathan ushers me in to the restaurant area to order for me but every one of the sandwiches on display contains meat. He has a lengthy discussion with the woman serving, who seems very reluctant to provide anything 'off-menu' until finally one of the other people working at the counter snaps something at her and she stomps away, muttering to herself.

I ask Jonathan, 'What did he say to her?'

'He said, "Just go into the fucking kitchen and ask the cook. He'll make one."'

I see the word *lomo* on the menu and ask what it is. Jonathan grimaces. 'TV, you don't wanna know.'

'I do want to know,' I say. For this is what was in the so-called vegetarian sandwich in Castellon.

'Well…it's like, the skin from a pig's back…'

Right. So in future when I want so order something vegetarian I must remember to say: no meat, no fish, no skin from a pig's back. A sandwich eventually arrives, and Jonathan also buys a large bag of honey-roasted peanuts in case of hunger later.

We continue our journey, hours over the high mesa, then straight into heavy traffic on the outskirts of Madrid. I'm met outside the club by a fanzine writer who tried to interview me last time I was in Spain. On that occasion we trudged from place to place around the festival I was playing to try to find somewhere quiet enough to record, and finally ended up down the road in his car, where he discovered that batteries in his cassette recorder were flat and he didn't have any spares. This time we try the dressing room, which is nice and quiet until Tommy starts the drum check, then we move out into the street, where we are disturbed by two boys kicking a ball against a metal door opposite us, and end up doing the interview on the move, trying to make ourselves heard above the traffic.

After sound bleak the promoter takes us to a packed tapas bar, but there is no room to sit down, and it's too near gig time to eat anyway. Jonathan, too, is pacing the street outside the bar—he'll be on stage with Suzy & Los Quattro right after me and I'll be joining them for some songs at the end of their set.

The club is looking pretty empty when we get back so we wait a bit longer. We had been hoping for a good turnout—Friday night and good promotion for the gig—so it's a bit disappointing, but then again it is the first time I've played in Madrid.

I'm up at the microphone and just about launch into the first song, when a couple of German guys start calling me from right in front of the stage. I break off and bend down to hear what they have to say. They're on holiday, they tell me, and heard I was playing, but haven't got any money left and had to talk their way past the doorman to be allowed in the club for a few minutes…can I get them in for free? It's not a great time to ask.

I was hoping for an excitable reaction from the Madrid crowd, but actually they are quite reserved. It's the same when Suzy & Los Quattro play, and things only really get going when we're onstage together at the end. Then afterwards at the bar I'm showered with compliments and everyone tells me how much they enjoyed it. I meet a guy who drove six hours to get here. He says, 'Madrid. Valium audience.'

Jonathan introduces me to the guy the band will be staying with tonight. He tells me my hotel is pretty much in the centre and well-placed for a look around the town in the morning, but I point out that by the time I wake up I'll probably only have about twenty minutes free before we have to leave for the next gig. 'Hmm…twenty minutes,' he ponders, then whips out a piece of paper and quickly sketches out where I can walk in twenty minutes, complete with places of interest and alternative routes.

Jonathan peers over my shoulder, knowingly. 'We call him The Human Map,' he says.

The manager of the club couldn't care less that not as many people as expected turned up: we broke even anyway, and more importantly he was very impressed: he says he had goose flesh all the way through my set, and if we don't play in his club again next time he will 'kill us.' I'm invited to drink quite a few beers, and on an empty stomach it's having a distinct effect by the time I get dropped off at the hotel, figure out how to check in, collect my keys and wobble up the stairs to my room. Aware that it's 3:30 in the morning I try to keep quiet, but drop the keys with a sensational crash on the wooden floor while trying to get my door open, then spill the nearly full bottle of beer I had in my pocket over myself while bending to pick them up, leaving a give-away puddle on the floor right outside my door. Once I'm in the room and have rinsed the beer off my jeans and jacket a hunger hits me of the type that only no food and much alcohol can bring. It's still noisy out on the streets—I seem to be located in the middle of the late-night bar area—but my clothes are wet so I can't go out and look for anything to eat. Instead, a quick search through my bags turns up the emergency honey-roasted peanuts, which I eat all of, after which I put in the earplugs and let the coma descend.

15th May

I complete the twenty minute walk in about fifteen—I'm a fast walker—and have time to sit outdoors with a coffee just up the road from the hotel while I wait for the van to arrive. It's a public holiday in Spain today, and a brass band is warming up just over the road, straightening their uniforms and parping tentatively away at their instruments. After a few minutes they begin playing and march in formation at a smart pace towards Plaza Sol, the large town square nearby. It's all very atmospheric, slightly spoilt by the choice of tune: *Y Viva España*.

There is a huge traffic jam, thousands of cars trying to leave Madrid for the holiday, and we sit static in the mounting heat for ages until we are finally out of the worst and on the way to Vitoria, my first visit to the Basque country. Jonathan managed to get a good deal on a four star hotel and we had been looking forward to relaxing there after the journey, but four hours later when we finally get there, there's no time to do more than dump our bags. I'm immediately whisked off with Jonathan and the promoter to play a song and a do a quick interview with a local radio station, while the rest of the band go straight to the venue.

There's less than half an hour before the programme finishes, so the promoter drives us at a fair lick through Vitoria, which is sparkling under its first sunshine of the year. 'It's been very depressing,' says the promoter, 'Six months of grey skies and rain. Now this! Even the priests will be fucking tonight!'

Back at the venue, we rejoin the rest of the band and meet up with the Basque-based punk band Nuevo Cataclismo Catolico, who will be headlining tonight. I met them first at a festival a couple of months ago, and they turned out to be fans and asked me to sing a few Adverts songs with them. Jonathan asked if they'd come and play with us tonight in Vitoria so we'd have a strong enough line-up to draw a crowd. Oh, and could we borrow all their gear?

Once again fewer people come than we had hoped for. There are probably a couple of hundred in, and once again the response is more reserved than I expected, but—once again—as soon as I get a chance to chat with people after the show I get some great feedback. The promoter is totally bowled over and tells us if we don't play at his venue next time we're in Vitoria he will kill us.

Then it's back to our luxury four star hotel, where we will be able to appreciate approximately one hour of sleep per star before setting off on tomorrow's seven hour drive to the last gig of the tour back in Castellon.

16th May

Breakfast isn't included in the price of the hotel—fine by me, I'd rather get the extra half hour of sleep—but it does mean there will be the tricky business of finding something vegetarian on the road later. Unbelievably, the first petrol station we pull into has a pre-packed vegetarian sandwich in the fridge, something I've never seen before in Spain. True, it's bits of tinned vegetables in mayonnaise on dreary white bread, but it's better than the skin off a pig's back! Tastes rather strongly of vinegar, though; in fact as I get down to the bottom corner of the bread it's sopping wet and so acrid I'm almost choking. I'm rather alarmed to see that vinegar isn't actually listed on the ingredients, and spend the rest of the journey thinking, food poisoning here we come.

We arrive at the Ricoamor club with minutes to spare before the place opens. Although Suzy & Los Quattro won't be playing their own set tonight they'll still be playing a few numbers with me so they start setting up their gear on the stage, which is so tiny that most of the band have to stand in front of it. After hours sitting in the back of a van not really understanding any of the conversations going on around me I feel my spirits starting to slump and sit in a corner morosely and change the strings on the guitar. Theoretically I'm on stage in an hour. I do a quick soundcheck and everything sounds great but I can't seem to drag myself out of my bad mood and fatigue. There's only one thing to do: find coffee.

Outside the sun is blasting down and the streets are totally deserted. Apparently there's an important football game for the local team taking place right now; if they win they will be promoted, and it seems all of Castellon is following that. Eventually I find a bar and gulp down an espresso.

Back at the venue I start to focus on the gig, and as soon as I hit the stage I enjoy it. The only thing missing is the audience, with perhaps a scant twenty people there. Good job it's a very small club. Outside as we pack away the gear afterwards it seems the game has finished: the streets are packed with cars, people waving team scarves out of their windows and honking their horns.

And the final score: Football 1, TV 0.

The good news is, the gig finished fairly early. Uri has already taken the van back to the hire place, and is waiting outside with the car, the bottle of Ardanza still safely stored in the boot. Despite the long drive today he's up for getting behind the wheel for another hour back to Jonathan's parents' holiday place on the coast just down the road from Barcelona. It will mean we can sleep late in the morning without having to worry about a long journey to the airport for my flight to London. This tour has been quite short but still felt like a marathon.

We stop off at a petrol station—'the usual'—to pick up a veggie pizza because Jonathan doesn't think there's any food in the house. When we arrive back it turns out he's wrong. We throw open the windows to let the sound of the sea drift in, Uri uncorks the Ardanza while Suzy and Jon get to work in the kitchen. Then it's fresh Catalan Bread smeared with olive oil, tomato and garlic, manchega cheese, olives, pizza, and some good red wine. Sometimes being a vegetarian on tour really isn't so bad.

14. IN THE MIDDLE OF NOWHERE IN THE MIDDLE OF NORWAY (2004)

2nd July

Stansted airport, how I hate it—mainly for the fact that it takes me two and a half hours to get there compared to forty minutes to Heathrow. But Stansted does handle cheap flights to Norway—and as I'm going to play a festival being organised with no financial support by some kids in a Norwegian band called Algorythms we have to keep the costs down. I've offered to play on both nights of the festival for free as long as they can cover the price of the flight.

I have a few minutes of anxiety when I get out of the airport in Norway and find none of the band there to meet me. It occurs to me suddenly that it might have been a good idea to exchange phone numbers before I set out—but twenty minutes later guitarist Loco arrives. He's late because he and the rest of the band have been setting up things at the site all day,

Another forest, another festival (2)

Before we drive to the festival we have to go to a rehearsal room in nearby Larvik to pick up a bass guitar that one of the members in another band forgot. You have to wonder: if you're a musician and you're going to play at a festival, how disorganised do you have to be to actually *forget* your instrument?

So, on through the twisty country roads, forested hills with shelves of granite rising steeply on one side, a rushing river on the other, clouds lowering overhead and raindrops the size of pebbles beating down. It is, of course, an open-air festival.

The inclement weather does make me wonder if anyone will turn up. Another factor is the enormous Rosskilde festival in Denkmark which is being held this same weekend. Of course, our festival will be a different affair from a huge enterprise like Rosskilde. When we pull into the riverside glade that serves as the camping ground there are perhaps twenty tents there, as well as an enormous old bus with '666' written on the destination board.

666, the number of the bus

I go into the large open-sided wooden cabin next to the campsite, where Dan, the singer and guitarist with Algorythms, hands me a beer from the makeshift bar and introduces me to a few of the people helping out, mostly friends of the band. There are also two official security guys who it has been necessary to hire to comply with Norwegian law. They are responsible for making sure that drinking only takes place in the cabin—no drinks to be taken out to the nearby stage area—and that all the music finishes promptly at 1:00 a.m. even though there are no houses for miles around.

Over in the next glade where the stage is set up I can hear the first band starting, but for now I sit at one of the picnic tables while people come over and chat with me. They all seem really glad I've come. One girl wants to know all about English punk rock and in particular her favourite band, the Sex Pistols.

'Is it true you knew the Sex Pistols?' she asks.

'Well, yes.'

'Oh my God! Did you ever *touch* the Sex Pistols?'

Dan, who sports a red mohican haircut hands me another beer and tells me that he is going to get me drunk and then cut my hair like his. That would be something—a grey hair mohawk.

I get to put faces to a couple of my email correspondents when they introduce themselves. They point to the campsite and tell me that they have a *huge* tent out there if I need somewhere to sleep tonight. Which is a good point. Where exactly am I sleeping tonight?

A word with Dan confirms that I can sleep at his place, which is just a short drive away and will be completely empty. The only question is—looking at the rapidly increasing drunkenness around me—will anyone actually be sober enough to drive me back later? It wouldn't be the first time I've been stranded at a festival in a forest in Scandinavia.

Over the next few hours I wander over to the stage area from time to time to watch a few songs from the bands. The stage has a bucket in the middle of it to catch the last of the rainwater draining from the awning. The sound is very good, and the setting dramatic with the pines all around and a wide river at the foot of the hill.

'Don't be fooled by that river,' says Dan. 'It has a very strong current—if you went swimming in there you would be in Larvik ten minutes later.'

Hmm, I did bring my trunks, but…maybe not. Anyway, it's far too cold. I am already wearing every T-shirt in my bag (3).

Soon it will be time for Algorythms, to play, and I'll be on after them. When they first got in email contact, they asked me if we could play two of my songs together at the end of their set. We obviously haven't been able to rehearse them together so now we go to the back of the cabin with guitars and snare drum and have a quick run through. I'm quite surprised to find the arrangements and tempos are rather different from the way I've always played them. Drummer Andy explains that he hadn't actually heard the original records when he learned them, he was just going by the way Dan played them to him.

The Algorythms set goes down well. There are only about fifty people on the festival site in total, but they're all down at the front of the stage. I get up for the last two songs. The first one goes pretty well, the second is a bit of a disaster but nobody in the audience seems to notice and we bluff our way though to the end somehow and all finish at the same time.

Then I go straight into my own set. After the first song I start getting requests from the audience, quite a few of them from the people with the big tent. I notice other people singing along too, which I hadn't expected out here in the middle of nowhere in the middle of Norway, and it's very pleasing.

After about forty minutes I hurry off stage to give the last band of the night time to play before the one o'clock curfew, and make my way back to the cabin, where I get a lot of compliments. The good mood is only broken by a girl who is having an argument with her boyfriend and screaming non-stop at the top of her voice. It is the Sex Pistols girl.

The guys in Algorythms tell me how much they enjoyed playing the songs with me. It seems a pity we only got to play them one time so I bring up the idea that we could do them again at the end of my set tomorrow. They hadn't been intending to play tomorrow but seem pretty keen, drummer Andy included, even though he thinks he may have broken a finger during the set today. It's non-drinking Andy who now tells me that he can give me a lift back to Dan's place whenever I'm ready. Just then Dan returns and asks me if it would be alright if one of his friends who has been working on security by the river stayed in the house with me. It seems the girl who was having the argument with her boyfriend has just thrown herself in the river and Dan's friend had to pull her out. Luckily he was able to grab her before she was carried off to Larvik. The cost of being a hero is that now all his clothes are soaked and he needs a shower and somewhere warm to sleep. Dan decides that he doesn't need to stay on the site overnight either, so he and his girlfriend Camilla, the hero and me all end up back at his place with beer and pizza in traditional rock'n'roll fashion and I bed down on the mattress in the computer room at around 4:30.

3rd July

The house rouses mid-morning and we have a quick breakfast of bread, cheese and salad. Dan phones to arrange someone to give him and Camilla a lift back to the festival site where Camilla will start cleaning up and Dan will pick up his car and go and buy more supplies of food and beer then come back and pick up me and the hero.

When Dan and Camilla have gone, there's a slightly awkward silence between me and the hero as he speaks very little English and I don't speak any Norwegian. It's not a language I'm likely to attempt to learn. It took most of yesterday before I recognised the sound of Dan's name, which seems to be pronounced 'Doo-won.'

I go outside and sit in the sun with a book. Hours go by. Finally Dan is back with another of the security guys from the festival and his girlfriend and a carload of beer and food. Now we have the challenging prospect of squeezing all five of us, the supplies and my guitar into a rather small car. 'I am driving with my elbows,' says Dan from the front seat.

Even though it's Saturday there's not many more people at the festival site than yesterday. I see the guys who had boasted about their huge tent across the campsite and wander over to them. They are a bit bleary, just getting up. I look the tent up and down. 'It's not that big,' I tell them.

Nothing's really happening yet so I go for a walk along the river bank and over a graceful low bridge to a decked platform over a weir, where the water pounds by beneath me, throwing up a refreshing spray. The sun is hot. Black-throated swallows dart past. On one side of the weir the water is diverted through a cage-like arrangement of spruce branches, an old fish trap. Next to it on the bank is a ten foot long net on a pole for scooping out the catch. Would also be handy for fishing out heart-broken Sex Pistols fans.

Back at the festival site there's still nothing happening. The band due to play first haven't turned up and no one else can play instead because although the drummers in the bands were told to bring their own cymbals, hi-hats and pedals, none of them has.

Due to the late start the timings will all have to change and I find Dan at one of the tables in the cabin feverishly scribbling away at a revised running order for the evening. I'm being pushed back later than originally planned, partly because he doesn't want me on too early before there's a good atmosphere and partly because no one knows where Algorythms bass player Ciggy is and we can't play without him. He was last seen driving away from the site earlier in the day. His mobile phone is on the bar, charging.

Dan works out the new setlist

'I'm getting seriously worried,' says Dan. 'He hasn't drunk anything today, but if he gets stopped by the police he might still be over the limit from yesterday.'

The music starts up. The people with the big tent come over and one of them tells me that they have some hot dogs back at the tent if I want something to eat. I say I'm vegetarian and he suggests I could just have the bread roll. When I don't look too excited about that he adds, '…with as much ketchup and mustard on it as you want!'

I see the Sex Pistols girl, back together with her boyfriend. Throwing yourself in the river obviously works.

The sun has dipped below the top of the hill and it's rapidly getting cold again. I chat with a guy from one of the bands playing later, The Trashcan Darlings.

'So, what do you think of Norway?' he asks.

'Really, all I've seen is Oslo,' I reply, then gesture at the forest and the river, '…and this.'

'Well, if you've seen Oslo and this,' he says, repeating my gesture, 'that's pretty much all of it.'

I bump into an Austrian guy who I last met when I played his hometown, St Pölten. It's a small world. But big enough that Ciggy is somewhere out in it and we don't know where. Time for my set is fast approaching. Dan waves his mobile at me, 'We just phoned Ciggy's parents…he was seen in Svarstad half an hour ago!'

We arrange that I will start playing and when Ciggy arrives Dan will come to the stage and give me the thumbs-up so I know that I can invite the band on with me. The drama!

It all works out. My set goes down even better than yesterday, Ciggy arrives in time and we play the two numbers together, this time without any mistakes. We're all happy.

The last two bands play, then it's time to wind down. It's after one a.m. so the official padlock is on the drinks cabinet, but us musicians seem to have secret access. Unfortunately it's hard to relax—tonight is even colder than last night and pretty soon I am wearing the three T-shirts, a jacket, and someone has put a sleeping bag around my shoulders.

In a final effort to beat off the cold Camilla suggests some exercises, touching head, shoulders, knees, toes. 'Hode, skulder, kne og tå…'

It's time to leave. Dan and Camilla have decided to stay on site tonight. The job of sober driver has fallen to Ciggy. He's going to take me back to Dan's, then return for members of the last two bands who will also be staying at the house. I feel sorry for Ciggy, he looks pretty much dead on his feet already.

Probably the party will continue when the bands get back to Dan's place, but for me the festival is over. I close the door of the computer room, put in the earplugs and I'm out.

It's not THAT big...

4th July

I open the door of the computer room to find people sprawled all over the house among empty tins of beer, overflowing ashtrays and half-finished plates of food. A bleary eye opens from one of the bodies. 'I—ah—hope we didn't disturb you...we got back and decided to have a bit of a party.'

God bless earplugs.

Not sure how I'm going to get to the airport today. Ciggy, who lives in the downstairs flat, was going to drive me, but he's gone missing again. The drummer from the Trashcan Darlings tells me that that he can give me a lift though—someone is coming to pick them up and take them back to the festival site, he'll pick up his car from there and drop me off at the airport on the way back to Oslo.

At the festival site all the tents have gone, including the huge one. Ciggy is sitting at one of the picnic tables outside the cabin, looking tired. 'Did you see my car on the way here?' he asks. 'It ran out of petrol on the last trip back and I had to abandon it.'

I walk around to the stage area. All the equipment has gone, now there's just a large empty stage—empty except that Dan and Camilla are asleep in the middle of it. I say my goodbyes and head off with the drummer from the Trashcan Darlings. By the side of the road I spot a pair of shoes. How can anybody leave a festival and forget their shoes?

We stop at a petrol station to buy some food, but I can't find anything vegetarian. I realise that I've eaten nothing since breakfast yesterday and I'm seriously hungry. My first opportunity comes at the airport, where half a bread roll with a thin slice of cheese on it costs £2.00. One isn't nearly enough. Musing on this with a £3.00 cup of coffee, I realise that what with the train ticket to Stansted, the tube fares and all the other expenses, it's cost me quite a bit to come to this festival. But I'm glad I did. I got to play my songs, I met a lot of good people and helped get a festival off the ground that hopefully will become an annual event. This year not a lot of people turned up but those that did had a great time. Most importantly, in the middle of nowhere in the middle of Norway…something happened.

15. IF YOU GO DOWN TO THE WOODS… (2004)

24th July

There's a slight hold-up before we can leave for the gig. René just checked on the meal he's preparing for us tomorrow and he needs to do something to it. I'm banned from the kitchen because the dish he's cooking is supposed to be a surprise, but I gather that 'something that should have happened overnight has already happened.'

I'm here in Switzerland to play a private birthday party in a hut somewhere in the woods near a village called Birmensdorf, which I couldn't find on my atlas at home. It also gives me a good excuse to stay with my friends René and Mariann. When the crisis in the kitchen is sorted out, we set off, following a map I'd been sent a few weeks ago. We finally find Birmensdorf, and take a country road out of it, following a pencil line marked on the map. At the end of the pencil line the instructions say, 'Turn left at the tree.'

We turn off at a likely-looking tree and head off up a track. Soon we find some parked cars, and just beyond them we see a timber hut on the edge of the woods with a long view over the fields to a distant hillside. The rain has cleared away and it's a damp, warm evening. A few people are sitting at tables and some punk music is playing loudly from inside.

A hut in the woods

A guy wearing a kilt comes out of the hut and sees me carrying my guitar up the track. He mimes an air guitar, and shouts in a heavy Scottish accent, 'Hey, Teevee! THERE'S GONNA BE A BORSTAL BREAKOUT—NERRR, NERRR!—THERE'S GONNA BE A BORSTAL BREAKOUT…!'

He's a friend of Alan, whose 40th birthday party I'm here to play. Alan is Fin's boyfriend. Fin is a Swiss girl who lived for a couple of years in England, ending up in Hull, where she stayed with my friends in the housing collective there, including Danny—who once drove me and Attila around Germany on tour—and Eddie, who has made it over for the party. Eddie and I discovered a couple of years ago that we both have Huguenot ancestry. After a quick soundcheck I go outside to the barbecue to give him a couple of postcards from the Huegenot House in London that I've been saving for him and find him nibbling at something vegetarian while being harangued by the man in the kilt, who is explaining that *his* idea of a barbecue is to go out into the woods, drag back a deer and throw it on the flames whole.

A right couple of Huegenots

There's a wood fire blazing away around the side of the hut and I sit by it for a while to collect my thoughts. A Scottish woman comes over and hands me a beer. She tells me that today was the first time she'd been in an airplane. She took binoculars with her in case she got a window seat. She did, but was then too scared to look out of it. She tells me that the guy in the kilt is her boyfriend and a huge punk fan, really excited to get the chance to see me play. At that moment he walks up and glares at me.

'AH YOUSE CHATTIN UP MAH BURD?'

I ask where they're intending to stay the night and they tell me that they did bring a tent but never actually got round to putting it up, they started drinking instead. They might do it later. 'The Swiss, though,' says the woman, 'they drink three tinnies and that's it. We'll be drinking all the night!'

I suppose at some point I should play some songs as that's what I've been invited here to do. Man In Kilt gets wind of it and starts rounding everyone up to go inside the hut. He doesn't know I need to tune up first. I slip into the kitchen to do it, where it's quiet, and hear him roaring from the next room: 'TEEVEE, WHIR AH YEW, YER OVERSTUFFED TURKEY?!!'

There's a small noisy crowd, and quite a bit of good-natured heckling between the songs. I play for two hours, checking the clock occasionally to see when it's midnight and the official start of Alan's birthday. Between songs, on the dot of twelve, someone shouts 'Happy Birthday!' and I pass over the microphone as a round of 'Happy Birthday To You' starts up. The girl who began the song then suggests we have a break for the birthday cake and everyone wanders outside to where it awaits on one of the picnic tables.

As I'll be carrying on with the set shortly I don't get involved with the celebrations; instead I go back over to the fire to have a think about what songs I might play in the second half. René and Mariann come over and chat with me, then Eddie arrives. Over the hillside in the distance, some fireworks erupt. I speculate that they were hired for Alan's party but the people in charge turned off at the wrong tree. Gazing over at the display, Eddie tells me about the time he saw the Northern Lights in Hull. 'No-one else seemed to notice, they were all walking around looking at their shoes,' he says.

I'm edgy and wound up, itching for the cake break to be over so I can get going on the second half of the set. But…am I actually supposed to play again? I seem to have been sitting here for quite some time, nursing the odd beer, and—hang on—a few people are saying their goodbyes and have started leaving. I check inside the hut. The only person in there is Man In Kilt, crashed out along one of the benches like a big ol' teddy bear. Looks like I might as well stand down and pack away my guitar.

Outside, as I'm preparing to leave, Alan comes over and thanks me for the gig. 'Hope you enjoyed yourself too,' he says.

'Nah, I can't wait to get away,' I deadpan. He looks upset. 'Don't worry, just kidding,' I reassure him.

'All those years ago, when I was just a young kid going to see the Adverts play,' he mulls, 'I never thought that one day TV Smith would come to play my birthday…and take the piss out of me…'

I say my goodbyes, then head off up the track with René and Mariann. Alan walks a few paces with me. 'You were at the WASTED festival in Morecambe last weekend?' he says.

'Yeah.'

'How many people were you playing in front of there?'

'Oh, I guess about two thousand.'

'And today you played for about twenty-five…'

I think he's pleased I came. I'm pleased I came—it was something special.

What's more, I have a day off before my flight back on Monday. Tomorrow will see René and Mariann and me on a *Touristenprogramm* that will have us driving to a two thousand meter high mountain near Luzern, going up it on a thirty-five minute cable car ride, having a go on 'Switzerland's longest Summer toboggan run,' riding a toy duck for some silly photos, looking for wild blueberries, and finally finding out what René's mystery meal turns out to be.

And I'll tell you all about it right after this cake break.

The end of the run

16. El TV (2005)

10th February

Jonathan phones up while I'm in the queue at the coffee shop in Heathrow. 'Hola TV! Do you have your passport this time! HA! HA HA!!' Honestly, lose your passport once and they never let you forget.

When we've landed I take the shuttle into the city and at the second station from the airport a conductor clears the train, shouting 'Barcelona!' and pointing to another platform. A crowd of confused foreigners, including me, heave their luggage down a flight of stairs, along a subway and up another flight of stairs then stand around looking lost, wondering which of the two trains now standing there they should be on. The one I get on proves to be the right one, but obviously no one told the people waiting at the next station there's been a change. When we pull in many of them jump off the platform and cross the rails on foot to get over to us. Spanish people: please don't try this in London. You will be electrocuted.

I endure a few attempts by a dodgy looking woman to sell me a dodgy looking gold ring outside Sant Station, then Jonathan arrives and we run through the plans for the coming few days. Right now I have an appearance on local television, later this evening a solo show in a small bar called the Barbara Anne, a radio show and another TV show tomorrow, then a gig with Suzy & Los Quattro the day after.

We head down town to the TV channel and meet the presenter and the production team. I've decided to play Gary Gilmore's Eyes as it's probably the only song anyone knows by me round here, and the crew seems to enjoy the run-through.

'Must have gone well,' says Jonathan afterwards. 'They've offered to pay for us to have a coffee.'

Before the live recording we have an hour to kill, so we get the coffee, then go for a walk to distribute some flyers for Saturday's gig to the local record shops.

By the time we get back, the audience is in and the show underway. Suzy turns up to see what's going on. I leave her and Jonathan in reception while I get taken to make-up. There I'm left in the hands of a girl who speaks no English. As I speak virtually no Spanish (and certainly none of the 'hey, what is that foundation you're using?' variety) there is a rather uncomfortable silence while she performs the strangely intimate act of delicately applying creams and powders until I look like I have a magnificent complexion. At the end she gets out a tiny brush and combs my eyebrows.

Back outside in the reception area the other guest is pacing around nervously. Jonathan whispers to me that she is a hugely famous flamenco singer who sells 300,000 copies of her records. But she is also wearing a white fur coat so I won't speak to her. In fact, when she goes in to the studio and leaves the coat on the seat—ranched mink, I checked—I'm tempted to do something terribly punk rock to it.

I'm ushered in as she is finishing off her interview, then it's a commercial break, my guitar is plugged in, the microphone is placed in front of me and we're ready to go on air. Before I start I turn round to the small studio audience and say 'Hola!' with a wave. They all smile and shout 'Hola!' back, and I get the feeling this is going to be good.

We're on. To my surprise the presenter is bigging me up like crazy in his introduction. I don't understand a word of it but he gets very excited and mentions the words 'Clash' and 'Sex Pistols.' Then I'm into the song, I throw in a few leg kicks and hear the crowd laughing and enjoying it. The song ends, there's huge applause and the presenter falls to his knees in front of me in mock worship.

I'm ushered off, then a 'Pipi Longstockings' type character comes on in little girl dress and pigtails and starts doing some acrobatics.

I pack the guitar away and a few minutes later we're outside waiting for Jonathan and Suzy's friend Uri to drive us over to the Barbara Ann. Jonathan works at the bar when he's not out with the band, and tonight is the first time he's tried putting on a gig here, so we're not expecting a huge turnout. The place only holds forty people in any case. We arrive at around 10:30 to pull the shutters up and get the bar ready for opening at 11:00, and there's time for a very quick soundcheck on the raised area that usually houses the table football. The table has been pushed to the back wall and opened up so that a backdrop can be hung on it. In the workings—ooh, I've never seen the insides of a table football game before—I notice the coin counter is on the number 1975, so I click it on two for good luck.

A few people drift in to the bar and at midnight it's time to start. Only twenty-one people there, but Jonathan tries to encourage me a bit. 'Nineteen of them are here just because of you,' he tells me. I wonder who the other two are? Anyway, the gig is fun and a nice warm up—my first full length show this year.

11th February

Today's radio interview has been cancelled so I have the whole day to be a tourist before the television appearance at eleven tonight. I take the metro to La Sagrada Familia, Gaudi's visionary cathedral, more than a hundred years in the building so far, and no end in sight—the central tower, which will be the highest, hasn't even been started yet. At this time of year the place is mercifully free of crowds and the entrance fee is a couple of euros less than in the summer. Inside, massive newly sculpted blocks of masonry and delicate mosaic panels, all conforming to Gaudi's original plans, lie scattered around the floor in various states of readiness to be incorporated into the structure. It's the most beautiful building site in the world. Despite the lack of tourists there's a thirty minute queue for the lift to the top so I take the steps, and some considerable time later emerge from the dark and cramped spiral staircase into a sunlit fairy-tale word of intricate spires. The English tourist in front of me says to her husband, 'It should be nice when they've finished it.'

One word of advice for anyone else thinking of taking the stairs to the top of La Sagrada Familia instead of the lift: don't. Back on the ground I can barely stand, and stagger off to the nearest metro with cramping pains shooting up and down my legs.

In the metro I happen to notice a sign saying that if you travel without a ticket you're liable to a fine of forty euros, and if you smoke you are liable to a fine of thirty euros and five cents. Five cents is about 3p. How exactly did they arrive at that figure?

It's pleasant to be out in the warming Mediterranean sunshine after the long grey English winter. By late afternoon I get back to Suzy's flat, where Jonathan cooks a triumphant tortilla. Tommy Quattro arrives and at 10:00 we take a taxi to the Barbara Ann where Jonathan is working again, and Tommy will be doing a DJ spot. It's just like yesterday as we arrive in the deserted back street and pull up the shutters. I'll be returning later, but for now take the taxi on to a local TV station for the interview.

I really don't have much idea of what this programme is going to be like except that I've been told it's very popular with young people and that I'm going to be asked a few 'stupid' questions and then play one song. Walking through the production room on the third floor the first thing I see on the screen is a guy getting his trousers pulled down to great applause. The two presenters of the show greet me politely, tell me they speak a *leedle* bit of English, and hurry me into the studio which has a desk with two microphones on it, placed in front of a window looking out over the street.

As soon as the show starts the presenters transform themselves into fast-talking entertainers, joking around and working off each other. I can't understand what they're saying, but it all seems rather juvenile, with every smart comment punctuated by comedy sound effects triggered by someone in the production room. They're also mentioning my name quite a bit, apparently commenting about how difficult it is for a Spaniard to pronounce. Anyway, I assume that's what they're doing—I can't think of any other reason they would keep saying 'TV Smith' very fast three times in a row.

Suddenly I'm on. I'm handed a microphone and go to stand at the desk between them while they joke around in stilted English and ask me a few flippant questions. I try and match their style, but the language problems mean that my attempts at humour aren't understood by anyone. However, let me recreate a few of these scintillating moments for you.

Presenter 1: Is this your first time in Spain?

TV: No, I've been here three times now.

Presenter 2: And you still don't speak any Spanish?

TV: No, but every time I come here my English gets a little better.

Presenter 2: TV is a strange name. What's your real name?

TV: The 'T' stands for Tim.

Presenter 1: So why did you call yourself TV?

TV: I thought with a name like that I would get invited on lots of television programmes. This is the first time it's worked.

Presenter 1: Do you like Bryan Adams?

TV: No.

Presenter 2: I like him! I can do an impression of him! *[leans into mic and sings a few bars of Bryan Adams song, followed by canned applause from production room]* Just like Bryan Adams, no?

TV: Yes. That's why I don't like him.

Presenter 1: TV, do you prefer the sex, the drugs, or the rock'n'roll?

TV: The rock'n'roll.

Presenter 1: I prefer the sex! *[makes comedy leering face. Wolf whistle sound effect from production room]*

TV: *[turns to presenter 2]* And by the look of it you prefer the drugs.

Presenter 2: When did you start playing in a punk band?

TV: 1977

Presenter 2: The year I was born!

TV: Yes, I'm old enough to be your dad, sonny, and you'd better remember that the next time you try any of that 'TVSMITH-TVSMITH-TVSMITH' shit.

Actually, that last one wasn't very funny but I was getting a bit bored with it all by then and wanted to play the song and get back to the bar.

So then I'm storming through 'Gary Gilmore's Eyes' for the second time this weekend, but trying not to move about too much because I'm aware that there's just one static camera and if I dance around I'm going to disappear off the screen, which is not the intended effect.

The presenters give me lots of applause, then they're back into their routine, directing a few more jokes and references about me over to where I'm sitting, behind the camera. During one routine they shout, 'Hey TV, are you going to come out drinking with us after the show?'

I shout back 'YES!' with as much enthusiasm as I can muster but only afterwards realise that my lie must have been rather transparent as the camera would certainly have caught me flagging down a taxi outside the building five minutes later.

Back at the Barbara Ann there are a scattering of people in, Tommy's playing some good records, and I happily down a few beers, but there are hardly any English speakers here and it's going to be a hard slog through to 3:30 when the place will finally be cleared. I'm disappointed to see some people playing table football and unknowingly clicking forward the 1977 coin count.

'I'll let them get away with a couple of games,' I say to Jonathan, 'But if they take it through into the 1980's I'm going to get angry.' The Eighties were a very bad period for me.

Things must have got a bit vague after that. When we checked the counter at the end of the night it was 1992, which is okay.

12th February

Pretty hard to wake up this morning but after a shower and a coffee (not at the same time) I feel almost human. We need to head straight out for a rehearsal before tonight's gig and by the time we get to the rehearsal room my body is demanding breakfast so I go for a walk in the morning sunshine to find some food while the band set up and run through their stuff—I won't be needed for at least another hour. I end up in a pleasant pedestrianised area, manage to make myself understood in a traditional style Catalan café and sit at an outside table in the weak sunshine for a while.

The rehearsal is fine, and by three we are loading the equipment into the venue through a door at the back, over pools of urine and used condoms. The venue itself is very nice, with a great sound system and room for a few hundred people. Which means we have to start worrying again about whether anyone will turn up.

We drive back to Suzy's place to kill the remaining four hours before we are due to play, dropping briefly into a supermarket on the way to pick up something to eat. I notice a brand of bread called 'Bimbo,' and one particular loaf named 'Bimbo Sandwich' which conjures up the idea of rather more than a light snack.

I suppose I should also mention that when we drive back to the gig I notice a café called 'Bracafé' and find myself wondering what size cups they have.

We arrive at the venue to find that there's already been one show this evening, some kind of disco. Quite a few drunken drag queens are staggering out into the street on their high heels, and inside the mops are out and everything's being furiously prepared for our show—the barrier removed from the stage, the mixing desk wheeled back into the room from somewhere behind the bar. We have a strictly allotted playing time because we have to finish promptly for another disco to start at one in the morning.

Although it's good to know that the night is going to finish reasonably early, it's hard for audience and band to get in the mood for a gig so quickly. We gulp down some beers in the cramped dressing room, then barely half an hour later Suzy & Los Quattro get on stage. At least there is an audience: about a hundred people are in, which is more than any of us expected and despite the cold start the band are going down well. Then I'm up for my solo spot, the band join me for our songs together and suddenly it's all over. There's plenty of applause, easily enough to justify an encore, but we haven't learned any more songs together so that's it.

Outside, while the van is being loaded, I start thinking to myself how nice it will be to relax back at Suzy's with that bottle of wine Jonathan bought earlier when I realise the band are discussing something and making some kind of plan. It's easy to miss these trigger points when you don't understand a language. Jonathan comes over.

'Now we are going to go to the Barbara Ann,' he tells me. I think he notices that I'm slightly surprised at the idea of going there yet again, and laughs. 'This tour you cannot escape the Barbara Ann. Of course, you have your keys if you want to go back to Suzy's, just tell me.'

Hmm. To get some much-needed rest on my own, perhaps a nice relaxing glass or two of Spanish wine then a welcome sleep…or to wind up in a dirty, smoky rock'n'roll bar until the early hours with a bunch of drunken people talking in Catalan all around me?

'So, TV, what's it to be?'

'The Barbara Ann. I'm in.'

17. A DUCK FLIES IN (2005)

22nd February

If you were to want to enter America on a tourist visa without drawing attention to the possibility that you might be playing a few gigs while you were there, how should you go about it? Well, don't act like a musician: don't for example spill wine over yourself in the airplane so you're stinking of booze by the time you land.

Oops.

Don't meet another musician with a fierce reputation for drug taking and misbehaving—let's say, ooh, Ian Brown—get chatting and end up going through customs with his band in the queue in front of you wheeling all their instruments through on trolleys.

Oops.

But luckily I get through faster than ever before, only mildly scolded by the Immigration guy because I try and do the fingerprints in the wrong order, then blink when he takes the photo.

While we're waiting for baggage Ian tells me that he brought in John Leckie to produce the Stone Roses because he liked what he'd done with the first Adverts album so much. Then he and the band go off to catch their stretch limo into New York and I wait in the Arrivals hall for the Midnight Creeps to come and pick me up in their band van.

I attempt a quick re-pack while I'm waiting, get out of the soft shoes I'd been wearing for the flight and back into my DM's, which are somewhere in my suitcase. I'm not in a very organised frame of mind after seven hours in the air, and I'm crouched on the floor in bare feet with most of the contents of my bag spread out around me when I hear a scream over my head.

'AAAAAAAH! HE'S DOWN HERE!!'

It's Jennie from the Creeps. They almost walked right past.

'Jennie, please don't scream when you see me.'

She puts a hand to her mouth. 'Sorry. How embarrassing.'

But what a welcome!

We drive down to the rehearsal room in New Jersey and get caught up in the evening rush hour traffic, crawling through the depressing industrial wasteland and on into suburbia. On the way we pick up Adi, whose band The New York Rel-x usually use the room and are lending us drum kit and amps tonight, saving us having to unload all the stuff from our van in the snow. We also stop off at a liquor store because when Jeff sent me the itinerary for the tour it said for tonight 'Pick Tim up from airport. Practice. Drink.'

It's getting on for eleven by the time we start, that's around four in the morning UK time, but it's soon clear that the band has really learned the songs well, and it's just a question of running through them for fun. It's a very nice rehearsal, and with Adi and Jennie singing along plus a couple more people listening in it starts to feel more like a gig than a practice.

It's past two before I get to the motel, around the time I would be waking up if I were home. We're all pretty hungry but there's no time to stop at a diner because the band have to get to their friend's place where they're going to be spending the night. That means a vending machine meal for me. I go for a pack of: enriched flour (wheat flour, niacin, reduced iron, thiamine mononitrate [vitamin B1], riboflavin [vitamin B12], folic acid), partially hydrogenated soybean and/or cottonseed oil and/or liquid soybean oil, whey, sugar, high fructose corn syrup, butter (cream, salt, annatto color), cheddar cheese (made from cultured milk, salt and enzymes), buttermilk solids, salt, leavening (baking soda, calcium phosphate), disodium phosphate, natural flavor, soy lecithin (emulsifier), maltodextrin, artificial color (includes yellow 6), modified cornstarch, malted barley flour, peanuts.

All this for a dollar!

Then it's just a matter of rinsing out the wine from my trousers and hanging them over the back of the chair so they're in the updraught from the fan heater and I can get to bed.

23rd February

I'm up and showered by 9:30, when the Creeps are due to get kicked out of their friend's house because she has to go to work. I can see a familiar-looking white van in a quiet spot off across the parking lot, so I guess they drove over here and are getting some more sleep.

I'm in no hurry so I relax for another hour. Breakfast is calling, though, and eventually I decide to go out and see what's happening. Unfortunately, when I peer through the shaded windows I find out that it's not the Creeps' van after all, so I move off pretty quickly before someone shoots me. This is America.

Jeff phones the room to say they were able to sleep longer than expected at the place they were staying and we're all going to meet up for breakfast in the IHOP around the corner from the motel. I don't know what an IHOP is—maybe some trendy diner version of the iPod and iMac?—but it turns out to be an International House Of Pancakes, where they serve astonishing amounts of sugar and cholesterol disguised as pancakes with various toppings. The desperately bland veggie burger I find on the menu, called a Garden Burger because it has a leaf of lettuce in it, is very welcome despite the lack of any discernable flavour—the first warm food I've eaten since the aircraft meal a day ago.

We drive into New York City to while away the afternoon before the gig, which is only about two miles from the motel. The sun is out but an icy wind is shafting through the streets. We wander around St. Marks Place, Jami and Jeff sticking up flyers for next Saturday's gig in CBGB's, then head through the Holland tunnel and back out into New Jersey.

In the venue the first of the five bands playing tonight is already soundchecking. On bass is Jimmy Pogo, who came to see my first ever gig in the States a couple of years ago, and was so impressed that he wrote a song about it. He is pretty excited that he's going to be able to play it tonight with me in the audience.

There's going to be a quick turnaround of bands and no time to soundcheck the rest of us, so we go down into the basement dressing room, where a couple of sofas and a table are set up in an alcove past all the beer pumps. At least it's warmer down here. Four huge pizzas are ordered in but I'm not really hungry, and starting to feel the jet lag again.

If you don't know what jet lag is like, it's like this: I go up to watch Jimmy Pogo's band and take a place at the back near the side wall. As I'm focusing on what's happening on stage I become aware that some guy covered in tattoos leaning on the wall by my side is staring at me the whole time. I don't want to get into a confrontation so I try to ignore it but after a while I just have to turn and see what he wants. But it's not a person at all: for the past fifteen minutes I have been intimidated by a large red pipe running up the wall, covered in stickers marked AUTO SPKR—FIRE DEPT CONNECTED.

Back down in the dressing room, promoter Phil has a chat with me. I'm interested in how he came to be promoting a club here in Passaic, which I looked up on my atlas before I left and couldn't find. He tells me he's not from Passaic but has been trying to build up Wednesday nights here for over a year, after he took the booking over from Adi. Seems to be working by the look of the crowd in tonight. The only problem, he says, is the toilets. He recommends that if I need to use the toilets I should go to Dunkin'

Donuts up the road. 'We're the CBGB's of New Jersey when it comes to the toilets,' he says.

But somehow it's often true that the worse the toilets, the better the gig. And so it proves tonight.

When it's all over I go out into the front bar. Jennie is sitting there arranging a lewd tableaux of model cowboys and Indians. In this version of the Wild West, the Indians definitely win.

Phil tells me that he's really happy about tonight's show. Somehow we get talking about bands cancelling gigs. The strangest excuse he ever got was when one band phoned up the morning of the show to say they couldn't play because their drummer had been mauled by a seal.

Talking of which, the woman behind the bar tells me about the time she went for a romantic evening walk in Central Park with her boyfriend and got attacked by a racoon. They were next to a wall, it poked its head over, she thought it was a mugger and screamed, and it went for her. Jeff joins in the conversation and says that a few years ago there was another problem with the wildlife in Central Park—there was so much residual crack cocaine around in the undergrowth from illicit drug use that the squirrels started getting addicted to it.

Mauled by seals? Crackhead squirrels? It's time to leave.

By the time I get back to the motel at 3:50—that's, oh God, nearly nine in the morning UK time—the pre-show slice of pizza that I smuggle into the room in its embarrassingly outsize box bearing the legend 'oven fresh hot delicious pizza' is cold and strange looking, and even after resting it on the fan heater for a few minutes to take the chill off, it doesn't live up to the promise of any of its adjectives.

24th February

Jeff's friend in Baltimore just phoned to tell him it's snowing heavily down there and a big winter storm is forecast—are we still coming? Of course. We only cancel gigs when we get mauled by seals.

I check out of the motel and we drive over to Jeff's friend Mary-Beth's house where the Creeps are just waking up. Mary-Beth is trying to carry her dog upstairs as I come in because she's heard I'm allergic to them, but I tell her not to worry—that's only cats. Soon the dog is all over me and belly-up at my feet. Dogs go all soppy when they see me.

We gather ourselves together and drive over to Adi's house, where she whips up breakfast for everyone and then on the spur of the moment decides to come to the Baltimore gig with us. Voluntarily getting in the van and driving through a snowstorm for four hours for a gig she's not even playing? That girl is rock'n'roll.

I join Jennie out on the front porch where she has gone to smoke a cigarette and try to recover from last night's alcohol-fuelled excess. Jennie has a voice and attitude that could knock walls down, and counterpoints it with the skimpiest of stage clothes. She once showed me a tiny suitcase and told me it had fifteen of her outfits in it. I see her sitting there on the steps with the first of the snow fluttering down around her and say, shouldn't she be wearing something warmer? She shudders and says, 'At least now I can pretend I'm shaking because of the cold.'

It's going to be a nerve-wracking journey to Baltimore in this bad weather, so it's good to find out that the strange noise we think we hear coming from the engine is actually Jeff's electric toothbrush which somehow got switched on in his bag. We power through the gloom, the snow warnings flashing all the way down the highway, snowploughs throwing up sparks as they race past us. Despite the weather, we make it to the venue pretty much on time. Jeff has been telling me that Baltimore is not a city I'd really want to walk around in—murder capital of America with some dangerous areas, pimps and drug dealers on the streets. I'm not going to be doing much walking around anyway, as after we've loaded the gear in with the snow cascading around us all I want to do is I get out of the sub-zero temperature and warm up.

The venue is a small bar with a very low stage at one end. I've heard that the good folk of Baltimore seriously know how to drink and I have a feeling this could be quite a rowdy one. I have some issues with the promoter here though. He printed a poster advertising the gig as 'The Adverts' and I told him if he called it that I wasn't coming. So the posters were destroyed and it was changed on the website. Okay. But now I'm very annoyed to see flyers around the place advertising the gig as 'TV Smith's The Adverts.' Significantly, the promoter hasn't come to the venue.

I take a chair, and get into a bit of a bad mood about this, cheered up only by a dog that comes bounding up and goes all soppy on me.

When the audience starts coming in I slip down to the dressing room, which like yesterday is in the cellar, an old sofa and a couple of chairs, large pans arranged about the place to catch the drips from the ceiling. Guitarist Jami braves the snow and brings back a sandwich from a nearby Subway, the only place open, then it's time to crack open a can of the local beer, 'National Bohemian'—or Natty Bo as it's referred to here—which bears the slogan 'from the land of pleasant living.' That's not what I've been hearing about Baltimore. I'll probably never know why the logo on the can shows the head of a man with a large moustache and one eye.

Despite the snow there's a good turnout to the gig and we get a great response. Quite a lot of people want to talk to me at the bar afterwards and tell me how much they enjoyed it. 'No wonder my dog loved you!' says one girl.

A tall skinhead guy tells me about the time he met one of his favourite singers when he was over in Europe and was crushed when the guy refused to speak to him because he was American. I agree with him that you can't judge people by what country they're from. Then he gets kind of intense.

'That's right! I mean, this guy, he was, like, a HERO to me and it's like…he insults me and like…how can he talk to someone like that? He ain't even anything SPECIAL, he's not even like TOUGH, I mean…I'VE STABBED BIGGER GUYS THAN HIM!!'

Uh huh. Right, I'll just be off to pack away my guitar and stuff.

A bit complicated now: The Creeps will be staying with a friend of theirs called Chris and I'm supposed to get a motel, but Jeff didn't want to book one in advance because he thinks it's extremely advisable to actually look at the rooms round here before handing over the money. So while they finish loading the van, Chris is going to drive me up to a motel near his place and check me in. If it really turns out to be a dump I can stay at his place too.

Baltimore isn't accustomed to snow, so the streets are deserted as we drive out of the centre and into the better neighbourhoods, past where the mayor lives. Despite his claims that crime in Baltimore really isn't so bad, the mayor has a police car parked at the end of his street every night.

The motel is fine, but a bit cool. The room has a giant fan heater unit against the wall, which really blasts the air out—though unfortunately not of the hot variety. I'm ravenously hungry now and roam the motel corridors for a chemical snack vending machine, but all they sell is coke.

25th February

It was the jet lag night, where you lie down dead tired, sleep for two hours then wake up and can't get back off again. I get up early and set the coffee machine brewing, then take a shower. When I get out, the coffee still hasn't filtered through, even though the water seems to be boiling away. Reception sends someone up to have a look and he finds that someone has taken the tube from the water tank in the back. I say to the repair guy, 'Why would anyone steal the tube from the back of a coffee machine?'

He gives me a look. 'You wouldn't believe it. I've had people here steal light bulbs.'

Jeff arrives a little later than we planned. The party went on long into the night over at Chris's place. As we drive back over there I mention the coffee machine and Jeff points out that the tube was probably stolen by someone to make a crack pipe. I'm so naive. When we arrive at the apartment there are bodies sprawled out all over the room. I'm starving, and scour the kitchen but can only find some *Mini Chew-rific* beef and cheese flavour dog biscuits. 'There's probably not actually any beef in them,' say Jonas helpfully.

Well, I am hungry, but not actually dog-biscuit-hungry.

The original plan to drive to a diner for breakfast then head straight for New York hits a snag when Jennie has to pop upstairs for a lengthy retching session after an ambitious selection of fancy drinks yesterday. After a couple of hours the rest of us head out to the 7-Eleven round the corner for coffee. There are no sandwiches or hot food of any kind there that is vegetarian. I buy a croissant and a banana for now and an emergency energy bar for later.

Never before have I heard anyone throw up for that long. Respect.

The snow has stopped and the skies are a limpid late afternoon blue when we finally set off—good driving conditions and Jeff makes up some time. I read a list of America's top ten sandwiches in a magazine lying around in the seat pocket. Number one is the chicken fingers, mozzarella sticks and French Fries sandwich.

I'd like to know what the top ten vegetarian sandwiches are, or even if they go as far as ten. When I ask at the food stand in a rest stop if they have anything without meat they look at me as if I am mad. Back in the van I open the emergency energy bar, which is called a Detour—presumably because it detours any concept of flavour—and has the consistency of congealed glue. It also contains gelatine, which I only find out after reading the ingredients list while trying to chew my way through the first bite, so I put the rest aside. It's my first UCMM (Unexpected Confectionary Meat Moment.)

CBGB's is packed by mid-evening. Jami, who plays guitar for me and the Creeps on this tour, is also playing tonight with his regular band The Sleazies, and with two more groups stacking the bill there's plenty to keep the audience entertained. At the back of the club I bump into Jon and Sophie, a couple of fans from Florida who have a present for me: my favourite Spanish wine, right year and everything. They found out I liked it by reading my tour diaries on the internet. Jon tells me he felt a bit strange sneaking a fine wine inside his jacket past the doorman of CBGB's.

Soon after 11:00 the Creeps hit the stage. Jennie is giving it full power up there; you wouldn't know that a couple of hours ago she was stretched out unconscious in the back of the van. She's a tough cookie alright, or as we say in England: a hard biscuit. I get to play at around midnight. It's a very exciting gig, although I'm finding it hard-going after the first half hour; the stage is a sauna and I'm gulping for air and not finding any. Towards the end I'm happy to pass the microphone to the audience and let them sing while I try to breathe.

Then we have to pack away for the drive through the night back to Providence. Within a couple of hours Jeff and me are the only ones left awake in the van. It's a punishing five hours after everything we've done today and a relief when we finally get into the city as the dawn starts to break. We drop off the band members to their various homes—Jennie is going to have to head straight out to work—then Jeff shows me round his apartment which he's handing over to me for the next couple of days while he goes to sleep over at Jami's place nearby. It's seven in the morning, that's—mmm—midday UK time, and I had two hours sleep last night. Over the last few days I must have lost an entire night's worth. Best not to think about it.

26th February

It's a hometown gig for the Midnight Creeps tonight, and Jeff's last gig here drumming with them. After tomorrow's he's going to be quitting to concentrate on booking and managing the band, so it's a very special evening for him and he's been working on it for a while. The Creeps will play the headline slot, there's a supporting line up of five of his favourite bands and we're all hoping for a great night.

The venue is inauspiciously situated away from the city centre in a parking lot between a garage and a Dunkin' Donuts, but looks promising inside. The Dunkin' Donuts is the only store open in the area so I head over there with Mark, a Creeps fan who's been travelling with us the last couple of days. We make a complicated order of various coffees for ourselves and the band but the girl serving gets a bit confused. I point out that she hasn't rung up some of them and she huffs, 'Oh, just take them.' So bored and underpaid that she doesn't really care if I pay or not.

'Well, OK,' I say, with a laugh. 'I'll come again!'

She looks at me. 'I won't be here.'

Walking back across the parking lot clutching a tray full of free coffee, Mark says, 'I love America.'

Back in the club, we get our first soundcheck of the tour, then the promoter brings in some trays of food and we have a hot meal—a buffet at the bar with enough time to digest it before the show, what a treat! I really feel a lot better afterwards and it occurs to me that the simple equation 'food = energy' is true.

The room fills up fast and soon there are over 400 people in. The first band on is from Boston. They get onstage and to my surprise the singer announces how thrilled they are to be playing on the same bill as me. He counts in the first number and the sound immediately cuts out. Technical problems dog them through the first few songs, then they hit their stride and put in an enjoyable high-energy set.

Next up is Jami's band The Sleazies, followed by a band with the ex-guitarist from L7, an old friend of Jeff's, then it's a psychobilly band called Sasquatch. I've been talking to Sasquatch in the dressing room (which by the way had one of my favourite pieces of graffiti up on the wall: 'Jesus is coming—try to look busy') and the singer and guitarist of the band was lovingly showing me his vintage Gretsch guitar. A few bars into the first song, it cuts out and he has to borrow a guitar from Jami.

These things tend to go in waves so I'm wondering what's going to go wrong when I start playing, but apart from me falling over during the first song, everything is fine. Falling over on stage is cool.

It's my favourite gig of the tour so far and as an added bonus I can relax and watch the Creeps knowing my gig is finished.

It's all back to Jami's apartment for a few beers. A case of Miller Lite has appeared and the guy from Sasquatch tells me he's a bit uncomfortable drinking it after his band got banned from a festival sponsored by Miller last year.

'Why did they ban you?' I ask.

'Oh, nuthin' much. I was sick into a cup onstage and set my pubic hair on fire, but they didn't need to ban us...I mean, I was *holding back...*'

27th February

Jeff arrives mid-afternoon with Mark. They're carrying in coffee and bagels from Dunkin' Donuts.

'How do Dunkin' Donuts make their coffee taste so bad' I ask, taking a sip.

'It's not as bad as McDonalds,' says Mark. 'I had a coffee there once and it tasted like shoes.'

Just two hours down the freeway to New Haven for the final show. We stop for fuel on the way and I nip into the 7-Eleven to see if I can find something a bit more substantial to eat. To my amazement there is an egg salad sandwich on the shelves so I snap it up. Healthy food at last!

'Wow, you found something, dude!' says Jeff, impressed, when I get in the van.

But the Egg Salad Sandwich turns out to be a bit of a disappointment—when I read the ingredients I see that there is no salad whatsoever in it. However, it does have: Enriched flour (unbleached wheat flour, malted barley flour, niacin, reduced iron, thiamine mononitrate [vitamin B1], riboflavin [vitamin B2], folic acid), water, cracked wheat berries, stone ground whole wheat flour, honey, high fructose corn syrup, yeast, wheat gluten, partially hydrogenated soybean oil, salt, raisin juice concentrate, distilled vinegar, yeast nutrients (monocalcium phosphate, calcium sulfate, ammonium sulfate), baking soda, dough conditioners (may contain one or more of the following: mono and diglycerides, calcium and sodium stearoyl lactylates, calcium peroxide), amylase, cornstarch, eggs, mayonnaise (vegetable oil [soybean, canola], egg yolks, sugar, spice, salt), premium mayonnaise (vegetable oil [soybean, canola] egg yolk, vinegar, water, corn syrup, whole eggs, salt, lemon juice, natural flavors, calcium disodium EDTA [to protect flavour], modified food starch, mustard (white distilled vinegar and water, mustard seed, salt, turmeric, onion powder, spices, natural flavoring), sodium benzoate, potassium sorbate [as preservative], spice, salt, mustard seed.

The New Haven gig is a last minute replacement for Philadelphia because the club there got closed down. It's a lot smaller than the clubs we've been playing so far, and we have to finish by 9:30 because there's the weekly open mic spot already booked in after us. Secretly, I'm pleased. Last night really felt like the end-of-the-tour gig, so tonight will be less pressure, and I'm keen to get it over with and drive back to Providence for a last night party.

These intimate gigs can be the best though: the small crowd surges forward and sings along and it's a very nice show.

It feels late by the time we're back in Providence but in fact due to the early start it's only just after midnight. Pete, one of the guitarists in The Sleazies, works in a bar so he slips over there to grab a few cases of beer and then we all sit around at Jami's place drinking and winding down from the tour. Jami tells me that one summer he held a party which was slow to get going until suddenly a duck flew through the open door. The duck ended up being handed around and petted and stroked by everyone, and it really broke the ice. The party only really starts when a duck flies in.

Beer starts getting spilt. At some point Jeff insists that I try some whisky from the South. The talk around me is in full flow. It starts off with vomit stories and then moves on to an improbable lexicon of terms for deviant sexual practices. I'm going to gloss over most of this. Suffice it to say, I'm not often likely to be requiring the phrase 'donkey punch.'

On into the wee hours and the drink is running out, until we are pouring the last can of beer into shot glasses so we can toast the tour and Jeff's last night with the band. Then they all take turns to say how much they have enjoyed touring with me and how much the Adverts meant to them as they were growing up. It's very touching, except that I feel a little bit as if I am present at my own funeral.

The rest of the details of the evening are a bit hazy, but I do know one thing—a duck definitely flew in.

Time for some sleep. A four-hour drive to the airport tomorrow, seven inches of snow forecast.

18. THE RETURN OF THE EMERGENCY SANDWICH (2005)

6th August

A twenty-four hour trip to the Czech Republic to play Antifest, a yearly open air festival which attracts four thousand punk rockers from all over Europe. My flight leaves Gatwick at five in the afternoon, I play at two in the morning, then fly back shortly after noon the next day. It's a lot of travelling for forty-five minutes on stage, but at least on a short hop like this is I only need to take the guitar and a small carry-on bag with a few T-shirts and other bits and pieces with me. I'm not even bothering to bring merchandise—last time I played this festival, anticipating the potential four thousand customers, I took a full box of CDs and didn't sell a single one. I also had some of the worst vegetarian food I have ever tasted, so this time I have packed an emergency cheese sandwich.

On the way to the airport I get a text from my friends Carl and Paul from Poulton-le-Fylde, near Blackpool. They are at Antifest! They have a merchandising stand! Bring lots of CDs!

Too late!

The recent bombings in London have raised the security levels at the airport to paranoid levels. Even though I get to Gatwick two hours early there's still a risk I could miss my flight and I'm getting increasingly nervous as I shuffle along down the massive queues. At least I remembered not to pack the string clippers in the guitar case: there have been a few occasions where they've been picked up on the X-ray machines and I've been sent back out to queue up again to check in the guitar with the hold luggage. Everyone knows that if a terrorist gets hold of a pair of string clippers he could give the pilot a nasty pinch.

On board at last, I realise that I forgot to order a veggie meal and am seriously tempted to break into the emergency sandwich already but I resist the temptation—it's going to be a long day and I'm sure I'll be more in need of it later.

My Czech promoter Petr meets me at the airport and takes me out to the van where a band he manages called SPS are waiting. Then it's a journey at breakneck speed down the motorway and out onto the country lanes, and we are at the festival in just over ninety minutes.

The dressing room is a sort of large shed behind the stage, and there are a few English bands around—among others, Peter And The Test Tube Babies. Peter tells me that he flew in this morning from a festival in Sweden. At first they refused to let him on the flight because his passport was peeling away at the corners on the photo page and looked like it could have been tampered with. He went away, fixed down the corners with superglue, changed clothes with one of his band members, put on sunglasses and a hat, then came back to the counter and got checked in without a problem.

I wander out into the festival area to find Carl and Paul at the merch stand. Carl gets the beers in. 'What's this?' he says, waving a flyer with the festival timings at me. 'All the bands have start and finish times, but for TV Smith it just says *2:05 until ?*'

That's not the only question hanging over the evening. I was supposed to play a song with Czech band NVU but haven't been able to find anyone here who speaks enough English to let me know when or if this is going to happen. One thing's for sure, it's going to be a late night: Peter and the Test Tube Babies are just starting now, 999 will be next, then after them comes a Czech band called Green Monster, so it will be some time yet before I get to play.

Backstage there is a Czech journalist who wants to do an interview with me, but the problem is finding anywhere quiet enough. He says we could do it in his car, parked some way outside the festival area, but neither of us feels like battling through the crowds to get to it. One of the festival organisers eventually finds a tiny two-bed caravan, already crammed with three people, where we can sit in relative quiet and record the interview. The journalist speaks pretty good English and we have an interesting chat. After I've been going on for a while about how punk means expressing yourself and talking about the real world he says, 'You know, you are the first of all the musicians I have spoken to in the last two days who has said that. All the rest said that punk is just about drinking and having fun.'

Well, I like doing that too.

The Test Tubes are just coming back into the dressing room, sweaty and elated after a good gig. 'Beat that if you can, Mr Smith,' says Peter. Still two hours to go before I even start. As I'm higher up on the bill, Peter is curious to know how much I'm getting paid. I tell him it's supposed to be a benefit concert so I said I'd do it for 300 euros. His eyes widen in disbelief.

'No! Never!' He shakes his head. 'You need a manager.'

Hmm.

It's getting cold now. I take the guitar out of its case to acclimatise, then get two more T-shirts out of my bag and put them on over the one I'm already wearing. The emergency sandwich is still in there. I am pretty hungry now but it's too near show time to eat it, I'll save it for afterwards. Meanwhile there is a never-ending supply of beer in the dressing room. The Test Tube Babies are in party mood now their set is over and numerous bottles of wine are being opened.

I go out into the chill air and meet some Italian fans by the merch stand, who want their photos taken with me and offer to try and set up a tour in Italy. Sounds interesting, would be my first ever gigs there. I ask Paul what hotel he and Carl are staying in. He looks amused, and points behind him, to where his car is parked.

It's past midnight now, the bands are running late, and 999 are only just starting. I'm still totally in the dark about whether NVU are playing a song with me or whether I'll just be playing solo. After asking around, the guy who found me the caravan for the interview tells me that the drummer from NVU has disappeared. 'He is very drunk last days, everything wrong, he go, all here want…erm, not war…' he mimes a punch, '…him.'

The drummer who all here want punch is also the guy who asked me to play the song with NVU and arranged for me to play at 2:00 in the morning. I may want punch him myself. My translator friend tells me that Stepan, NVU's singer, is very sorry for the confusion, and wants to apologise. I tell him that it's not necessary, but he insists: 'No, Stepan come here apologise want must.'

Stepan then arrives and makes a lengthy formal apology, translated line by line by the other guy. It's all rather embarrassing, but it's nice of him to take the trouble and it clears the air.

All the same, I wish I could get on with my set. People in the audience are starting to drift away back to their tents. I'm freezing despite the three T-shirts, and distressed to see that the musicians now preparing to go on stage are a full-on psychobilly/punk band, exotic multi-coloured Mohawks, double bass, the lot. I'm supposed to follow that with just an acoustic guitar.

I watch a bit of the set with Carl. The band have extravagant pyrotechnics, twenty foot flames shooting up from the stage at regular intervals, explosions, light show… I turn to Carl, 'I think I'd better get another beer.'

'Don't worry,' says Carl, with a heavy note of irony in his voice. 'Remember, you're *headlining*.'

It's a fine line between headlining and the graveyard shift.

Back in the dressing room I'm alarmed to see Arthur from 999 has my guitar and is entertaining the assembled bands with a variety of Country'n'Western versions of punk tunes. I really wanted to keep those strings unplayed to avoid snapping them later, but everyone is laughing and clapping along and I'm not going to be the killjoy who breaks up the party.

I wander back outside and watch some more of the band. It's 2:15, I should have been on ten minutes ago, but Green Monster show no sign of finishing.

Through the dressing room window I can see Arthur passing the guitar round so some of the Test Tube Babies can have a go. I love Arthur, but at this moment I could happily kill him.

Nick from 999 walks past with some food he's bought from one of the stands out in the site. It's a whole fish on a stick.

The party in the dressing room is winding down. People are apologising to me that it's got so late they're going to have to miss my set and head back to their hotels. I don't blame them.

Okay, we're getting there. Green Monster are off stage, I have the guitar back and tuned up, I've stripped back to one T-shirt. It's nearly three in the morning and the audience have dwindled to a few hundred but they are crowding right up to the front of the stage, twenty deep, and that's enough to make this work. I'm ready and can't wait to start, I can feel it bursting to get out of me.

Right from the first note the crowd are on it, and I know this is going to be good. This is what the waiting around has been leading up to and what I'm here for. The cold air means that I feel perfectly comfortable up there on stage, rather than superheated like usual, and I can sustain the energy, barely breaking a sweat. The guitar strings don't hold up quite as well: the first one snaps after three songs, and another a few songs after that, but the audience stick with me while I hurriedly change them. Wish I had those string clippers though—if only those terrorists knew the trouble they cause. There are a few requests for songs being shouted up from the crowd, which I pick up on and play. I lose track of time and am thinking I should probably start finishing the set with a few favourites when one of the stage hands comes over and says, 'Just one more song.' I belt out Gary Gilmore's Eyes, people singing along, dancing, climbing over the barriers. A great atmosphere.

They applaud so long that I'm eventually allowed back on for a quick encore, but that's it, even though the crowd chant my name for another ten minutes before they eventually start to disperse.

Fatigue washes over me as people shake my hand and slap me on the back. Petr congratulates me, and says 'Okay, Tim, all tired, we go back now to hotel, must leave 9:30 for fly.' Good news, looks like I will get a few hours sleep after all. Carl gathers my things from the stage, a big smile on his face, and we take them back to the dressing room, now deserted.

Too deserted. My bag's gone.

That's the bag with my passport and return flight ticket.

It's 4:00 in the morning.

Paul and Carl ask around, and find someone who thinks they saw Peter carrying out the bag when the other bands left during my set. If that's true, it's better than it being stolen, but how the hell am I going to get it back?

I love Peter, but right now I could happily kill him. If I knew where he was.

Petr says that Peter (pay attention at the back) could be in any one of four hotels, but no one from the festival organisation knows who is staying where. He says, 'All hotel nothing reception, nothing room numbers.'

We drive back to our hotel, a couple of kilometres away, but there is no bag lying around, nothing stashed behind the unmanned reception counter, no sound of any parties going on in the rooms, no one around.

'Now is too tired,' says Petr, 'We wake eight, have breakfast in restaurant, then people reception, give list of rooms.'

If that doesn't work, I'll have to go to the embassy to get a new passport on Monday, then find a new flight. Looks like I'm going to be here at least another two days.

The room is surprisingly nice, and normally I'd be happy to relax back here after a good gig. It's warm, and there's even a television and a bathroom. The bathroom door won't shut though, because—in an interesting deviation from the non-lethal—the power cable from the television leads through the doorway and plugs into a socket in there.

I am devastatingly tired now, and my stomach is churning. Somewhere in the Czech Republic, maybe in this hotel, is a bag with my emergency sandwich in it. There is a lot to think about as I settle down for three hours sleep.

7th August

The alarm rings and it is the meanest, most despicable sound in the world. I stagger down to reception. There is no one around, and the door to the restaurant is locked. Back up the stairs to my room. Ring Petr, no reply. Down the stairs. No one there. It's 8:20. If I am to have any chance of getting home today I will need to be out of here in less than two hours and I still don't know where the bag is. Back to my room. Ring Petr. He answers, 'Tim, five minutes okay, I am in shower.'

At 8:30 the door to the restaurant is unlocked and we can get a coffee. I start to feel almost awake. Petr orders up some breakfast. It's plate of bread and cheese slices, sprinkled with chopped herbs. For one paranoid moment I suspect that my bag must have been handed in to the hotel last night and they are playing a cruel trick on me by arranging my own emergency sandwich onto a plate and serving it back to me for breakfast.

Petr comes back to the table with a list of room numbers scrawled onto a piece of paper, no names to go with the numbers. Eight rooms full of punk rockers sleeping off the effects of the night before and we will have to wake up all of them. We don't even know if Peter is staying in this hotel.

I ask Petr if the Test Tubes are leaving today, and he tells me they are. 'If we can't find the bag here,' I say, 'maybe we can go straight to the airport in Prague and meet them there. Then even if I can't get on my flight, I will at least be able to get my passport.'

Petr says, 'They flying Brno airport. 200 kilometres other way.'

So we rap on doors. Some are opened by empty-eyed hungover punk rockers, some aren't answered at all. A few are unlocked and I just walk in and look around while the punks sleep on oblivious, but there's still no sign of the bag. The next-to-last room is occupied by a band called Sick 56 who are surprisingly alert and helpful. They think Peter is staying in Hotel Herman, a few kilometres down the road. 'I know this place,' says Petr, 'But just hostel, nothing reception, not possible get in.' One of the guys from Sick 56 suggests setting off the fire alarm, then everyone would have to come out. I find myself seriously considering this idea. It could work.

Perhaps it's lucky that at that moment Petr calls me from out in the corridor. He has just tried the last room on our list, and the woman inside has come to the door but can't understand what he's saying. I rush round there. A bleary red-haired punkette looks at me inquiringly. 'I'm looking for a bag,' I gasp, 'a grey shoulder bag. Someone took it out of the backstage last night.'

She glances behind her. 'Oh, you mean *this* bag…'

Right now she is my favourite person in the whole world.

A quick check through. It's all there, passport, tickets, emergency sandwich. It's now 9:40, if we leave right away we could still get to Prague in time. But we can't leave yet—first Petr has to drive SPS to the festival site for their gig this afternoon, so he goes to round them up and I go back to my room for a lightning-fast shower. I've no appetite for the emergency sandwich at the moment, but I'll be lording it up on the plane when all the rest are given their dismal Czech Airline meals. If I make the flight.

Soon after ten we're on the road, but time is going to be tight, very tight. We drop off SPS and their equipment at the festival and it's nearing eleven before we leave the site, past dishevelled punks camped in the verge next to the cornfields, just waking up and emerging from their tents. From the number of them heading off into the thickets of corn to relieve themselves it's going to be a bumper crop this year. We barrel down the country roads towards the motorway, Sunday drivers everywhere, taking their time, Petr swearing loudly at them in Czech. At least, I assume he's swearing—it certainly doesn't sound like he's saying 'have a nice day.'

Swearing seems to particularly suit the Czech language, robust and guttural, and I get to hear quite a lot of it as we drive along. We hit every delay imaginable: traffic lights, road works, sudden downpours. At one point we get stuck behind a monster combine harvester which takes up half the road and trundles along at 20 kilometres an hour. When we finally get round that we find a large van driving along in front of it to warn oncoming drivers of the wide load, and we get stuck behind that as well.

Petr makes a call on the mobile to find out how the traffic is flowing on the motorways around Prague, where road works have been causing five hour delays recently. A delay of just five minutes could ruin my chances of catching the flight. He puts the phone back in the cradle. 'No traffic, good, you have still twenty minutes in airport.'

Twenty minutes! It's a good job they checked me in for both flights yesterday so I already have my boarding card. I could just make it.

The phone rings and Petr grabs it, listens for a moment. 'Traffic!' he shouts, and swings off onto a slip road, bouncing over the cobbles into Prague city centre.

Okay. That adds ten minutes to the journey. Ten minutes to get through the airport? It's past midday, my flight is at 12:30. Really, we might as well forget it and give up now.

But no, on we go. I can feel the anxiety rising and I'm trying to push it back down. 12:10, through Prague and heading out the other side. 12:15 and the airport is in sight across the fields. Just this one time, let the plane be delayed.

12:20, we screech to a stop in front of the terminal building. 'You miss flight, book new one, many flights Sunday, festival will pay,' says Petr.

The briefest handshake and I grab my bag and guitar and am running through the terminal, heart pounding. Why am I doing this? Is it really worth it?

Through security, 12:25, I glance at the screens as I run past, my flight flashing red, last boarding. One minute to go.

Never again.

Never, never again.

Until the next time.

www.ingramcontent.com/pod-product-compliance
Ingram Content Group UK Ltd.
Pitfield, Milton Keynes, MK11 3LW, UK
UKHW051248180426
11947UKWH00020B/1604